THOMAS HOOKER
1586–1647

Frank Shuffelton

THOMAS HOOKER
1586-1647

PRINCETON UNIVERSITY PRESS

PRINCETON, NEW JERSEY

For Jane, For David

vos, o clarissima mundi
lumina, labentem caelo quae ducitis annum

CONTENTS

PREFACE

THE most recent biography of Thomas Hooker was published in 1891, and Cotton Mather's short biography included in his *Magnalia Christi Americana* was the only previous original account of Hooker's career—other accounts being abridgments or padded versions of Mather's narrative. Mather's presentation of Hooker as a model of ministerial piety contains many useful insights into Hooker's religion, character and deeds, and George Leon Walker's *Thomas Hooker: Preacher, Founder, Democrat* (New York, 1891) shows a scrupulously researched mastery of the relevant facts concerning Hooker's life. Unfortunately, the strength of one biographer is the weakness of the other, and both writers have failed to give an adequate treatment of Hooker's published works—Mather, perhaps, because they were so familiar to his audience, and Walker because they were so foreign.

The absence of a modern treatment of Hooker's life is in itself a good reason to retell the story of this great preacher and leader of our first Puritan settlers. A deeper and more satisfying understanding of the Puritan enterprise has been created in the last eighty years; Hooker's career deserves to be reconsidered with the scholarly accessions of the twentieth century in mind, and a biographical study will further deepen our knowledge of the New England experiment. Walker perpetuated the misleading version of Hooker's significance so dear to nineteenth-century American historians. From George Bancroft to Vernon Parrington writers have attempted to portray Hooker's removal to Connecticut as a type of the American Revolution; Perry Miller has since shown us that this interpretation will not do. Hooker was a preacher first and foremost, a founder only in a secondary sense, and hardly a

ix

democrat at all. My study has led me to believe that Hooker's significance for New England and America was as a preacher and pastor, as a theologian, and as an architect of the religious community. I have attempted to explain Hooker's career within these guidelines and to integrate a consideration of his writings with a discussion of his activities in the hope that thought and action might illuminate each other. While Miller disproved the idea of Hooker as a democratic refugee, he did not give an explanation of Hooker's reasons for removing to Connecticut. I began this study in an attempt to discover in Hooker's sermons reasons for his emigration, and what I discovered there has importance for Puritan and American life on a much wider scale. His concern for men's troubled minds, for civil harmony, and for the practice of a meditative, intensive piety has reappeared throughout our history, although I have confined myself to a consideration of his significance for the Puritan experience.

Hooker's activities seem to me to fall into several phases which correspond to his cultural and geographic milieu at any given time. I have devoted successive chapters to Hooker's education, first pastoral experience, English preaching career, activities in the Netherlands, settlement in Massachusetts, resettlement in Connecticut, and his work in defense of the New England Way then being formulated in the four plantations known as the United Colonies. My final chapter attempts to suggest the lines of Hooker's influence through Cotton Mather and Jonathan Edwards; I must emphasize the term "suggest," for any attempt to cover a hundred years of New England church history in a short chapter can scarcely hope to do more.

A minor warning or two is due the reader at this point. First, I use the term *Puritan* within a historical, and hence shifting, context. In the first part of the study, involving Hooker's activities in England and the Netherlands, I intend *Puritan* to include all those men who wished to reform the Church of

England in a protestant direction, whether they were inclined to presbyterian, congregational, or separatist forms of church government. After Hooker's arrival in the New World, the opponents to the established church of England began to distinguish themselves in accordance with their preferences for various forms of church order, and hence in the latter part of the study, involving Hooker's activities in New England, *Puritan* refers to the particular variety of Puritanism and to the particular theories of church government practiced there. This is clearly a matter of convenience rather than of definition, and when obliged to distinguish between varieties of Puritan in Old and New England, I have referred to them as presbyterians or nonseparating congregational independents as the case might be. As I have used the term *Puritan*, I have had in mind Alan Simpson's useful study, *Puritanism in Old and New England* (Chicago, Univ. of Chicago Press).

Second, I have for the most part attempted to explicate Hooker's ideas within the narrative context of his life, but in two important, lengthy passages analysis has displaced narrative. In the second chapter I have made a detailed study of Hooker's *Poore Doubting Christian Drawne to Christ* in order to reveal the complex machinery of his cure of souls; as I indicate there, concern for the spiritually troubled was central to Hooker's entire career. In the third chapter I have analyzed Hooker's concept of preparation for salvation as he preached it in England; the overwhelming bulk of his published work deals with this preparationist theology, and it was through these writings that he gained his reputation and influence in New England. Chapter Three, in particular, covers ground already familiar to scholars steeped in the Puritan mind, but I hope they will discover some new insights there, and newcomers to the field should be able to find their way through the thickets of Puritan theology without extensive prior reading. Except for expanded abbreviations, all quotations preserve the original spelling and, unless otherwise noted, the original punctuation. All dates are based upon a January 1st New Year's Day; thus, February 12, 1633/34 is given as February 12, 1634.

I have been indebted to various scholars more than mere footnotes can possibly reveal. George and Williston Walker helped begin the spadework necessary for a reevaluation of the Puritan past. Perry Miller has revolutionized our knowledge of the American seventeenth century and has made possible most of the significant scholarship which followed his pioneering work. I have profited widely from the work of Raymond P. Stearns, Edmund S. Morgan, Norman Pettit, Larzer Ziff, Darrett B. Rutman, Sidney Ahlstrom, and Jesper Rosenmeier. David Hall's collection of documents on the Antinomian Controversy was indispensable. Winthrop S. Hudson has been extremely kind and patient as he listened to half-formed versions of my ideas and offered valuable suggestions. William A. Clebsch read an earlier stage of this work with an ear sharpened to theological overtones and distinctions. Above all, I owe an enormous debt to David Levin, whose suggestions and corrections have made this a much better study than it might have been and whose patience and encouragement have supported my carnal heart. Needless to say, any errors herein are my own. Helen Craven has spent long hours of typing, and the librarians of the Congregational Library and of Houghton Library made me comfortable during extended bouts of sermon reading. And finally, Jane Shuffelton has offered motivation, a sympathetic ear, and a keen sense of stylistic grace as she relived with me the intricacies of seventeenth-century thought.

THOMAS HOOKER
1586–1647

ONE

Education and Conversion

WHEN Queen Elizabeth I came to the English throne in 1558, she attempted a settlement of the religious controversies which had wracked that country ever since her father had repudiated the Pope's authority over the English Church. She supposedly acted for peace, unity, and the protestant religion—whatever that was—and placed the English Church half-way between Rome and Geneva, episcopal and traditional in form, Calvinist and reformed in doctrine. In the latter years of her reign, however, this characteristically Tudor compromise began to strain at the seams; the Roman Church still had great hopes of recovering England, and at the other extreme there were men who wished to press on with the work of the Reformation, still just begun in the established church, as they saw it. Elizabeth succeeded in maintaining peace for the whole of her long reign, but the unity she sought to maintain was only apparent, for beneath the surface, plots and counterplots to take over the English Church were being hatched.

English priests returned from the Continent and worked behind the front of conformity and obscurity to keep the Roman faith alive. In the year 1586, for example, "William Tomson, alias Blackeborne, made priest at Reims in France by the authoritie of the bishop of Rome and Richard Lea alias Long, made priest at Laon" were condemned for treason—their treason consisting principally in "remaining within this realme after the terms of fortie daies after the session of the last parle-

3

ment."[1] On the twentieth of April they were taken to Tyburn, hanged, and quartered. Hard times indeed for those who worked against the Queen's church; especially so, some patriotic Englishmen such as Raphael Holinshed thought, since God was on the side of English Protestants. In July of the same year the Babington conspiracy was discovered, "wherein, as the turbulent spirited did what they could to proceed, so it pleased God the author of peace to intercept them in the plot of their mischeefous devise." When the people of London heard of the conspirators' discovery and capture, says Holinshed, "the present occasion forced such a sudden impression of joie, that they made the bels in steeples witnesses of their inward conceipt; . . . some galled themselves with ringing, choosing rather to loose a little leather, yea a portion of their fat and flesh, than not . . . to give a signe of their good affection."[2] In September vast crowds turned out to watch fourteen of the conspirators be hanged, disemboweled, and quartered; the first seven of them had this grisly operation performed upon them after being pulled from the gallows still half-alive. The only results achieved by the plotters were to bring about the long-delayed trial and conviction of Mary Queen of Scots during the ensuing winter and to serve as terrible examples to any others who might choose to be "turbulent spirited."

While Elizabeth and her counselors were able to negate the Roman threat with occasional displays of vindictive justice and the enthusiastic cooperation of a large majority of the English people, the established church faced a threat from another direction, that vigorous left wing of the English Reformation which sought to further purify church discipline. During the short reign of Mary Tudor, many reformers were forced into exile on the Continent, and many of them brought

[1] Raphael Holinshed, *Chronicles of England, Scotland, and Ireland* (London, 1808), IV, 891.
[2] Ibid., 898–99.

back from Geneva and Strasbourg advanced ideas concerning the nature of a true, scripturally justified church. Beginning
in the late 1560s, Thomas Cartwright, then Lady Margaret
Professor of Divinity at Cambridge, advocated presbyterian
reform of the episcopal establishment, and after 1583 ever-in-
creasing numbers of reforming ministers, now being derisively
referred to as Puritans, surreptitiously passed around the Latin
manuscript of *The Book of Discipline*, a presbyterian manual
for a new church order.[3] The Tudor Puritans prudently
avoided such extravagances as plots to assassinate the Queen
or to blow up the Parliament; their quarrel with the church
was within the family, so to speak, and not involved with the
treacherous game of international politics. While their more
tactless and vociferous spokesmen might be barred from their
pulpits, they had no martyrs. By the end of Elizabeth's reign,
the establishment had seemingly reduced the cry for further
church reformation to a low murmur of discontent and a
sullen resistance to wearing surplices. As events would very
soon show, however, the Puritan movement begun by Cartwright and the Marian exiles was by no means dead; more
firmly entrenched than ever among the clergy, it had quietly
changed tactics and begun to win the sympathies and loyalties
of the laity by convincing them from the pulpit of the necessity of an inward, personal change in their spiritual lives as
a prerequisite to any further action.

In the latter years of the sixteenth century the new generation being born would be the first to come to maturity after
the external reformation of the English Church had been halted
and the Puritan movement had turned its attention to the problems of the heart. Born Elizabethans, these men and women
would come to discover themselves under the first two of the
Stuart monarchs. In the 1630s they would seek to evade the
heavy hand of Charles I and the corruptions of his imper-

[3] William Haller, *The Rise of Puritanism* (New York, Columbia
Univ. Press, 1938), 10-11.

5

fectly reformed church by taking both their vision of a more nearly perfect religious society and their memories of a happier England to a wilderness continent. Early in July of 1586 one of these men was born in Marfield, a small village in Leicestershire; when he came to manhood, he would become one of the most famous Puritan divines of his day and one of the chief architects of the New England experiment. Thomas Hooker was born the son of another Thomas Hooker, who was apparently an overseer of landed property belonging to the Digby family. Marfield was one of four tithings making up the parish of S⁺. Peter's in Tilton; since the church records before 1610 are no longer extant, and lacking other records, we do not know the exact date of Hooker's birth and baptism, or even the Christian name of his mother. The Hookers appear to have been respected members of the middle class; funeral records in the Tilton church refer to both Hooker's father and his brother, John, as "Mr.," an appellative awarded only to men of some standing. In addition to his brother, Hooker had at least two sisters surviving to marriageable age, one of whom married a Mr. George Alcock and emigrated to New England in 1630. A cousin married "a revolutionist by the name of Pymm," indicating that the whole family was more or less Puritan in its sympathies.[4]

Marfield was no more than a hamlet; a parliamentary return of 1563 listed only six households, out of a total of fifty-one in the whole parish. The focus of social life was a mile and a half away in the village of Tilton with its church atop a hill. A late nineteenth-century visitor admired "the picturesque old church of mottled gray on Tilton hill-top, compassed

[4] George Leon Walker, *Thomas Hooker: Preacher, Founder, Democrat* (New York, Dodd, 1891), 3–4. Walker claims Ann Hooker Pym as Thomas Hooker's sister, but Edward Hooker, "The Origin and Ancestry of Rev. Thomas Hooker," *New England Historical and Genealogical Register*, xlvii (1893), 191, shows otherwise. Edward Hooker finds only two sisters and correctly gives the Christian name of Hooker's brother-in-law as George Alcock.

round by the dead of the different precincts of the parish; the wide prospect of alternating woodland and open fields and spire-surmounted hills toward every compass-point . . . and the little Marfield hamlet embowered in trees down in the valley . . . approached through rustic gates and stiles which the visitor opens or climbs as he descends through the sweet green fields."[5] The pious and sober Hooker family walked every Sunday up the hill to Tilton, and the younger Hookers might well have made the trip again in the afternoon to be catechized by the rector. In the weekdays children might be sent on errands to the village, and almost certainly the Hooker sons went there to learn their ABC's. If there was no schoolmaster in Hooker's day, the rector of the church probably took it upon himself to prepare likely young sons of the parish for admission to a grammar school. By 1614 there was a regular charity school established in Tilton with its own master;[6] this may have been organized too late to benefit Thomas and John Hooker, but it clearly reveals that some men in the village took a serious interest in the minds of the younger generation.

However else he spent his earliest years, Thomas Hooker by the age of eight or so learned to read English prose with facility and to handle pen and ink confidently, if not particularly handsomely. These were the usual requirements for admission to a grammar school, and in addition the infant scholar may have begun learning his Latin accidence. It seems reasonably certain that Thomas Hooker attended and graduated from the grammar school at Market Bosworth, a town nearly twenty-five miles west of his home village. This school had been endowed by Sir Wolstan Dixie, a wealthy merchant who owned property in the area; this school was founded in 1586, the supposed year of Hooker's birth and the year in which Sir Wolstan served as the Lord Mayor of London. Sir Wolstan also

[5] G. L. Walker, *Hooker*, 3.
[6] *The Victoria History of the County of Leicester*, II (London, Oxford Univ. Press, 1954), 243.

established two fellowships at Emmanuel College, Cambridge, which were restricted to his relatives or to graduates of Market Bosworth. Hooker later came to hold one of these, thus giving us our only evidence of where he prepared for the university.

At grammar school Hooker tackled first, appropriately enough, grammar, Latin grammar, learned by heart from the rules laid down in the small, crabbed type of Lily. Latin was the passport to learning, and as soon as practicable became the language of instruction in the grammar school; even conversation between students was to be carried on in Latin, and monitors from the upper form reported breaches of the rule to the master. The first Latin readings were probably from one of the popular editions of colloquies, perhaps Corderius or Castellion; the colloquies were collections of dialogues, usually concerned with student life, although Castellion's presented sacred history. After the colloquies, the student went on to read a goodly amount of the best classical authors: Cicero—especially Cicero—Terence, Virgil, Ovid, Sallust, and Horace were among the most popular. The nearly universal reliance upon the colloquies as a basic pedagogic tool reveals important assumptions behind the education which Hooker received. Learning was a dialectic process between reader and writer, teacher and student, knowledge and ignorance, and the young scholar was implicitly encouraged to conceive of his studies as a training in the art of communicating truth to men.

At about the time Hooker began his first Latin readings, he began developing his Latin prose style. First, perhaps, he might translate some brief text into English and then after a suitable period of time be given the translated version to set back into Latin in order to see how closely he could capture the style of the original. In later years he might be set to writing letters in imitation of Cicero or the composition of themes in accordance with Aphthonius or Erasmus's *De Copia*. The end of all this practice was to produce a student able to write readily and elegantly—elegance being exemplified by Cicero and other select Latin writers—and to organize his thoughts on any subject into the classical patterns defined by Quintilian and, again, Cicero. In addition to this concentrated dose of Latinity, the young Hooker probably would have been introduced in the latter part of his stay at Market Bosworth to Greek, perhaps Hebrew, and almost certainly to the first elements of logic and a bit of mathematics.

School was kept six days a week, beginning at six in the morning and continuing until five or six in the afternoon; there was an hour off in the morning for breakfast and perhaps three for dinner. Discipline was maintained with a firm hand; the traditional image of the schoolmaster always showed him with his birch and rod, and pictures of schoolrooms of the time usually featured these implements in prominent display.[7] There were exceptions to this generalization, of course, but masters who couldn't control their students probably didn't last long, and it seems at least slightly significant that most educational theorists and reformers complained more of masters who used the rod too unsparingly than of those who used it too little. Hooker's master undoubtedly maintained an orderly classroom. Although Hooker always displayed a streak of stubbornness and had a temper he had to learn to control, the tone of his school life was probably not set by the rod and birch, but by the prayers which began and ended the day. Elizabethan grammar schools balanced their study of pagan rhetoricians with solid grounding in the truths of the Christian religion. The first-year students were allowed to relax from their assault upon Lily's Latin grammar by reading the New Testament and Psalms in English. All students were expected to attend Sunday services in the Market Bosworth church and to take careful notes on the sermon. In the succeeding week they were surely examined upon the sermon's content and its meaning, and part of the text might even be given to them in the regular

[7] J. Howard Brown, *Elizabethan Schooldays* (Oxford, Blackwell, 1933), 86, 108.

course of their exercises for translation into Latin. The students took notes of the sermon in order to assist their memories, thus initiating what for some of them would become a lifelong practice. By the end of their school careers the students would be expected to "dite" the rector's sermon completely; when Hooker in his own turn entered the pulpit as a minister, he would hardly be surprised to see pious and studious members of his congregation writing down his words.

The rector in Hooker's time at Market Bosworth, the Reverend William Pelsant, was also one of Sir Wolstan Dixie's first appointees to the school's board of governors, and he might well have taken a close interest in the proceedings of the school. He perhaps visited the school occasionally in term and examined the scholars upon their progress into the mysteries of grammar and rhetoric and their knowledge of the catechism. The master may also have arranged a yearly exhibition of his students' skills in declamation and disputation which the rector surely attended in order to deliver his approbation or criticism. Given some indication of Sir Wolstan's puritanical leanings in his benefactions to Emmanuel, the most notable Puritan college at Cambridge, his decision to erect his school under the protective eye of the Reverend Mr. Pelsant seems to argue that the doctrine preached every Sunday in the Market Bosworth church was solidly protestant in the Calvinist direction and probably of a reforming tendency, but not likely very radical. Hooker boarded in Market Bosworth while the school was in session, and since the minister often took in students for supplemental income, he may very well have lived with Mr. Pelsant during term. If not, he would have lived in town with some family whose reputation and piety were approved by the master, the rector, and the other governors.

After seven or eight years of this regimen Hooker would have been about sixteen years old and fitted for the university. It is not entirely clear that he went to Cambridge immediately after he graduated from his grammar school, however, for he matriculated at Queen's College in 1604, when he would have been almost eighteen, and his residence was given as Birstall, Leicestershire.[8] Hooker's putative age in 1604 unfortunately doesn't tell us much, since his birth year is uncertain, and we have no knowledge of his age when he began grammar school or whether his time there was interrupted in any way. On the other hand, his parents seem to have lived out their lives in Marfield, and we need some reason to explain his arrival at the university from Birstall, a village nearly ten miles from Marfield. A very possible explanation is that he was teaching school there; the older students in the grammar schools were often assigned to instruct the younger, and thus Hooker probably already had some experience in teaching. If the people of Birstall wanted a teacher of reading and writing for their children, they would probably have asked the master of some respected grammar school, like Market Bosworth, to recommend a promising scholar. Richard Mather, the first of the New England Mathers, became a schoolmaster in Lancashire at age seventeen and then went on to the university in a year or two. If Hooker did the same, his probable age upon entrance to the university would be explained; his status as sizar, a student who worked for his keep, might indicate that he would have wanted to set aside a bit of money before going up to Cambridge. Later on in his career Hooker definitely kept a school for a period, and he might well have gained his first experience as a teacher here in his home county.

I I

Thomas Hooker was admitted as a sizar to Queen's College in the Easter term of 1604 on the twenty-seventh of March. At this time Queen's was presided over by Humphrey Tyndall, who had revealed sympathy for the Puritan reform movement and had previously served as chaplain to the Earl of

[8] John Venn and John Archibald Venn, *Alumni Cantabrigienses*, Part 1 (Cambridge, The Univ. Press, 1922), II, 403.

Leicester. Tyndall's county connections and his reformist sympathies might in some way explain Hooker's initial attraction to Queen's but within a very few months Hooker migrated to Emmanuel College, where he was to spend his next twelve years. Emmanuel, established in 1584 by Sir Walter Mildmay, had already acquired a considerable reputation for puritanism. Its chapel was not consecrated and uncanonically stood north and south rather than facing eastward toward Jerusalem (and Rome!); unsurpliced clergy held services and conducted notorious communion ceremonies with participants sitting around a table. Nearly a third of the Cambridge men who eventually emigrated to New England came from this college alone, and its head, Lawrence Chaderton, was one of the divines who had pleaded the reformers' cause before the King earlier in the year at the Hampton Court Conference. This conference had been a serious blow to the hopes of the Puritans, some of whom had speculated that James might be more tolerant than Elizabeth of Genevan-style reforms in the English Church. After his experiences with presbyterianism in Scotland, however, James had determined to resist anything of the kind in England. The future for young Cambridge Puritans seemed unpromising after their hopes had been foiled by the Hampton Court Conference. James was obviously not going to permit any change in the English Church at large, and the university felt his policy as Valentine Cary purged Christ's College of its Puritan fellows. Cary's actions must have posed a warning for many godly young men. Chaderton, fortunately for Emmanuel, was a good friend of George Bancroft's, and his college enjoyed a certain amount of ecclesiastical protection. Hooker's enrollment at Emmanuel was simply part of a steady influx of undergraduates, and during his time at the university, Emmanuel enjoyed one of the largest undergraduate enrollments of all the colleges.

In his first year at the university, Hooker would have been directed by his tutor to spend much of his time on the study of rhetoric. Rhetorical studies were in some ways a continuation of the grammar school effort to develop a flexible and elegant Latin style. More attention was paid at the university level to rhetorical theory, and the student was expected to widen vastly his knowledge of the classical writers. University instruction was delivered only in Latin, and the various academic exercises which the students were to perform as the essential parts of their university education were also done in Latin. Hooker continued his readings in the classics under his tutor's direction, culling the pages of the ancients for passages of either exceptional grace or matter which might later be bent to his own purposes. The tutor undoubtedly advised him to keep a commonplace book in which to write down these notable fragments; later in the century a master of Emmanuel recommended to his students, "You will meet with many choice and witty sayings, sentences and passages which you are to gather into your paper books."[9] Hooker learned early the value of a well-kept notebook to a scholar and orator; when we read through his published works, we discover that he had favorite "witty sayings, sentences and passages" in the vernacular which he used again and again to bring home his point to audiences of sinners. This was exactly the purpose of the traditional study of rhetoric which he began at the university. In the traditional scholastic sense, rhetoric was the art of persuasion in speech or writing, addressing itself to a popular auditory; in the newer, reformed versions of rhetoric made by Peter Ramus and his followers, rhetoric was the art of speaking well. In both senses, rhetoric was the art by which a speaker reached the individual hearts of his auditors, and one chief end of education was to bring a student to mastery of this art of persuasion.

In his second year Hooker probably began an intensive

[9] Richard Holdsworth, quoted by William T. Costello, S.J., *The Scholastic Curriculum at Early Seventeenth-Century Cambridge* (Cambridge, Mass., Harvard Univ. Press, 1958), 56.

study of logic. Medieval and Renaissance logicians, when distinguishing between logic and rhetoric, were fond of using a traditional metaphor as an example; as Thomas Wilson, the author of the first logic in English, had it, "Zeno beyng asked the difference betwene Logique and Rhetorique, made answere by demonstration of his Hande, declaring that when his hande was closed, it resembled Logique, when it was open and stretched out, it was like Rhetorique."[10] The logic Hooker learned at Cambridge and used in his later sermons and polemics was the reformed science of Peter Ramus, although he was probably also acquainted with the scholastic logic it had displaced. Ramus claimed to have rejected the tortuous mazes of scholastic logic in favor of a more simplified, diagrammatic articulation of dialectic which was supposedly based upon the true meaning of Aristotle's *Organon*. Logic, speaking with the "clunched fist," was the art of disputing well, according to Ramus, and following his stated concern for the usefulness of the arts, he intended to lay out a practical system of dialectic comprehensible to nonscholarly as well as to scholarly minds.

Logic was central to Ramus's treatment of the arts, and in placing this emphasis, he followed the scholastics who had held with Peter of Spain that dialectic was the "art of arts and science of sciences, having the way to the principles of all methods."[11] Dialectic was the backbone of any rhetorical statement because it presented a system of forming and arranging arguments, thus producing a skeletal statement which rhetoric could ornament and make pleasing. One "invented," or discovered, one's arguments, judged their truth or suitability, and disposed them by method, arranging the most general positions first and moving to the most particular. Just as rhetoric persuaded like the stroking palm, so dialectic func-

[10] Quoted by Wilbur Samuel Howell, *Logic and Rhetoric in England, 1500–1700* (Princeton, Princeton Univ. Press, 1956), 14–15.
[11] Quoted by Neal W. Gilbert, *Renaissance Concepts of Method* (New York, Columbia Univ. Press, 1960), 57.

tioned in discourse by hammering the truth home to men's minds. His study of rhetoric taught Hooker how to make his arguments pleasing to the human affections, and his study of logic showed him how to dispose them methodically in order to convince effectually the fractious intellect. Hooker's sermons were delivered to popular audiences, but just beneath the persuasive rhetoric was always a logical core contributing its power to the charm of the tropes and figures. In a few treatises intended for a select readership such as his *Survey of the Summe of Church Discipline* he exercised the "clunched fist" alone with no concealing rhetorical art. These undergraduate lessons remained with him to the end of his career, and it is impossible to understand his influence over his contemporaries without recognizing the informing power of the rhetorical and dialectical arts.

This emphasis on two of the seven medieval liberal arts was preparation for the scholarly exercises which would have been expected of Hooker as an undergraduate. From the beginning of his career at Cambridge, he probably spent at least two afternoons a week composing and polishing rhetorical exercises for his tutor. These compositions would probably have been on topics suggested by his reading, such as "Priam's troubles exceeded his good fortune," or "Was C. J. Caesar justly put to death?"[12] He would be called upon to write declamations for his tutor, for delivery in the college hall, and perhaps also in the university schools. The education he received in early seventeenth-century Cambridge was above all theoretical, but it was never divorced from practical ends. The theories of logic and rhetoric flowered in the declamation delivered before a critical audience of students and fellows, thus giving the young sophister both a sense of self-possession and practice in writing for the ear, two requisites for the future pulpit speaker. The declamation was in its way the final pedagogic instrument to

[12] Quoted by Costello, 59.

teach smoothness, clarity, and force of style. When he had thoroughly mastered the art of logic, Hooker would have performed in disputations with his schoolmates. These were far beyond the simple acts performed in grammar school over points of grammar; university disputations consisted of lengthy set-tos between an answerer and an opponent which continued until one party had syllogized the other to a standstill. These formal disputations trained the students in close reasoning and the ability to develop their ideas with clarity and conviction.[13]

After the student had attained the necessary skill in the principles of communicating his ideas, he would turn his attention more fully to the sciences, particularly metaphysics, where he would discover matter about which to have ideas. The undergraduate sciences were three, metaphysics, physics, and mathematics, and in the traditional scholastic version of them still in force at Cambridge they were linked in this order. Metaphysics was the study of being *qua* being and its transcendental principles; physics concerned itself with the qualities of extended, changeable being; and, of least importance to most students and teachers of the early seventeenth century, mathematics studied extended being merely as quantified.

Metaphysics, the study of first principles, was most important to the undergraduate, and particularly so for the young scholar who wished to study theology after the B.A., for metaphysics was a companion discipline to that queen of sciences. The first object of both metaphysics and theology was the deity, but in the former science God was considered by human reason alone, as an *ens necessarium* merely, and in the latter his nature was considered as it was revealed to man in Scripture. Thomas Hooker probably mastered the complexities of potency and act, the four cases, the ten categories of traditional metaphysics as developed by generations of scholastic thinkers. We see little direct evidence of this study in his

[13] See Costello, 146–47; also James Bass Mullinger, *Cambridge Characteristics in the Seventeenth Century* (London, Macmillan, 1867), 25–75.

works, however, mostly because of the incredible intricacy of the system which could have only hopelessly confused his lay audiences. The humanist reforms of the Cambridge curriculum had preserved Aristotle—even Ramus was ultimately unable to do without the master of them that know—but they had rejected the scholastic commentaries and refinements upon Aristotle as irrelevant both to the original text and to practical life. Hooker certainly mastered what was passed off as metaphysical discipline, and in common with most educated men of early seventeenth-century England, he understood the philosophic proofs for the great chain of being. The most important fact about his metaphysical training was simply that it was there; he would never be tempted to discuss the spiritual realities of revelation separately from the intellectual realities of the creation.

The two other sciences were of less importance, although some parts of his study of physics were clearly of great use to him in later life. The physics of the time was rather a mixed bag, including in its realm, as William T. Costello put it, "legitimate philosophical speculation, excellent scientific observation, some quaint guess-work, not a little superstition, a bit of quackery, and much good intention in a sort of academic Czechoslovakia."[14] What must have particularly interested Hooker was the section of physics which discussed psychology. He would have learned how the rational soul of man operates through its faculties of understanding, memory, and will, and the ways in which these faculties act with each other. Of all his undergraduate studies in the sciences, this knowledge of psychology would perhaps be most useful when he came to his theological studies, for it gave him a working model of the rational soul which was transformed in the religious experience. As a part of his study in physics he would also have learned a bit about physic, the science of medicine; his sermons evince a knowledge of the physician's skills, and

[14] Costello, 83.

as a minister in a frontier town in New England, he occasionally treated his parishioners' bodies as well as their souls.[15]

Hooker received his B.A. in 1608 and in 1609 became a Dixie fellow in Emmanuel. As he entered upon his graduate career, his attention turned to theology, and by becoming a fellow, he began to take an active role in the religious life of his college. Before he left Emmanuel in 1618, he served as lecturer and catechist, and it was in the college hall that he first began expounding his favorite topics of divinity. After three years spent in the study of theology and further researches in the sciences, he acquired his M.A. in 1611, and a year or two thereafter he began to experience the most important event of his entire life, his conversion. His effectual calling and implantation into Christ, as he later referred to it, determined the whole tenor of his career, for, as he felt, it initiated the genuine possibilities of life in him. His life to date had been the consequence of his birth in Marfield; his activities from about 1613 on would be the result of his new birth into grace, transporting him beyond the Kingdom of England into the Kingdom of Christ.

III

When Sir Walter Mildmay had founded Emmanuel, he ordered one of its statutes to correct an abuse all too common in Cambridge, the turning of fellowships into snug sinecures for life. "We would not have any fellow suppose that we have given him, in this college, a perpetual abode," said Sir Walter. "We have founded the college with the design that it should be, by the grace of God, a seminary of learned men for the supply of the Church, and for the sending forth of as large a number as possible of those who shall instruct the people

---

[15] On Hooker's medical knowledge, see Richard Condon, "Thomas Hooker and the Angelical Conjunction," MSS in Congregational Library, Boston.

in the Christian faith."[16] While the production of a learned clergy had been one of the university's chief functions from its beginnings, this was the first explicit dedication of a college toward training preachers of the gospel. As early as his migration to Emmanuel in the first year of his studies, Hooker must have made some sort of choice about his eventual career. When he began his graduate studies in theology, he had definitely committed himself to a life in the pulpit, but the responsibilities entailed in that decision only became clear to him a few years later.

His home life, his education, and his natural propensities must have directed him toward the religious life and led him to consider piety the most important human virtue and activity. To choose the ministry as a career would be easy enough under these circumstances, but when he came to ask himself if Christ had truly chosen him for the ministry, the whole ground of his life must have been shaken, for this question would have inevitably led to the ultimate uncertainty, "Am I saved?" As he read more deeply into reformed theology, and as he observed the behavior of the men about him whom he most respected, his understanding of the nature of true piety was deepened. The religious doctrines which he had heard preached and had studied most seriously from his youth on would have been basically of a Calvinist or Augustinian orientation, but in the years of his Emmanuel fellowship he came to realize the full extent of their meaning. The faith which saved man was not a simple faith of the understanding, an acceptance of the historical truth of the gospel, but an experimental faith, resulting from the divine gift of saving grace, and renewing the will as well as the understanding. This he would have learned from reading Calvin, Bullinger, Peter Martyr—all the great names of the Genevan wing of the Reforma-

[16] James Bass Mullinger, *The University of Cambridge from the Royal Injunction of 1535 to the Accession of Charles the First* (Cambridge, The University Press, 1884), 314–15.

tion—and, closer to home, from the works of William Perkins, the English divine most respected by men of Puritan persuasion, from the discourses of Lawrence Chaderton, from the sermons and writings of men like William Ames and Paul Baynes.

In his vacations at his home in Leicestershire, he might well have journeyed the thirty miles or so to Ashby-de-la-Zouch, where one of England's most famous Puritans held forth. Arthur Hildersam had been active in presenting the Millenary Petition, which led to the conference at Hampton Court; from 1605 onward he was in constant trouble with the bishops because of his reforming views, and he was a respected figure to whom concerned young men often went for spiritual counsel. Hildersam was actively preaching from 1609 to 1613, between suspensions, so to speak, and Hooker might have heard him deliver some of his famous lectures on the fourth chapter of the gospel of John. Interestingly enough, for one of his own last major books, Hooker would choose his text from the fourth of John, perhaps realizing for himself the vision of spiritual bliss which must have seemed so distant in these years at Cambridge. William Perkins had died two years before Hooker came up to Cambridge, but his memory and influence were a powerful stimulus for students and fellows committed to the idea of reformed men in a reformed church. If and when Hooker read Perkins' treatise *Of the Calling of the Ministry*, this statement must have caught his attention:

> . . . we live as it were in a Seminary, and many of us are hereafter by Gods grace to be framed to the Ministry, as some of us already are. Now here we have many occasions to be puft up in self-conceit: we see ourselves growe in time, in degrees, in learning, in honour, in name and estimation: and to many of us God gives good portions of his gifts: What are all these, but so many baites to allure us to pride, and vaine opinions of our owne worths?[17]

[17] William Perkins, *Of the Calling of the Ministry* (London, 1606), 16–17.

A minister, Perkins said, was obliged to preach the Gospel with power, and "a powerfull ministry appeareth in this," Hooker himself noted years later, "when there is a kind of spirituall heat in the heart, when there are holy affections, and the heart of the minister is answerable to that he communicates and delivers unto the people."[18] Once Hooker had made the decision to enter the ministry, the nature of his own heart would have become particularly crucial to him. The question, "Am I certain of my salvation?" once asked, initiated a period of terrible doubts and anxieties.

The exact circumstances of Hooker's conversion are unknown, but by some means, as Cotton Mather recorded, "It pleased the *spirit* of God very powerfully to break into the soul of this person, with a sense of his being exposed unto the just *wrath* of Heaven, as filled him with most unusual degrees of horror, and anguish, which broke not only his *rest*, but his *heart* also, and caused him to cry out, "While I suffer thy terrors, O Lord, I am distracted!"[19] The type of Christian conversion was that of Paul in Acts, being violently struck out of the course of worldly life by a divine thunderbolt, but, as many Reformation divines observed, the usual experience of regeneration was rarely so instantaneous as Paul's. Hooker's own conversion seems not only to have been accompanied by a great deal of spiritual and mental anguish but to have taken considerable time to work out. According to Mather, "He afterwards gave his account of himself, 'That in the time of his agonies, he could reason himself to the rule, and conclude that there was no way but submission to God, and lying at the foot of his mercy in Christ Jesus, and waiting humbly there, till he should please to perswade the soul of his favour: nevertheless when he came to apply this rule unto himself in his own condition, his reasoning would fail him, he was

[18] Thomas Hooker, *The Soules Implantation into the Naturall Olive* (London 1640), 76.

[19] Cotton Mather, *Magnalia Christi Americana* (1852; rpt., New York, Russell and Russell, 1967), I, 333.

able to do nothing.'[20] The failure of his reason to help him in his predicament would only have confirmed his awareness of his unregenerate will at this time. When Christ did choose to persuade Hooker's soul of His favor, He would recreate the fallen will, thus giving his reason a solid basis to operate on.

In the course of this trial of his heart, Hooker must have gone on many long, lonely, meditative walks in the lanes and fields outside of Cambridge, leaving behind the distractions of the town "to retire under hedges and other secret places, there to lament his misery before God," as Richard Mather was doing elsewhere at almost the same time.[21] Certainly, meditation became one of the most important helps Hooker recommended to men seeking assurance of their salvation, and he later warned, "There is no casting up of account in a crowd; but if a man will cast up his account, if hee will see his sinnes, and consider his base practices, hee must goe aside by himselfe; loose occasions and vaine occasions withdraw the minde, and plucke off the soule from seeing the evill, and affecting the heart with it."[22] In addition to casting up the account of his sins, he meditated on those many hopeful verses of Scripture which he later came to refer to as the promises. These were the various statements, most often taken directly from Christ in one of the Gospels, which explicitly held out to men the pos-

[20] Ibid. Unless otherwise noted, Mather in these notes is always Cotton Mather, and the work is always the *Magnalia*.

[21] Increase Mather, *The Life and Death of That Reverend Man of God, Mr. Richard Mather*, Collections of the Dorchester Antiquarian and Historical Society, No. 3 (Boston, 1850), 48.

[22] Hooker, *The Soules Preparation for Christ* (London, 1632), 92. This quotation is from the text in the Houghton Library at Harvard. Although the Houghton copy has a title page identical with the copy contained in the University Microfilms series of English texts before 1640, it is from an entirely different typesetting. It has different pagination and a list of errata which have been corrected in the microfilmed version. The Houghton version is not distinguished in Pollard and Redgrave. I have quoted from the microfilmed version as more universally available, except here, where this particular comment is dropped from the later printing.

sibility of salvation. "When we are going to the Land of Canaan," Hooker would later say, "the promise of grace and mercy is the staffe which wee leane upon."[23] Frequently in his mature sermons, after holding out to men the terrible consequences of their sins, he would offer them this staff of grace and mercy, thus giving many of his writings an unusually hopeful tone when compared to those of some of his colleagues. His frequent depiction of Christ's offer of mercy to fallen men would lead to charges of being somewhat less than orthodox when he found himself entangled in New England's first heresy trial years later.

Twentieth-century men can scarcely understand the intense, radical, spiritual experiences which Hooker and many of his Puritan colleagues underwent. Even they were hard put to explain exactly what happened in the process of regeneration, but it was real enough for all that. This restructuring of experience, willed by a human will that could not will, was the most profound fact of Hooker's life. His later attempts to explain what had happened to him became the sermons he preached to audiences for whom, he hoped, the same experience was happening or about to happen. The experience of conversion was a means of resolving an untenable situation produced by the central paradox of Calvinist theology: how could a man seek salvation when he knew that his efforts could not possibly save him, and at the same time realize that not to seek salvation was to risk eternal damnation in the pains of a vividly imagined hell? Caught in this bind, Hooker first came to recognize the utter inability of his soul, as he then understood it, to do anything other than sin. Having undercut all confidence in the ability of the ego to sustain spiritual life, he became aware of the cosmic scheme of divine power and majesty of which he was such an infinitesimal part. He later came to state that a soul truly humbled would be content to

---

[23] Hooker, *The Soules Vocation or Effectual Calling to Christ* (London, 1638), 303.

accept damnation for the glory of God; the human mind can go no further in imagining its own insignificance in the world which it inhabits. Being thus emptied of self-esteem, he experienced the mysterious presence of an inhuman power, a divine power which could call him out of a meaningless life and save him from himself. Once he had genuinely experienced his faith in this manner, he was able to draw upon it as a principle of life, for it authenticated his actions, and the rest of his career was spent in transforming himself upon the basis of this experience.

This is a somewhat secularized description of Hooker's discovery of grace within himself, and, as such, it reveals an inner identity between Hooker's experience and other men's experiences of a conversionary nature.[24] It is important, however, that Hooker's was a specifically Christian conversion, an experience restrained and directed by a formidable body of dogma and tradition. Conversion understood as a psychological phenomenon is a raw fact and can include experiences as diverse as brainwashing or a chemically induced hallucinatory episode. This raw fact is essential for understanding the pattern of a person's life, but the specific pattern of a man's life is knowable only in relation to the context of this critical event. Hooker came to understand his conversion not in secular terms but as a theologically defined process of the soul's moving and being moved through steps of preparation, humiliation, vocation, and adoption. In succeeding chapters we shall examine the significance of his particular description of his experiences and the importance of the Christian context.

Hooker's conversion was the climax of his years at the university; it confirmed him in his choice of a vocation, for he was assured that he had been called to the pulpit by Christ. His experience was apparently so intense, so difficult, that he was never able to shake the memory of it, and the work of his

---

[24] The ultimate secularization, perhaps a foolish one, is demonstrated in R. D. Laing's *Politics of Experience* (New York, Ballantine, 1967).

pastoral career is marked by a tender consideration for the spirits of men and women undergoing like experiences. During his time of trial, he had been sustained by "the prudent and piteous carriage of Mr. Ash, who was the Sizer that then waited upon him; and attended him with such discreet and proper compassions, as made him afterwards to respect him highly all his days."[25] This sizar, Simeon Ashe, was himself a godly young man and followed Hooker to the pulpit; once when Ashe was to preach to an audience which included Hooker, the older man is said to have encouraged him, "Sim, let itt bee hot."[26] Emmanuel was an especially suitable location in which to be converted because the presence of men like Ashe provided the comfort for an anguished soul that only a holy community could offer. The lesson implicitly taught by Simeon Ashe was one Hooker never forgot, and his actions as a minister were guided by the awareness that, in addition to being a humble tool used by God to convey His Word, he was a man able to give a uniquely human compassion and encouragement to his parishioners.

I V

Hooker's conversion seems to have been marked by no radically new pattern of external behavior—John Cotton, fresh from his experience, stunned the university community by suddenly changing the very style of his sermons—but he must have discovered a new significance and purpose in his duties as a catechist. After 1615 Hooker had probably begun to feel some assurance that he had been saved, and he would be able to face the prospect of embarking upon a pastoral career with some equanimity. Furthermore, the situation for Puritan preachers and fellows in the university was beginning to look bleak as

[25] Mather, I, 333.
[26] Raymond Phineas Stearns, *The Strenuous Puritan: Hugh Peter, 1598–1660* (Urbana, Univ. of Illinois Press, 1954), 5.

the second decade of the seventeenth century wore on. In 1610, William Ames, one of the most promising and most radical of the fellows, was driven out of the university for demanding in imprudently harsh terms a reform of student morality. The case of Ames was only the most notable example of an implicit program of harassment aimed at those who would criticize the established church or the established political order. Ames was shortly after forced to flee to the Netherlands where he became a professor of theology in the university at Franeker.

Emmanuel and Sidney Colleges provided havens for young men who wished to further the reform of the English Church, but even these havens were under attack later in the decade. The distance between Emmanuel and the rest of the colleges was all too obvious when James I paid his first visit to Cambridge in 1615. There were great preparations made for the royal visit, including refurbishing and decorating the exteriors of the colleges:

> But the pure House of Emmanuel
> Would not be like proud Jesabel,
> Nor show herself before the King
> An hypocrite or painted thing
> But that the ways might all prove fair
> Conceived a tedious mile of prayer.[27]

This stiff-necked refusal to flatter the King did not make life easier for the residents of the notably Puritan colleges. In the years to come the Crown began increasingly to exert its authority over the universities, and Emmanuel was among the first to feel royal and episcopal displeasure at its dissenting ways. Overt resistance was impossible; any good Englishman would know from reading Foxe's *Acts and Monuments* that in days past the tortures imposed upon the Catholic recusants of the 1580s had been used to make protestant martyrs. The King

[27] Quoted by Mullinger, *University of Cambridge*, 517.

had not yet resorted to the gallows, but prolonged residence in a Jacobean prison could be equally fatal.

As conditions in the university became less promising, Hooker would have begun to think about obtaining a place in the larger world beyond Cambridge. He had been at Emmanuel for over thirteen years, and he must have felt the justice of the founder's desire that the fellows meet their serious obligation to become missionaries to the English. In 1618, having completed his formal initiation into the arts and sciences and having discovered empirical evidence for his calling, Thomas Hooker was ready to become "one of those who shall instruct the people in the Christian faith."

TWO

Pastoral Beginnings

In 1618 the village of Esher in county Surrey was a quiet, rural backwater; surrounding manorial estates prevented its further growth and kept it off the main thoroughfares even though it was situated near London. One of these estates, Esher Place, sheltered Cardinal Wolsey after his disgrace, and another was occupied at a later date by Lord Clive, the founder of Britain's Indian empire. At the end of the nineteenth century Esher's picturesque qualities were still apparent, and the old parish church of St. George's was still standing, although no longer used for worship. An American visitor of the time described the building: "It is very small, with a nave and chancel only. . . . The glass of the chancel windows is said once to have been fine, but no vestige of its former glories remains. At the west end the nave is surmounted by a low pyramidal tower in which formerly hung three bells, one of which was understood to be a war-trophy brought by Sir Francis Drake from St. Domingo."[1] The origin of this bell remains uncertain, but one reason for this attribution may be that in the early seventeenth century a prominent resident of the parish was a Mr. Francis Drake, a distant kinsman of the captain of the Golden Hind. But more important for the career of Thomas Hooker, he held the privilege of choosing the rector.

A donative living such as this was one of three possible havens for a ministerial candidate inclined toward puritanism, the other two being a privately endowed lectureship or a position as a family chaplain. Donors of these livings were not required to present their appointees to the bishop, and many a

[1] G. L. Walker, *Hooker*, 35.

promising young man from Cambridge was willing to escape the notice of an ecclesiastical superior. Bishops often asked awkward questions about matters such as the surplice and the liturgy, and they sometimes discovered all too quickly which pastors in their dioceses were not satisfied with the established course of the church. After William Laud came to power, he submitted to King Charles lists of clerical names with symbols after each name indicating the man's orthodoxy or his puritanism. It was difficult for a man to be admitted into a better living or to retain his current one if the wrong symbol followed his name. Often the best thing a graduate of Emmanuel College could hope for was obscurity.

The living of Esher was small but comfortable; in 1618 it was worth forty pounds, and about that time Mr. Drake offered it to Thomas Hooker. His motive for appointing Hooker was rooted not so much in his preference for a godly and powerful ministry as it was in concern for his wife. Mrs. Joanna Drake was a religious melancholiac with suicidal tendencies, and she required a great deal of care. The congregation of the Esher church was apparently very small, as the size of the building attests, and the rector would be able to spend a large part of his time counseling Mrs. Drake. To facilitate this intensive exercise of pastoral care, Mr. Drake invited Hooker to live as a member of his household. Since Hooker's experiences at Esher were in many ways essential in confirming his future pastoral thought and practice, as well as the only extended example of his practice of the cure of souls, we are fortunate to know a fair amount about Mrs. Drake's problems and about the passages between her and her religious advisers. A certain Jasper Hartwell published an account of her life based upon his own observations and his direct knowledge of the members of her family. His little book is almost forgotten, but it is notable among seventeenth-century biographies for the psychological perception shown by its author.

Joanna Tothill was the only child of a well-to-do civil servant; her father was one of the six clerks of chancery, and he maintained an estate at Amersham in Buckinghamshire. She was spoiled by her parents, "whose too great indulgence towards her in her youth (by her own confession) occasioned so much sorrow unto her in riper years."[2] Her religious training was inadequate from the viewpoint of a Puritan minister, but "though then shee were unacquainted with the power of godlinesse, yet had shee it in admiration, where she saw it shine forth." In accordance with a custom still common in the seventeenth century, her parents had arranged her marriage with Mr. Drake, but their choice of a husband for her was possibly not so well made as it should have been. Mr. Drake was most eligible economically and apparently a well-intentioned and decent man, but he was, unfortunately, a man "whom at first shee could not affect, so as she was married against her will . . . wherein though shee were obedient and dutifull unto her Parents; yet it stuck close unto her."[3] She tried to make the best of the unpleasant situation that her father had created for her, and she succeeded for almost ten years in living with it.

Affairs took a turn for the worse with the birth of her first daughter (she had already had two sons), for "in that delivery being very much wronged by her Midwiffe, she was ever after troubled with fumes and scurvie vapors mounting up into her head, . . . which no physick could remove." Her parents came down to Esher to attend her in her illness, and her mother slept in the same bed with her. This evidence of maternal love seemingly came too late, for one evening, "in the first part of

[2] Jasper Hartwell, *The Firebrand Taken out of the Fire. Or, the Wonderfull History, Case, and Cure of Mis Drake* (London, 1654), 6. This book has traditionally been ascribed to John Hart, but I follow George H. Williams' convincing argument which identifies the author as Hartwell. See "Called By Thy Name, Leave us Not: The Case of Mrs. Joan Drake, a Formative Episode in the Pastoral Career of Thomas Hooker in England," *Harvard Library Bulletin* 16 (1968), 111–28, 278–300.

[3] Hartwell, 8; 9–10.

the night," Mrs. Drake woke up, screaming that "shee was undone, undone, shee was damned, and a cast away, and so of
necessity must need goe to Hell, and therewith shook, dropt
down with sweat, and wept exceedingly." Mrs. Tothill prayed
with her daughter, calmed her, and soothed her back to sleep,
but she was again awakened, this time with an account of a
glorious angel bearing assurance of salvation. Again, prayers
and soothings followed, and again Mrs. Drake slept. Then
toward morning the convincing vision came; and she once
more awoke in terror: "Now shee was a forelorne creature,
being assuredly damned; . . . with shricks and loud Cryes, the
bed shaking, yea, the whole chamber seeming to rock and
reele."[4]

From the effects of this last hysterical vision Mrs. Drake
was never fully to recover. She was now "far from her former naturall constitution," for she made "strange desperate
speeches," and "had an unruly carriage." All the locks were
removed from the doors, and she was carefully watched by the
family and servants. She swallowed pins, attempted to steal
knives from the table, and furtively gorged herself on oranges,
forbidden to her by attending physicians, but "they proved
excellent medecines unto her." Guilty of not loving her husband, she manufactured both justifications for herself and
further motives for guilt by provoking everyone around her.
When her husband brought down a famous minister from London to counsel her, she saw them coming and barricaded herself in her chamber. "Whereupon her Husband took the great
iron fork" from the fireplace, "and run up after her, threatening to beat down the door if she would not open it." Since she
was now convinced of her eternal damnation, she would neither
pray "nor ever goe to Church againe." She was certain that
"in all her actions shee but heapt up wrath against the day of
wrath to her further condemnation; and that in that shee could

4 Hartwell, 10–11; 12; 13–14.

not grieve, nor be sorrowfull for that wofull estate shee was now in, this shew the desparatenesse thereof."[5]

Doctors and their physic gave her no relief—indeed, to survive a course of seventeenth-century medication was a sign of remarkable health—so ministers were called in to attempt a different sort of cure. Use of ministerial counsel in cases such as this was not unprecedented, for it was possible that Mrs. Drake's melancholy was of spiritual rather than of physical origin. The usual Galenic theory of melancholy as a disease was that defects of the body hindered the natural working of the mind, but countering this was the traditional Christian theory, ultimately stemming from Plato, that held melancholy vapors to be an effect and not the cause of intellectual disorder. William Perkins had advised the prospective young ministers of Cambridge, "Some thinke that all trouble of mind is nothing but *melancholy*, and therefore thinke nothing needes but Phisicke and outwarde comforts, but he that considers in what case the *Prophet* [Job] heere was, . . . will be of another mind, and will find that nothing can *properly* trouble the *mind* but sinne."[6] If God chose to afflict a conscience for sin, melancholy could arise as a physical disorder whose real cause was not a natural malfunction of the body but a malfunction of the soul:

> Conscience terrified, is of such nature, so beset with infinite feares and distrust, that it easilie wasteth the pure spirit, congeleth the lively bloud, and striketh our nature in such sort, that it soone becommeth melancholicke, vile and base, and turneth reason into foolishnesse, and disgraceth the beautie of the countenance, and transformeth the stoutest Nabucadnezar in the world into a brute beast.[7]

Timothy Bright, one of the various Elizabethan commentators on the subject, wrote his *Treatise of Melancholie* to counsel

<hr>

[5] Hartwell, 44; 31; 22; 23–24.   [6] Perkins, *Calling*, 36.
[7] Timothy Bright, *A Treatise of Melancholie*, ed. Hardin Craig (1586; facsimile rpt., New York, Facsimile Text Society, 1940), 195.

a friend whose condition was similar to, but not so far gone as, Mrs. Drake's, "mixed of the melancholicke humour and that terror of God."[8] Melancholy presented an "opportunity Sathan embraceth to urge all terror against you to the fall," and the cure for this affliction of mind and soul was not to be found in "philosophical and humaine preceptes, and consideration of naturall causes, and eventes," but in persuading the patient to lean "upon the maine pillar of God's promises, of mercy and grace, and waight with patience the appointed time of his release."[9] Mrs. Drake's care was not to be obtained from a physician but from another sort of healer, a godly minister for whom the care of souls was a traditional pastoral responsibility.

The ministers who attempted to counsel with her were sure that Satan had taken a hand in the business, for Mrs. Drake refused to hear them, derided their efforts, and scornfully sent them away. Her husband was finally advised to consult with the Reverend John Dod, rector of Canon's Ashby in Northamptonshire, and one of the most respected Puritan leaders in England. Dod agreed to come to Esher, and he was apparently more clever in dealing with her than the previous ministers had been. Although he found that "the Devill's rhetorike taught her against herself," he began to meet with some success by treating her gently and lovingly. Mrs. Drake seemed to need a constant reinforcement of her self-esteem, and Dod discovered that "giving her good words, using much meeknesse, affability and service unto her, even in her most untoward crosse carriages, . . . got much ground upon her spirit, and brought her to doe many things which no harsh crossenesse could possibly effect with her."[10]

Dod persuaded her to give over her suicidal attempts, to sit quietly while others prayed for her, and to join in group prayers, but even so the "Devill's rhetorike" grew more forceful.

---

[8] Bright, 191.
[9] Bright, 192, sig. *6ʳ.
[10] Hartwell, 22; 38.

She was stubbornly argumentative; she now accused herself of "that great unpardonable sinne against the holy Ghost,"[11] and she occasionally relapsed into mocking Dod's efforts on her behalf. Dod was more than seventy years old at this time, and, although he was a spry old man who lived to be ninety-five, the travel down to Surrey must have been almost as exhausting as arguing with Mrs. Drake. About the year 1618 he seems to have told her husband that he would be unable to continue as her counselor, but he remained interested in her spiritual progress until her death.

Mr. Drake learned upon inquiry that Thomas Hooker was "a great Scholar, an acute Disputant, a strong learned, a wise modest man, every way rarely qualified."[12] His abilities as an acute disputant were deemed especially important, for, as Mrs. Drake's behavior became externally more regular, the "Devill's rhetorike" appeared more frequently in her discourse, and she became more controversial and stubborn in her theological quibbles. The solution seemed to be to call in a more convincing advocate of God, one who could answer her objections once and for all. What none of her previous counselors, except perhaps Dod, seem to have recognized was that Mrs. Drake thrived on argument; a new opponent only caused her to go back over all her objections of the last few years:

> For now having a fit person to rough hew her (as it were) whom shee could neither weary nor overcome in Argument, but was able to discerne and catch Satan in all his Sophismes, there every way fell out strong disputes betwixt them; But all within the compasse of those former things wherein Mr. *Dod* before had convinced her; Satan delighting to raise new uprores in her.[13]

The "new uprores" were obviously not all of infernal origin, for to be taken seriously in the course of debate by men like

[11] Hartwell, 41.   [12] Hartwell, 117.
[13] Hartwell, 120.

Hooker and Dod went a long way toward reassuring her that she was indeed loved and respected despite the seeming callousness of husband and parents.

But the appeal of her new spiritual adviser consisted in more than just his willingness to deal with her intelligently and kindly:

> For Mr. *Hooker* being newly come from the University had a new answering methode (though the same things) wherewith shee was mervellously delighted. And being very covetous of knowledge, was pleased with new disputes and objections to fasten further upon her selfe those forementioned things [her convictions of her own damnation].[14]

The key to Hooker's eventual success seems to lie in this ambiguously described "new answering methode." This intriguing phrase probably refers to Hooker's training in the new Ramist logic and rhetoric which purported to cover the same material as the more complex scholastic arts. Ramist logic was intended to be of practical use, and in dealing with Mrs. Drake, Hooker would have been able to apply it to the practical business of pastoral care. This phrase may also refer, however, to Hooker's training in the casuistical divinity of William Perkins and William Ames. While the study of cases of conscience was a traditional part of Catholic theology, it was first thoroughly pursued in Reformation England by Perkins; Ames in the preface to his own casuistical text recalled "the time, when being young, I heard worthy Master Perkins, to preach in a great Assembly of Students, . . . How with the tongue of the Learned, one might speake a word in due season to him that is weary . . . by untying and explaining diligently Cases of Conscience." Along with Ames, Perkins "left many behind him affected with that study."[15] Casuistical divinity was usually

---

[14] Ibid.

[15] William Ames, *Conscience with the Power and Cases Thereof*, in *The Workes of the Reverend and Faithfull Minister of Christ William Ames* (London, 1643), sig. A4ᵛ.

defined as the resolution of ethical dilemmas, but, since "the Conscience of man . . . is a mans judgement of him selfe according to the judgement of God of him,"[16] Hooker's problem with Mrs. Drake was both casuistical and catechetical. He had to work with her understanding in order to correct her faulty notions of Christian doctrine, but he also had to clear her conscience so that her judgment of herself truly accorded with God's judgment.

The technique used both to inform her understanding and to resolve her conscience was a close and thorough application of Ramist logic in framing answers to her questions and objections. The new logic was able to analyze each "argument" of a question, to divide the answer into multiple, finely reasoned parts, and to carry on the entire discourse without the use of unfamiliar or confusing philosophic terms. Since Hooker was trained in the sermonic use of Ramist logic, he gave Mrs. Drake both reasoned answers to her objections and applications of the truth revealed in these answers. The rationale of the answer worked as an immediate corrective to her understanding, and the application of the truth served as a continuing guide to an errant reason. Hooker's arguments thus not only refuted Mrs. Drake's errors but also provided methodically organized formulae which, if observed, would help to maintain her in the truth.

Mrs. Drake's biographer related many passages between her and Dod and relatively few between her and Hooker, but since she argued anew with Hooker what she had formerly disputed with her first adviser, her side of the struggle seems clear. To discover Hooker's replies and his method of pastoral care our best source seems to be his earliest published work, *The Poore Doubting Christian Drawne unto Christ.* This text first appeared in a collection of sermons entitled *The Saints Cordials* (London, 1629); most of the sermons in the collec-

16 Ames, *Conscience*, I, 2. Each of the five books of this treatise is separately paginated.

tion were by Richard Sibbes, who was also interested in the strange case of Mrs. Drake. Hooker's contribution, although numbered "Sermon XXIII," does not follow in any significant way his usual sermonic form, but is a sort of manual of practical devotion or a guide for conduct when in spiritual distress.[17] Its message was designed for someone in a psychological situation very like Mrs. Drake's, for the voice of the woman who accused herself of the unpardonable sin echoed in that of the poor doubting Christian: "My sinnes are worse, not onely because they are many, but because of the grace and salvation that I have rejected, which hath beene offered me from day to day."[18]

Hooker defined the purpose of his treatise in the first sentence: he would describe "divers lets and impediments which hinder poore Christians from comming unto Christ" (347), and he would go on to prescribe remedies for the impediments in order to help the distressed soul find a saving faith. He stated that these hindrances were of two differing kinds; the first sort, of which there were four subtypes, "really keep men from comming to take hold of Christ at all" (347). After enumerating and briefly describing these, he passed to the second sort of hindrances and found here three subtypes. This second kind of hindrance to conversion did

> not indeed deprive a man of title from Christ, but it makes the way more tedious, that hee cannot come to Christ so readily; and the ground of this hindrance is this, when men out of carnall reason contrive another way to come unto Christ, than ever he ordained or revealed, when wee set up a standard by Gods Standard, and out of our owne imagi-

[17] See Shuffelton, "Thomas Prince and His Edition of Thomas Hooker's *Poor Doubting Christian,*" *Early American Literature* 5, No. 3 (1970-71), 68-75.

[18] Hooker, *The Poore Doubting Christian Drawne unto Christ,* in Richard Sibbes, *The Saints Cordials* (London, 1629), 349. Further quotations from this work will be identified in the course of this chapter parenthetically in the text.

nation wee make an other condition of beleeving than ever
Christ required or ordained. Thus wee make barres in the
way, and manacle our hands, and fetter our feet, and then
we complaine we cannot goe. (348)

The first sort of hindrances prevented a man from ever beginning upon the work of regeneration, and the second sort
deluded him into strange byways, dead ends of the soul. It is
simple enough to understand Hooker's first sort of hindrance,
a mental block to the whole idea of being converted, but to
understand the second sort, which "makes the way more tedious," we must be sure to understand his theory of conversion.
This concept has already been touched upon in the account of
his own conversion, and more of its complexities will be unfolded in the next chapter, but a summary account is necessary
here in order to explain how man can impede a divinely ordained event.

When Reformation theologians began to consider the precise
nature of conversion, they faced a unique problem; they were
talking about a new kind of conversion. In the early days of
the church men were converted from paganism to Christianity,
but Reformation divines sought to convert men who already
considered themselves to be Christian. Conversion had become
redefined as the transformation from historical faith to experiential faith, the saving faith of the elect. The experience
of Paul on the road to Damascus proved that this sort of faith
could come in a sudden flash, that conversion from the old
Adam to the new life in Christ could be instantaneous and
constituted a radical break in one's life. These post-Calvinist
theologians realized, however, that for most men the regenerating experience did not happen as the result of sudden divine
illumination but as a change in the condition of the soul which
could take years, even a lifetime to accomplish. Although there
was no sudden awareness of God's gift of saving grace, the
presence of grace in different forms could usually be de-

termined at each step of the process, and since the experience of conversion was articulated in time, many Puritan divines felt that they could denominate these steps with some assurance.

Because conversion was an experiential process, one problem that the theologians had to face was the nature of the part played by man. The complexities of this question must be deferred to the next chapter, but it is important to realize that Hooker and most of his colleagues held with St. Augustine that the God who made man would not save him without his cooperation: "Faith is the free gift of God; it is GOD that must doe it, and yet hee will not doe it without us, because wee are reasonable men and women" (361). The typography alone makes the priorities clear, but since man did have some part to play in the drama of conversion, it was obvious that faith was not usually so immediately and surely effective as in St. Paul's case. "Carnall reason" and "imagination" could create hindrances to the smooth fulfillment of regeneration at any number of places, as anyone who had to deal with Mrs. Drake would have been well aware.

English Puritan divines agreed that the first gracious act of God in leading man to salvation was to make him feel "legal terrors," to make man aware of the demands made by the law of God, of the punishment set for the inevitable failure to meet these demands, and of man's absolute inability to meet them.[19] Ames, the master theologian to the New England Puritans, stated, "Yet that man may be prepared to receive the promises, the application of the Law doth ordinarily goe before to the discovery of sin, and inexcusablenesse and humiliation of the sinner."[20] Hooker was clearly certain that Mrs. Drake had be-

---

[19] Norman Pettit, *The Heart Prepared* (New Haven, Yale Univ. Press, 1966), 64. Pettit's book has been invaluable to me, far beyond what any footnotes can indicate, for his treatment of Hooker's predecessors and followers. It is important to note that not all of Hooker's colleagues agreed about the significance of legal terrors. See my Chapter Eight for a discussion of Cotton's dissent.

[20] Ames, *The Marrow of Sacred Divinity, Drawne out of the Holy*

gun this first step in the way to conversion. Although her initial experiences were unusual, to say the least, they did not fit the description of the carnal man laboring under the first sort of impediment. Her condition was not characterized by "presumptuous security, whereby men content them selves in their present condition," for she saw the need of conversion, nor had she made the last shift of the natural man, to

> attend upon the ordinances, thinking that if hee doe labour and bestirre himselfe hard, he shall hammer out a faith at last of his owne making, and here he rests, and so as it were hangs upon the outside of the Arke, . . . till at last the waves and windes are so fierce and violent, that he is beaten off from his hold, and so sinkes forever. (347)

Her sense that "in all her actions shee but heapt up wrath against the day of wrath" revealed that she had begun the work of contrition. Her position on the way to Christ was similar to that of Bunyan's Christian, who a few decades later found himself in the Slough of Despond.

I I

Hooker's first problem in dealing with a poor doubting Christian, such as Mrs. Drake, was to persuade her to interpret her past experience correctly; seen in the proper light, her "legal terrors" were gracious signs, for "a wounded soule is the gift of God" (350). Natural man's intellectual and spiritual weakness often increased the difficulties of conversion by creating a false view of reality; as Richard Sibbes observed, "It would prevent many crosses, if we would conceive of things as they are. . . . The best way of happiness is not to multiply honours or riches, but to cure our conceits of things."[21]

Scriptures, and the Interpreters thereof, and brought into Method, in *Workes*, III.

[21] Richard Sibbes, *The Soul's Conflict with Itself, and Victory over*

Hooker's initial problem was Mrs. Drake's understanding of her own condition, and he attempted to correct this failure of reason by describing in detail the three main hindrances which now barred her way to Christ. These impediments had the character of "fears and doubts and discouraging apprehensions," in Bunyan's words, but they were not laudable symptons of true Christian humility. Bunyan identified them as the "scum and filth" which made up the Slough of Despond.

Hooker stood upon a long Christian tradition of seeing sin as a product of self-love; at the center of all the impediments man put up to his own regeneration was this *philautia*. Pride in one's own presumed natural abilities to atone for sin caused the first set of hindrances, and more subtle manifestations of pride were responsible for those now affecting the distressed soul. The first expression of this pride occurs, Hooker argued, when the soul, laboring under legal terrors,

> takes notice of the beauty of holinesse, and the Image of God stampt upon the hearts of his children, and of all those precious promises which God hath made to all that are his; now the soul seeing these, begins thus to reason with himselfe, and saith, Surely if I were so holy and so gracious, then I might have hope to receive the pardon of my sins; for were my heart so inlarged to duties, and could my heart bee so carried with power against corruptions to master them, then there were some hope; but when I have no power against corruption, nor any heart to seeke so importunately for a Christ, how dare I thinke that any mercy belongs to mee, when I see so many wants? (348)

To the diseased and corrupted soul the vast distance between itself and the healthy and regenerate soul is an immediate discouragement. Seeing what the love of God could do and had

Itself by Faith, in *The Collected Works of Richard Sibbes*, ed. A. B. Grosart (Edinburgh, 1862), I, 190. Also, John Bunyan, *The Pilgrim's Progress* (London, Oxford Univ. Press, 1945), 19.

41

done in others makes the distressed soul feel even more distant and rejected, and the mind interprets this imputed rejection as genuine reprobation. This grasping after damnation, as it were, provides a crutch to injured pride; the sickness of the soul is not caused by its own faults, the sinner tells himself, but by the action of an outside agency, by God's withholding of His healing love.

To this complaint the *curator animarum* replied, "This doth not hinder, wee make it a hinderance, . . . nay, who made this a condition of the covenant, that a man must have this inlargement before he come to the promise" (348). As we have seen in the account of Hooker's own conversion, he held the scriptural promises of grace and mercy to be the greatest help in the agonizing process of conversion, particularly when his own reasoning failed him. Immediately after denying the validity of the doubting Christian's hindering argument, he quoted two such promises and explicated them to bring the point home, e.g.,

> Buy without money, saith the text; you must not thinke to come and buy a husband; the Lord lookes for no power or sufficiency of our selves, nor power against corruption, nor inlargement to duties; if you will bee content that Christ shall take all from him, and dispose of you, then, in truth, take a Savior and have him.   (348)

Frequent recurrence to the promises is the most important duty of the wounded soul, but this soul must first order its errant mind aright so that it can profit from them. For the moment, however, the sick soul needs a godly minister to explain the word: "Men oft are not able to read their own evidences without help."[22]

This first impediment is briefly handled in *The Poore Christian*, and it was not one of Mrs. Drake's overriding problems.

[22] Sibbes, *Conflict*, 194.

She was more preoccupied with her own sins than with the examples of piety displayed by others, and the second hindrance described her condition more closely. Here the sinner "lookes upon his own sinfulnesse and worthlessnesse, and therefore dares not venture upon mercy" (348). In this shift to avoid conversion, as in the previous one, wounded pride operates, but here more than a merely human cause could be found for the soul's rebelliousness. When the soul grieved for sin "viewes the number of his sinnes, so many and vile, and the continuance of them so long, and he seeth the floods of abomination comming in amine upon his soule, . . . Sathan helpes him forward hereto; for this is the policy of the Devill" (348–49). Hooker here brought home to the doubting Christian the manner and method of the "Devills rhetorike." Satan takes advantage of the unregenerate man's lack of saving faith in Christ and plays upon his natural pride. The "Devills rhetorike" was not merely supernatural manipulation of the mind but human rhetoric arguing from fallen, natural reason.

Just as Hooker had implied in the beginning that the two different kinds of hindrances to salvation had human pride as a common cause, here he showed how the devil insinuated himself into human life by using this pride. Satan's first tactic was to persuade man that he was already good enough to presume upon Christ's mercy, but if the sinner would not be tempted into presumption and insisted upon proclaiming his faults, Satan then attempted to convince him that he was so wicked he could not be saved. Pride in the first hindrance was like that of a sullen child; here it inverted itself in an odd way, leading the sinner to exclaim, "What . . . should I thinke that there is any mercy for mee, and that I have any interest in Christ, that were strange" (349). In this complaint of the poor doubting Christian we hear again the voice of Mrs. Drake; Hartwell reported her reply to Dr. James Ussher, who wished to console her with the goodness of Christ, in very much the same terms: "All these were excellent things he spoke of touching Christ, for them unto whom they belonged, but shee had no share in them for aught shee knew."[23]

If the sick soul could not become an eminent saint, she was willing to become a great sinner for the sake of the distinction. As Hooker pointed out, pride allows the soul to consider only itself, its own self-esteem, and not the order of the world surrounding it. Hooker's view of the psychopathic morbidity of this introspection is implicit in the imagery he chose to realize it. "And thus the soule is here poring and fastened, and setled upon his corruption, and is ever stirring the wound, and never goes to the Physitian: for a sinner is as well kept from looking to Christ by despaire as by presumption" (349). The cure that this soul seeks was not to be discovered by a self-destructive reasoning from pride but by looking outside of the self and making a realistic appraisal of God's universe and man's place in it. "For, . . . (observe it) for whom did Christ come into the world, and for whom did hee die when he was come?" (349). Man is a reasonable creature and, while subject to "the policy of the Devill," is in the end responsible for his own actions.

As the soul "ever stirring the wound" of sin became "fastened, and setled upon his corruption," he also confirmed himself in his inherent depravity, holding out against God, continuing to be deluded about the nature of creation. The heart hardened and turned aside the gracious message of Christ; after being admonished for his errors in creating hindrances to salvation, the poor doubting Christian complained, "Ah, that is true, . . . had I but a heart to mourne for my baseness; see my sinnes I doe, but this is my misery, I cannot bee burthened with them, I have a heart that cannot breake and mourne for the dishonours of God" (350). The spiritual counselor replied, "This hinders not neither, provided that thy heart is weary of itselfe, that it cannot be weary of sinne; . . . so the churlish Jaylor, when he was most opposite against the meanes of

[23] Hartwell, 69.

44

grace, the Lord then showed most compassion upon him, he that resists the meanes of grace, is now brought home by those meanes" (350). The commission of sin produced a psychological pattern of guilt and justification leading to a further involvement with evil, or, as Hooker would have said, the heart was framed for sin. Conversion was approached through the tension of rejecting the means of grace while futilely willing to reject sin. The only solution was to submit to the divinely appointed means of enlightenment, for man had to both act and be acted upon in order to break his established pattern of wickedness and misery.

This mention of the appointed means to grace, God's ordinances which were designed to soften the heart and to change the life of man by conversion, in conjunction with repentance, provoked the doubting Christian to his most plaintive objection:

> But woe, saith the poore soule, you are now come to the quicke, this very word is like a Millstone about my necke, to sinke my soule for ever; for this is the depth of that basenesse that lies on mee, that all the meanes doe not better me. . . . is there such a heart in hell? how ill am I, when all the meanes in the world will doe mee no good? but, me thinkes, I feele my heart more hard and stubborne under all Gods Ordinances, and therefore my condition is hopelesse, when the meanes that should soften me, doe but harden me, and make me worse. (350)

Here the soul stated for himself the last hindrance which prevented its continuance in the way of regeneration. Although he could articulate for himself this "last plea whereby the Devill holds downe the heart of a poore sinner" (350), he had again failed to see the situation in its true light. Mrs. Drake's biographer revealed that the principal question she opened for the first time with Hooker was this problem of repentance. Since one of the specific goals of *The Poore Doubting Christian* was to open the way to contrition, and given Mrs. Drake's obsession with the inability of the "means" to affect her hardened heart, it once again becomes clear that the doubting Christian of this book had many correspondences with the troubled lady of Esher. Hooker apparently resolved Mrs. Drake's questions about her inability to feel true repentance for her sins by correcting her vision of God and her self. Her biographer gave the sum of Hooker's answer to her objection of a hard heart:

> For, shee could not deny, but her wishes were that she might repent, and she was in some sort sorry for her indisposition and hardnesse of heart, which being a burthen and a kinde of griefe unto her, was so a kinde and sort of repentance: Therefore was shee exhorted to be patient, and not to limite the Holy One of *Israel*.[24]

The reply given to the poor doubting Christian was similar in content and phrasing, but it was considerably more elaborated, being disposed into "three passages by way of answer."

For both Mrs. Drake and the poor Christian the first course taken by the spiritual counselor was to correct their mistaken notions of their own experiences. Sin, or melancholy caused by a dwelling on sin, had so confused man's reason that he was unable to judge rightly what happened, even within himself. Hooker advised the poor doubting Christian:

> First, the Word and meanes doe worke good if it make thee more sensible of thy hardnesse and deadnesse, though happily it worke not that good, and after the same manner that thou desirest, . . . then the word works in the best manner, because it is after Gods manner, howsoever not after thine.
>
> (350)

While the distressed soul could formulate its problem for himself, this particular answer could only come from one who had

[24] Hartwell, 124–25.

himself been converted and enlightened. Only in regenerate man had the reason been sufficiently restored so that the mind could perceive for itself, although only vaguely, in this material existence, the workings of God in man. What was bewildering and distressing to the natural man, the poor Christian, became just and reasonable for the saint who had arrived at some empirical knowledge of God. Hooker believed that the God whose conservation of man's world "is nothing else then as it were a continued Creation"[25] was the same God in whom "as sinne was a perpetuall act in us, . . . there was a perpetuall act in pardoning of sinne, not transient, but in a perpetuall constant currant."[26] Although the soul on the way to Christ theoretically became aware of God's forgiveness of his sins at a point in time, he went on to realize that God's forgiveness was for all time, absolving all the past and disposing all the future. Only by turning itself toward God and away from its corruptions could the soul hope to understand its own sorrows, for man's sensibility of the divine presence was mutable and uncertain, but the regenerate man, in looking back on his own experiences, could recognize the continued recurrence of divine providence.

Hooker, the regenerate pastor, could thus clear the mind of a reprobate sinner like Mrs. Drake by giving her a speculative notion of the manner of God's working in the soul, but this was not all the answer, for if "there bee some lust of distemper that the heart hankers after, . . . then the Word will harden thee, because thou hardenest thyselfe" (350). Not only the mind had to turn to God, but also the will, for it was not rational acceptance of God's truths that would serve but complete submission to them. Again the sin of pride was pointed out as the chief hindrance to salvation underlying all the others, and Hooker called the doubting Christian's attention especially to the second passage of the answer:

[25] Ames, *Marrow*, 42.   [26] Hartwell, 126.

Secondly, (marke this I beseech you) thou art the cause why thy heart is not softened, and why the Word workes not upon thy soule; this distemper of thy heart hinders the working of the word, and dispensation of Gods providence, and the tenure of the Covenant of Grace; thou must not thinke to limit the Holy One of Israel, for it is the Covenant of Grace; the Lord will not stand bent to thy bow, and give thee grace when thou wilt; it is not for us to know the times and seasons. (350)

If man were to live in joy and assurance, he had to live by God's terms and not on his own. But even if truth were being slowly unfolded in the soul of man, the truth of the regenerate heart could only be an imperfect model of a larger external truth. The "dispensation of Gods providence" which re-created the human heart was only one expression of a providence engaged in a continual creation of a universe, His Israel. To find "peace of conscience and assurance of his love" in a divinely created universe, Mrs. Drake's soul had to patiently submit to its Creator, for "the Lord deales equally and lovingly with you, and as shall be best for you; God gives what, and when, and how hee will, therefore waite for it" (351). Submission to the omnipotent truth had to be perfect, but acceptance of human notions of truth could only be provisional.

Mrs. Drake's distressed soul should not, then, simply accept the objective universe as it appeared to natural man. God was not found in external objects which men could manipulate, as she attempted to prophesy her condition by manipulating Bible verses, but in the spiritual action through which He created and sustained those objects. Human pride, the desire to preserve our self-esteem, led men to believe that their actions, dealing with objects as material, had some intrinsic value and importance. As the third part of his answer, Hooker thus warned the poor doubting Christian that he has "rested upon thine owne duties and indeavours, and thou doest not goe to

God, that blesseth both the meanes and indeavors" (351). This spirit to use the means ordained by God was a gift of God; it was God's love, the same providential love which maintained the universe and forgave sin, working in the soul. The vision of reality presented by Hooker contemplated simultaneously a cosmic and a personal God; He was not only the act and the acted upon but also the actor. "Look as it is with two clockes that have the selfe same poizes, and the selfe same wheeles, they will strike both together, so it is with the heart of a Christian, the spirit of Christ is the poize of the heart, and his grace the wheele, therefore he performes duties like *Christ*."[27]

This argument led to the central paradox. The sinner was required to pray and to use the means of grace in order to go out of himself to the divine source, and he was simultaneously forbidden to believe that his actions were of any value in accomplishing this self-abnegation. As Hooker made clear, this was a difficult point, and, with human cooperation, Satan took full advantage of its complexity: "The Devill . . . makes us beleeve (and wee out of ignorance are deluded) that we have power in our owne hands to goe out of our selves" (351). Taking the devil's advice, the advice of natural reason, was the source of a great many of the soul's problems, for the true answer was not self-affirmation but self-denial. "Now (observe it) whiles that I thus thinke with my selfe, that I have ability to goe out of my selfe, which is quite contrary, for to deny a mans selfe is to know that hee hath no power in himselfe to doe any spirituall duty" (351). Commenting on Matthew 16:25 ("For whosoever will save his life shall lose it: and whosoever will lose his life for my sake shall find it"), Hooker said that self-denial "is the way to have our selves, and whatsoever is in us (not sinfull) our safety, comfort, sufficiency, credit, it doth not remove these, but onely rectifie them."[28]

Mrs. Drake's mental disorder had its roots in her personal

---

[27] Hooker, *The Christians Two Chief Lessons* (London, 1640), 27.
[28] Ibid., 61.

inability to cope with her private vision of reality; much of Hooker's treatment as already outlined aimed at correcting her diseased alternate reality, her fantasy of reprobation. The counselor's injunction to learn self-denial worked in this direction by cutting against her pride and deluding imagination which forged such "monstrous fictions." More important, however, this injunction was also conducive to healing through restoring her self-confidence to act in a significant manner. To reject oneself is to reject all human weakness, guilt, and anxiety, but a crucial element of this self-denial for the poor Christian was the affirmation of Christ, who was beyond the sick personality, although able to enter into it and support it. Self-denial is what Hooker called humiliation, and he said of a humbled soul, "The Lord Jesus will not delay to come into the heart truely humbled."[29] Through identification with Christ the sick soul was healed and given the ability to face daily troubles with equanimity; to deny that the soul could overcome its own misery was to affirm that only Christ could forgive sin and dispel evil. "Therefore wee must looke only to the voice of Christ, and know, hee that cals us from the wayes of darknesse, and from our selves, must also bring us to Christ" (351). As Emerson would realize two hundred years later, man in "obeying the Almighty effort and advancing on Chaos and the Dark" practiced not self-denial but self-reliance. Men found true strength when "we lie in the lap of immense intelligence, which makes us receivers of its truth and organs of its activity. When we discern justice, when we discern truth, we do nothing of ourselves, but allow a passage to its beams."[30]

The poor doubting Christian raised one more objection under the rubric of this third hindrance, apparent hardness of heart; he complained of his "want of sense and feelings" of God's love and argued that this proved he has no "worke of

[29] Hooker, *Implantation*, 106.
[30] Ralph Waldo Emerson, "Self-Reliance," in *Essays First Series* (Boston, Houghton, 1903), 47.

faith to come to Christ" (352). Hooker replied to this with an answer phrased in three succinct parts. First, this "joy is a fruit that proceeds from faith after much wrestling; it doth not follow from faith at the first." Secondly, a "man may have a good faith, and yet want the rellish and sweetnesse which he desires." Thirdly, the "Saints of God many times are deprived of comfort, not because God with holds it, but because they put it from them and will not have it, though he offer it" (352). Since Hooker returned to the problem of sensible evidence of faith later in his preaching and treated it in more detail, this summary of his answer will do for the present.

This brief passage, completing the first part of *The Poore Doubting Christian*, was basically diagnostic, although curative suggestions were part of the diagnosis. The academic version of Renaissance psychology, as learned by Hooker in the university, tended toward a mechanistic and simplistic model of human personality; Hooker and other practical observers of the religious phenomenon of conversion realized, however, that human personality and behavior are bafflingly diverse and complex. Good pastoral psychologists such as Dod and Hooker respected this diversity by refusing to use force upon wayward and contrary minds, but at the same time their theoretical knowledge of the mind urged them to emphasize characteristics of behavior common to all men. Thus Mrs. Drake's disturbing behavior was unique in the annals of sinful man, but she was motivated by the same pride that has led man into sin and misery ever since the fall. By discovering these motivations of the diseased soul, the pastor could then prescribe a cure already proven to be efficacious in dealing with pride. Indeed, the prescription of the cure had already begun, for the articulation of the causes of the disorder was the first step toward recovery.

As the hindrances affecting both Mrs. Drake and the hypothetical poor doubter were described, Hooker indicated solutions of a general and theoretical nature. Next he proceeded to prescribe as therapy a practical course of conduct which would serve, with God's grace, as a way to salvation. He first offered four "Helps to come to Christ" which were essentially particularized advice developed out of the general suggestions already made. The first "cure and help" was a warning against morbid introspection: "We must not looke too long, nor pore too much or unwarrantably upon our own corruptions, so far as to be feared or disheartened from comming to the riches of Gods grace" (352). This advice was particularly designed for someone in the situation of Mrs. Drake, for Hooker's usual, and equally authentic, demand was for the soul to labor to get a "clear sight of sin." This demand, however, was usually made upon the "carnal" man who had not yet wholeheartedly entered on the way of salvation. The dangers of the tender soul's introversion were not only that he might turn away from Christ but that, by thinking only of sin, he opened "the streame and fludgate of corruption" (352). Mrs. Drake, thus faced with her own guilt, announced that "shee was resolved to spend the remainder of her time in all jollity and merriment, denying her self of no worldly comforts."[31] It might have been better for her if she had acted upon this resolve, but her idea of jollity continued to express itself as spite and perversity; psychological patterning in the form of a "streame . . . of corruption" caused not only a surrender to sin but also subjection to the misery and melancholy that follow. Hooker completed the negative injunction against morbid introspection by giving positive instructions "to see sin aright." The poor doubting Christian was urged, "away to the throne of Grace, and dwell no longer on thy sinnes, for there is pardon enough to remove the guilt that sinne hath brought upon thy soule" (353).

The last three helps are perhaps best discussed as a group; the first help immediately concerned the soul's conflict with itself, and the last three involve its confrontation with something beyond itself. "The second meanes of cure is this, take heed of judging thy estate by carnall reason without the rule."

[31] Hartwell, 23–24.

By "the rule" Hooker meant the rule of Scripture; the way to subjugate the old Adam was portrayed in God's revelation and was not discoverable by natural reason, which listened to "those carnall pleas which Sathan helpes us to invent" (353). As a third help, the poor doubting Christian was enjoined to "bee marvellously wary and watchfull that wee enter not into the lists of dispute with Sathan, upon those points which are beyond the reach of man" (354). Mrs. Drake had been warned again and again that the workings of election were God's secret, and that no man could truly know he was among the reprobate until he appeared before God for judgment. The fourth and last cure was "specially to be observed above all: In thy proceeding with they selfe in judgement, . . . passe no judgement against thy soule but according to the evidence of the Word" (355).

As the distressed soul considered each of these helps in turn, it would be progressively led away from itself toward God. The intellectual program of each help built upon what had gone before and prepared the way for the next step. Thus, in the second help the soul which had previously been shown how "the Devill keeps us in sinne" was shown again how Satanic intervention in man led fallen, natural reason to frame "carnall pleas" against salvation. This observation led to the third help, in which the distressed soul was warned against being tricked by Satan into a reenactment of the debate in the garden between the Serpent and Eve. Furthermore, the second help offered to the soul, already warned away from unwarrantable introspection, both a guide for healthy self-judgment and an object worthy of consideration outside of himself. This part of the help laid the foundation for an understanding and acceptance of the fourth help in which the distressed soul was explicitly urged to give up all self-judgment by natural reason and submit to judgment by the revealed truth of the Word. In the first three of the four helps to Christ the injunctions were essentially negative, and in each of them, culminating with the third, Satan and evil were identified with an unrestricted operation of natural reason. In the last three of the helps an increasing emphasis was placed by Hooker upon the extrapersonal truth which could correct and supervise natural reason.

The whole movement of this complex persuasive structure tended to lead the poor doubting Christian to a consideration of God's laws and promises contained in the Word. Hooker's helps to come to Christ, if attentively followed, could produce a new order in a disordered mind, such as that of the doubting Christian or of Mrs. Drake, and this order would be a Bible order. If the distressed soul was genuinely on the way to conversion, it was about to enter a spiritual realm the principles of which were not to be determined sensationally from the material universe but directly from God. The soul's earlier expression of anxiety for his inability to feel repentance and grace had been partially answered by showing the inherent paradox in his statement; here Hooker revealed to the sick soul that all its self-impeachment was ultimately irrelevant. The mind and the soul were not to be regulated by autistic standards but by the divine gift of truth, experienced in the soul as grace, and the ultimate means of grace was the Word. "Learne of the lord Christ, for his word is faithfull, and his promise sure, and there you shall finde rest as strong as Mount Sion; it is that word whereby thou shalt bee judged at the great day, when sense and feeling shall bee cast out for wranglers, and never come into Court" (356).

Although the poor Christian had been directed out of himself to an external truth, Hooker realized that his patient could not be left alone before the Word without additional help. Mrs. Drake's condition appeared hopeful to herself so long as she was being harangued by her favorite divine, but, left to her own devices, she lapsed into melancholy and terror. Submission to the "evidence of the Word" was not enough when she did not know how to find that evidence nor understand how to use it. She had in her most querulous moments a deplorable way of using the Scriptures; she would choose texts for guidance by arbitrarily opening her Bible and putting her finger on the page. Whichever text she came upon she presumed applicable to her condition, and she usually labored to put the worst possible interpretation on it. By supplying an ordered method of approaching the Word, Hooker was apparently able to direct the misguided procedure of Mrs. Drake into a more profitable course and to persuade her to leave off this business of tempting God. Properly read, the Bible provided an account of human sin and divine redemption which was a more stable basis for living than her diseased fantasies of human and divine rejection.

In a very restricted sense, the process of conversion for Hooker was synonymous with learning the skills of authentic exegesis of Scripture. The experiential apprehension of the Word's truth, was not, however, a substitute for the linguistic and literary training which fitted a learned minister to explicate Scripture. Thus he laid down four "rules to direct a Christian how to use the word of God for the evidence of his assurance" (356): first, "As thou must in all conditions that concerne thy soule repaire to the word, so thou must consider thine owne uprightnesse, and what worke of grace is in thy soule, that will answer the word, . . . bee sure to take they soule at the best" (356); "Secondly, labour to have thy conscience setled and established in that truth which now out of the word thou has gotten," for "if there is some guilt of sinne still remaining, then conscience will breed new broyles, and continually nip and disquiet the heart" (357); "Thirdly, we should strive mightily to have our hearts overpowred with the evidence which reason and conscience makes good to us, that so we may quietly receive it, and calmly welcome it, and yeeld and subject our hearts to that truth" (358); "The last rule is this, Maintaine the good word which thy heart hath submitted to, and keepe it as the best treasure under heaven, and when thou hast this evidence heare nothing against it, but sticke fast to it, which is good in Law" (359).

The phrasing of these rules seems to betray what would be for a Puritan an excessive value placed upon human action. While Hooker shared with men of his time, Calvinist and non-Calvinist, the belief that man had retained at least a portion of his natural abilities after the fall, he never lost sight of the essential fact of human depravity. Sibbes had observed, "We carry about with us a double principle, grace and nature,"[32] and Hooker himself would say later in his career that "sinne is called the old man in Scripture, as if sinne were another man in us."[33] This nature of contrary doubles could not continue as a permanent principle of existence for men, and God would nourish the seeds of righteousness in some and allow others to perish deservedly in their wickedness. But if righteousness were to become dominant in man, he himself must also strive to preserve and increase it through God's grace. Hooker intended by these rules to urge the poor Christian to turn his attention away from the old Adam and seek in himself the clouded and imperfect image of God which was also revealed in the Bible. In explaining the first rule, he pointed out that it is with man's soul and the Word

as it is with a mans hand and the staffe, I compare the promise to a staffe, you know the backe of a mans hand cannot take hold of the staffe, but let him turne the palme of his hand to the staffe, and then he can take it; . . . but we turne the backe-side of our hearts to the promise, when the soule saith, Oh my stubbornnesse is great, and mine inabilities and corruptions are many; this is the wrong side of thine heart, and this will ever hinder thee from taking hold of the promise, but thy soule hates these, and is weary of them, this is the right side of the heart, turne that to the promise.   (357)

[32] Sibbes, *The Bruised Reed and the Smoking Flax*, in *Works*, I, 50.
[33] Hooker, *The Unbeleevers Preparing for Christ* (London, 1638), 62.

Hooker's argument to his enunciation of the rules to use the Word had been framed to convince the poor Christian that the source of all good, the cure for his distress, was outside himself. Here, in an elaborate intellectual minuet, he has led the soul back into himself by means of the rules in order to discover there the seeds of goodness implanted by God. In his discussion of the four rules, Hooker aptly unified his dramatic argument by casting the distressed soul as a defendant before a court. This trope, as it was used to explicate each of the rules, obviously served to reveal the organic nature of conversion, but more important it at once portrayed the soul from both an internal and external point of view. The soul was to sit introspectively as a judge upon himself to decide the case between his righteousness and his sin, but at the same time he had to remember that God judged him from above. In order to nourish righteousness, to achieve salvation, and to find "constant comfort" in this world and the next, the decisions of both judges must coincide. God was all-loving as well as all-just—"the Lord doth not lye at catch with his children, but he takes them at the best" (356)—and man must temper his judgment to God's.

After Hooker had subtly directed the soul's attention inward to the possible presence of "Gods free grace in Jesus Christ," he once again guided him out of the self to the external good. He did this by urging upon the poor doubting Christian four "meanes whereby a man may so improve his time that at last hee may obtaine this blessed grace" (361). Hooker's four "meanes to obtaine grace and faith" provided directions for something approaching a course of meditation which, similar to the four helps and the four rules described above, operated to impress a new order on a disordered mind. The tendency of all Hooker's suggestions to the poor Christian was increasingly conducive to orderly initiative, perhaps looking forward, as in the case of Mrs. Drake, when he would no longer stand by his or her side. If the doubting Christian used the means described by Hooker, he would begin to act upon a new, gracious principle rather than out of pride, caprice, or self-will. If apparently sanctified behavior did result from a use of these means, Hooker would of course not see it as an effect following from that particular cause; the use of the means in no way limited God, and sanctified behavior was a sign of grace rather than a result of carrying out a prescribed set of actions.

The development of sanctified behavior which would argue the prior presence of saving grace occurred even in the first of the means, and this means established the operative pattern for the whole set of means.

> First, we must as much as in us lyes, labour to pluck away all those props that the soule leanes upon, . . . that when all these are taken from us, wee may bee forced to goe for suc-cour there where it is to bee had. (361)

This first means functioned by limiting the soul's intellectual and spiritual alternatives to Christ alone. If the soul consistently rejected the equivocal comforts of the world, it inevitably discovered in itself a compensatory faith in sure and eternal comforts. If the soul rejected "the gods of this world, honour, and profit, and pleasure" (362) as potential saviors or sources of comfort, then it also repudiated sin; if sin were repudiated, then only Christ remained. "Therefore let us take our hearts off from these things, and have a base esteeme of them, that wee may bee forced to seeke to Christ" (362). The transformation of the distressed soul's values led to a change in the personal significance of his deeds. Aware of fallen man's inability to do good, Hooker held that the Lord demanded from men not good acts but good desires.

The intellectual reorientation which led the poor Christian to faith was effected by meditation upon the promises. Hooker affirmed, of course, that any genuine progress toward conversion was caused only by grace, but, nevertheless what (humanly speaking) altered the consciousness of a sinner was the intense concentration and direction of thought required by Hooker's means. The "labour" demanded in the first means was an intellectual labor, an intense, deliberate managing of the mind, and the same labor was required of the sinner in the second means to improve his time:

> Therefore labour in the second place to have your hearts possessed throughly, and perswaded effectually of the fulnesse of that good which is in the promise, . . . leave not thy heart till thou see the promise of grace most beautifull in thy eye, and that thy heart may gaine some earnest touching the goodnesse of God, and the riches of his grace towards thee, and bring thy heart to know and see, that the promise is better than all the riches and honours that thou canst have, or the world can bestow.   (362)

In accordance with the insight gained in his own experience, Hooker directed his patient's attention to the scriptural promises, the source of our knowledge of God's dealings with His elect. Each of Hooker's four "meanes to obtaine grace" detailed a manner of approaching the promises, and if the doubting Christian concerned himself with one promise at a time, as we are told Hooker himself did, the posing of the selected text would engage the whole mind, including both the faculties of reason and will ("the heart") and the subsidiary parts of the mind such as memory and imagination ("see the promise of grace most beautifull in thy eye").

Much, perhaps too much, has been made of Ignatian meditation as an imaginative exercise, and the imaginative strategy of Puritan meditation has been perhaps correspondingly undervalued.[34] Hooker did encourage a restricted use of the visual imagination, but for him imagination was of only limited use in grasping the promises since it was merely an unreliable ad-

---

[34] Cf. Louis Martz, *The Poetry of Meditation* (New Haven, Yale Univ. Press, 1962), 154.

junct of the understanding. At this point in the poor Christian's spiritual development, he stood more in need of motivation of the will than of enlightenment of the mind. "Content not your selves that you are able to dispute somewhat fully of the excellency of the promise and of the riches of God's free grace; What is this to the purpose that the heart knowes this, and yet is forestalled that it comes not to the promise?" (362). It was the heart that was to be persuaded, the heart that was to "see the promise of grace most beautifull." The imagination was only a mediator between the memory and the understanding and had no direct effect upon the will. Hooker's conception of meditation involved the imagination only insofar as it was a necessary epistemological tool; he was less concerned with imagination, the mind's eye, than with the affections, the eyes of the heart. The heart, the seat of pride, was the last carnal holdout against faith and saving grace, and the object of meditation, the promise contained in the Word, was immediately present to it. No need to summon up imagined visions out of the memory, for the object of meditation, according to Hooker, was to fill the mind with a present and not a remembered promise.

Hooker's kind of meditation had at the center a double dramatic confrontation, one between the understanding and the will and the other between sinful man and divine truth. This double confrontation between the self and the divine was the whole aim of meditation, and it was intended to be a motivating experience. The confrontation between man and God should indeed be comforting: "Wee dare trust a friend whose faithfulnesse we have tryed; and to rest upon that which it knoweth" (362). The dialogue between reason and the corrupt will, however, was not such an inspiring event: "Wee should deale with our hearts as a man would doe with a corrupt Justice, when hee would have him to be on his side, the onely way is to bribe him, though that is sinfull, yet it is good to bribe the corrupt heart with the goodnesse of the promise" (363). To face the heart was to face the seat of sin in man directly. The "corrupt Justice" attacked the soul with the "Devills rhetorike," and the soul needed all the strength he could draw from the Word in order to overcome the cavils of the unruly heart.

The dialectical manner in which the reason dealt with the will in meditation was very similar to the working of conscience within the soul. Ames stated that conscience was the exercise in the soul of the principle of synteresis, a "habit of the understanding by which wee doe assent unto the principles of *morall actions*." Synteresis operated by propounding syllogisms to the judgment, and, if the syllogism was correctly concluded, right action would follow. The syllogistic propositions framed by synteresis were created "partly of morall principles that are naturally in us, together with their conclusions; and partly, of those which God besides them hath injoyned."[35] Conscience, with its dependence both upon imperfectly understood innate principles and upon revelation, was thus related to the exercise in man of right reason. Ames defined right reason as

> that which . . . , if absolute rectitude be looked after, it is not else-where to be sought for then where it is, in the Scriptures: neither doth it differ from the will of God revealed for the direction of our life. . . . but if those imperfect notions concerning that which is honest, and dishonest, be understood, which are found in the mind of man after the fall; seeing they are imperfect and very obscure, they cannot exactly informe vertue; neither indeed doe they differ anything from the written Law of God, but in imperfection and obscurity only.[36]

The ability of right reason and conscience to order life aright obviously depended upon man's ability to clarify his imperfect and innate notions of God and to understand correctly God's will as revealed in Scripture. Intense meditation upon the Word could reveal to man a normative model of his mind as moral

[35] Ames, *Conscience*, I, 4–5.   [36] Ames, *Marrow*, 199.

instrument, and it could ultimately assure him of the congruity of his soul and the divine will. Hooker's brand of meditation was not intended to aid man to subdue the old Adam by his own efforts but to lead him to submit to the truth that can correct a sinful heart: "You must not stand struggling and striving with your owne hearts, and thinke to master a proud heart, that will not doe it, but let faith goe to Christ, and there is meeknesse, patience, humility and wisdome, and faith will fetch all these to the soule" (365).

If the soul desiring conversion was unable to comprehend God's will, either in natural "morall principles" or in scriptural revelation, it would be unable to proceed on the way to Christ, for "in such things as are necessary to salvation, and Gods worship, no opinion can be sufficient, though it have never so great certainty of reason; because Faith is required to these, and Faith takes only the infallible word of God."[37] In the first part of this treatise Hooker had shown that the poor doubting Christian had been indeed resting upon opinion, "a certaine judgement . . . arising from Reason,"[38] and these opinions formed the main impediment to salvation. Salvation could only be discovered through knowledge based upon facts and not by opinions founded upon "those imperfect notions" of the truth held by natural man. By catechizing the doubting Christian about the true method of God's working with man, the spiritual counselor had enabled the sinner to use his own conscience and right reason again. Hooker's meditative disposition of the "meanes to obtaine grace," building upon the catechetical process of the first part of the treatise, enabled the patient's

[37] Ames, *Conscience*, I, II.

[38] Ibid. Mrs. Drake's particular kind of misleading "opinions" were scruples. Ames's comments on the origin of scrupulosity throw light on Hooker's theory of pastoral care: "Scruples doe arise (God so ordaining) to the end he may either punish or try men: sometimes out of the suggestions of the Devill, sometimes from want of knowledge, sometimes from Melancholy, or some such like constitution of body." I, 13–14.

conscience to strengthen the soul. In meditation the soul went out of the self to the Word for truth and propounded the acquired truth to itself by synteresis; in the action of conscience the soul propounded to the self through synteresis truths based upon internalized grounds. Meditation was thus a method of providing internal, spiritual resources for the further exercise of conscience, and at the same time the meditating soul acted in a manner parallel to the working of conscience, in effect, teaching it the proper motions of a godly heart.

Cases of conscience were considered by Puritan casuists like Perkins and Ames to be "either about the state of man before God, or about those actions which in that state he doth put forth and exercise."[39] Professor Louis Martz has described Puritan meditation in terms of the latter of these concerns, immediate and particular acts of sin, but Hooker's concept of meditation, which was developed to understand "the state of man before God," belies this generalization.[40] If a contemplative soul addressed himself to the first of these problems, the effects of his meditation would be considerably more far-reaching than those following upon a simple thinking about his sins. The sort of Puritan meditation Martz described used the memory of past sins to impeach an errant will, but Hooker desired the doubting Christian to gain a forcibly present sense of God in order to change the will. As Timothy Bright observed, the minister's aim in dealing with a melancholiac like Mrs. Drake was to lead her to salvation and cause her to lean "upon the maine pillar of Gods promises." Reliance upon Christ became self-reliance, and the counseling minister was no longer a necessary psychological crutch. The type of meditation designed to consider sin was particular and situational, and it was most effective in keeping already converted souls up to a high pitch of righteousness. Hooker's sort of meditation was a general and autonomous exercise of conscience and right reason, brought

[39] Ibid. II, 2.   [40] Martz, 153–54.

to the Word, and it was crucial for the development of a regenerate personality.

The meditative element of Hooker's four "meanes to obtaine grace and faith" was thus intended to aid the distressed soul in finding spiritual help for himself. The meditative intent of these devices is most obvious in our somewhat complicated explication of the second means; the latter two means continued the process of submission to God's truth, and carry the soul to the threshold of salvation. The third means to obtain grace was to expect "all the good which thou needest or can desire from that sufficiency of the promise" (364). The doubting Christian was exhorted to speak to God and to himself: "Whatsoever frailties I find in my self, yet I will look to the Lord, and to his promise, for if I want faith, the promise must settle mee more and more therein" (364). The last means was to "labour to yeeld to the equall condition of the promise, and make no more conditions than God makes" (364). The "Devills rhetorike" raised debates of the soul with itself and with its God even here, and the exercise of these means resolved the debates in favor of God's plan for the salvation of man. There could be no arguments in God's court but God's arguments. Hooker summarized the means and then reminded the poor doubting Christian of the thrust of all his pastoral dealings with him: "Thus wee have seen the hindrances removed, and the meanes propounded, and now, wee may bee moved and perswaded importunately to seeke after the blessed grace of God" (365).

Hooker's pastoral care led the doubting soul out of its self-imposed mental labyrinth into a hopeful condition. The soul was no longer immobilized by sin, guilt, and fear, but was able to use its conscience and reason as grounds for significant action. Although Hooker of course denied that the exercise of these faculties by a natural man could by itself produce regeneration, nevertheless their use was necessary if a man would profit from the divinely appointed means of redemption. Most important for someone like Mrs. Drake, the soul was able to perceive that his actions had value and meaning, even if they showed no sign of being effective in the material universe, for meaning was an affair of the spirit. Although the sinner was rejected by men and as yet lacked convincing assurance of God's mercy, he was now aware that "wee are reasonable men and women, . . . [and must] waite upon the Lord in the use of the meanes, and let the Lord do what he will, and let us doe what we should" (361).

III

Hooker probably did not deal with Mrs. Drake exactly after the manner of *The Poore Doubting Christian*, for he spent several years with her, and the book is very schematic in its outline of pastoral procedure. The conversion of Mrs. Drake clearly took an exceptionally long time and was marked by her explosive outbursts and petulant regressions, whereas *The Poore Doubting Christian* unfolds the intellectual and spiritual development of the wounded soul concisely and rapidly. However difficult her case, he achieved more success with her than had any of her previous advisors. Her biographer noted:

> Yet being continually hammered and hewen with the tough acute disputations of this good man, Mr. Hooker, who was very assiduously industrious in watching her disposition, and various inclinations of her changes and tentations; by Gods mercy shee grew still better, using to present her selfe constantly to the use of meanes: having prayer, catechizing, expounding and reading of the word, and singing of Psalms constantly in the family, now with delight and willingnesse acted: yea, and in private spending some time by herselfe alone daily.[41]

41 Hartwell, 126–27.

While only God could give her the necessary saving faith, Hooker had so "acted his part with her, and done his best, to comfort, uphold and rectifie her spirit, so fitting her for mercy, as nothing remained to bee done but a full gaile of spirituall winde to blow upon her, to bring forth her fruit."[42] The "full gaile" did not come while Hooker was still with her, and, indeed, it did not come until the month before her death in 1625. At that time both Hooker and Dod returned to be with her, to witness her ultimate experience of grace, and to receive her apologies for her previous willful and slighting behavior toward them.

Hooker's experience with Mrs. Drake seems to have been extremely important in confirming the pastoral lessons he had drawn from his own conversion. The lady at Esher was also influential in shaping the direction of his future interests; throughout the rest of his life his sermons would be directed over and over to Christians in trouble or in doubt about the way to Christ. At times the image of Mrs. Drake reappeared in the sermons as a negative example for other doubting sinners; thus in the treatise entitled *The Soules Humiliation* he spoke of those that "have beene long over-whelmed with these cursed carnall cavillings, they will rather labour to oppose a direction, then to hold it and to walke in the comfort of it, onely because of the weaknesses of their understandings."[43] He went on to give a lengthy picture of such a person, and echoed again the complaints and objections of Mrs. Drake: "What mercy to me? Nay, it is prepared for those that are fitted for it; had I such a measure of humiliation, and so much grace, if I were so and so fitted; and if my heart were thus disposed, then I might have some hope to receive it."[44] Cotton Mather claimed of Hooker, "He had a singular ability at giving answers to cases of consciences; whereof happy was the experi-

[42] Hartwell, 129.
[43] Hooker, *The Soules Humiliation* (London, 1637), 174.
[44] Ibid., 175.

ence of some thousands." The "thousands" was probably Mather's somewhat enthusiastic conjecture, but Hooker did "usually set apart the second day of the week; wherein he admitted all sorts of persons, in their discourses with him, to reap the benefit of the extraordinary experience which himself had found of Satan's devices."[45] Mrs. Drake had been the mistress of an excellent school in the "Devills rhetorike."

The experience with Mrs. Drake not only confirmed the direction Hooker's interests were to take in his future ministry, but it also established the effectiveness of the rhetorical element of his "new answering methode." His "tough acute disputations" were apparently a main reason for his success with this contumacious lady, and the rhetorical fruits of his experience appeared in his first book. The argument of *The Poore Doubting Christian* was advanced by an interrogative dialogue between the doubter and the pastoral adviser; this use of dialogue was one of the distinguishing marks of Hooker's later sermons, and, as we shall see, it was one of his most effective rhetorical devices for urging sinners into the way of salvation. Hooker's dialogue was not, of course, the semidramatic dialogue employed earlier by Arthur Dent or later by Bunyan, but it was clearly recognized by the printer, who inserted marginal labels of "Objection" and "Answer" at the appropriate places.

This technique of introducing debate into a homiletic exposition was not original with Hooker; an English scholar has observed that

> some preachers, of whom "John Barlow sometime Minister of the word at Plimmoth" was one, interspersed their exposition with objections and solutions to such an extent as to earn from their theological critics the nickname of "obsollers." . . . Arthur Hildersam, a noted Puritan, is cited by Robinson as "one of these obsollers; he adds: "several of his

---

[45] Mather, I, 346.

lectures on the fourth of John are composed of *objections* and *answers*, and excellent sermons they are."[46]

Hooker would use this technique again and again in his sermons, and it would be a controlling method of argument in his great polemic work, *The Survey of the Summe of Church Discipline*. We shall later have occasion to consider the implications of the dialectic rhetoric in greater detail, but it is important to notice here that his "obsoller" technique enabled Hooker to recapture in a short treatise the essence of several years' experience as a healer of souls. Jasper Hartwell's narrative of *The Wonderfull History, Case, and Cure of Mrs. Drake* gave an account of the particular querulous objections and evasions of one sinner; Hooker's *Poore Doubting Christian* described a treatment applicable to all nominally Christian souls laboring under the guilt and anxiety of sin. The universality of Mrs. Drake's case was defined by the fears and objections which constituted her part of the dialogue; by identifying their complaints with the pleas of the doubting Christian, sinners unable to appear at Hooker's door on the second day of the week could be drawn into helpful discourse with the pastoral counselor.

In addition to valuable experience, Hooker found one other lasting benefit from his work in Esher, for it was there that he met and married his wife. Susanna Garbrand, Mrs. Drake's personal maid, had the spirit to speak up to her temperamental mistress, and her intellectual asperity was matched by her physical toughness. Once after Mrs. Drake had insulted an attending minister with a blasphemous remark, her maid reproved her, "Mistrisse, you have spoken some strange untoward things," and the lady submitted, "I think I did so."[47] Mistress Garbrand was from Amersham, Mrs. Drake's childhood home, and she was apparently an old and trusted companion. Her

[46] W. Fraser Mitchell, *English Pulpit Oratory from Andrewes to Tillotson* (London, S.P.C.K., 1932), 207–8.
[47] Hartwell, 101.

health was remarkable in an age of high female mortality, and she survived Hooker and married again in Connecticut. Her physical and mental qualities fitted her to be an excellent wife to a Puritan divine, for ministers were more often notable as scholars and preachers than as providers and managers. Richard Mather, for instance, especially lamented the loss of his wife, because "she being a Woman of singular Prudence for the Management of Affairs, had taken off from her Husband all Secular Cares, so that he wholly devoted himself to his Study, and to Sacred Imployment."[48] Hooker left his family well provided for at his death, but in the most trying years of his life Susanna must have conducted the household affairs with a sure and thrifty hand. In his will Hooker made her executrix of his estate, a not uncommon tribute to a wife's abilities, but it is perhaps more revealing that he also entrusted to her the disposition of his unpublished manuscripts.[49]

The marriage took place in Amersham on the third of April, 1621, about three years after Hooker had come to Esher. We know nothing of his courtship and very little of his family life, except through his sermonic use of certain conjugal and paternal images as tropes, but these generalized images could have been derived from observation of any family or from traditional Christian literature. One such image, at least, does seem particularized and personal enough to have a source perhaps in his own courtship:

> Looke as it is with parties that live in the same family, and their affections are drawing on one towards another in marriage; they will cast their occasions so, that if it be possible, they will be together, and have one anothers company, and they will talke together, and worke together, and the time

[48] Quoted by Edmund S. Morgan, *The Puritan Family* (New York, Harper, 1966), 43.
[49] Hooker, "The Last Will and Testament of Mr. THOMAS HOOKER," in *The Public Records of the Colony of Connecticut*, ed. J. Hammond Trumbull (Hartford, 1850), I, 500.

gocth on marvellous suddenly, all the while their affections are drawing on.[50]

Since the situation described here of living in the same family parallels Hooker's and Mistress Garbrand's, we may safely surmise that the marriage of Thomas and Susanna was not without tenderness and affection. Did not Hooker elevate his love for his wife so that after the moving description of human love just quoted, he turned to the soul's eternal love for Christ?

> So it is with the soule that loves Jesus Christ, and hath this holy affection kindled, it thinkes every place happy, where it hath heard of Christ, and thinkes that houre sweet, wherein it put up its prayers to the Lord, and enjoyed lovechat with him."[51]

In a successful Puritan marriage delight in one's spouse enhanced, and was enhanced by, a mutual love for Christ.

[50] Hooker, *Vocation*, 257.   [51] Ibid.

THREE

The English Preaching
Career

BY the middle of the 1620s Thomas Hooker had acquired a
fair measure of fame among the English Puritans, although his
activities had not yet come to the critical notice of ecclesiastical
authority. He had first made his mark as a catechist and lecturer at Emmanuel, and his successes with Mrs. Drake would
have called attention to the power of his ministry. Ministerial
and lay supporters of Puritan church reform noted the name
and accomplishments of John Dod's successor in counseling
that notorious lady. It also seems likely that toward the end
of his stay at Esher he was occasionally preaching in and about
London, and this activity would have offered a further opportunity to measure his talents. Cotton Mather wrote, without
citing authority, that "he did more publickly and frequently
preach about London; and in a little time he grew famous for
his ministerial abilities."[1] There were many opportunities in
London for occasional preaching, for example, those offered
by the church of St. Antholin. This church had an endowment
providing for six lectures a year, and the rector, Charles Offspring, was friendly to the Puritan cause; in 1626 he became
one of the feoffees for impropriated tithes, a group engaged
in buying presentations and lay impropriations in order to support Puritan preachers. After 1626 St. Antholin's was notorious
as a hotbed of Puritanism, and, while it is not known where
Hooker preached in London, this probably would have been
the sort of position open to him.[2]

[1] Mather, I, 334.
[2] Raymond P. Stearns, *Congregationalism in the Dutch Netherlands*,
Studies in Church History, IV (Chicago, 1940), 21-22.

Some sign of both his growing fame and his inclinations in the matter of church government appears in William Bradford's *Plymouth Plantation*. The Pilgrims were having serious problems with a scalawag named John Lyford, who had been sent over by their London backers in 1624 to be their minister. Edward Winslow returned to London later in the year on business and complained to the Adventurers about Lyford's conduct. Lyford's friends protested his innocence and threatened to prosecute Winslow for libel. Sometime in late 1624 or early 1625 it was "agreed to choose two eminent men for moderators in the business; Lyford's faction chose Mr. White, a counselor at law; the other part chose Reverend Mr. Hooker, the minister."[3] Hooker must have been relatively well known by this time if he was thus noticed by the Plymouth Colony's supporters in London. This incident also establishes that comparatively early in his career he was willing to be on friendly terms with the separatists; his toleration was to cause him serious problems in a few years.

In the years just before 1625 he was undoubtedly becoming restive under the burden of acute disputations with Mrs. Drake —not a misogynist, he later complained that "women that are weake in their reasons, are wonderfully refractory in their wills"[4]—and after the improvement in her spiritual condition he would have felt more free to expand the scale of his activities. Mrs. Drake died at her parents' home in Amersham on April 18, 1625, and although it is not clear whether or not Hooker was still rector at Esher, he did attend at her deathbed. Early in 1625 he probably began to look about for a new position. Although he was quite satisfied to remain within the wide circle of the Anglican Church, provided his own method of preaching God's word were tolerated, his opinions upon church organization were at odds with those of the Establishment. An anonymous contemporary noted:

[3] William Bradford, *Of Plymouth Plantation*, ed. Samuel Eliot Morison (New York, Knopf, 1952), 167–68.
[4] Hooker, *Humiliation*, 159.

His opinion about the Doctrine maintained in the Church of England, since the reformation thereof was *Orthodox*; but his conscience about the Discipline and Ceremonies thereof was scrupulous; yet so, as he loved such as he observed sincere and entire in the substance, though he differed from them in circumstances.[5]

The ecclesiastical powers had not yet interfered with his activities, and, since he believed the established church to be a true church, he felt no pressure to look for a position outside of England. His espousal of the separatists' cause in the Lyford case indicates that he had already begun to entertain some scrupulous concerns about discipline and ceremonies, and so he probably would have been interested in a position as a lecturer, one of the usual havens for a Puritan preacher. There is evidence to suggest that in 1626 he preached in "the great church of Leicester," the shire town in his home county, as a candidate for either the position of lecturer or that of pastor.[6] If so, nothing came of this episode.

One prominent Puritan who recognized the promise of the young rector from Surrey was the Reverend John Rogers of Dedham in Essex, who was the author of a treatise on conversion. Hooker had probably formed an admiration for the Dedham pastor sometime earlier, and he later attested his regard for Rogers by writing an introduction to the second edition of his treatise, *The Doctrine of Faith*, published in 1627. Cotton Mather has noted:

About this time it was that Mr. Hooker grew into a most intimate acquaintance with Mr. Rogers of Dedham; who so highly valued him for his multifarious abilities, that he used

[5] (Anon.), "Epistle to the Reader," in Hooker, *The Danger of Desertion* (London, 1641), sig. A2r.

[6] George Huntston Williams, "The Pilgrimage of Thomas Hooker (1586–1647) in England, The Netherlands, and New England," *Bulletin of the Congregational Library* 19, No. 1 (October 1967), 7. Professor Williams' very helpful article is completed in issue No. 2 (January 1968).

and gained many endeavours to get him settled at Colchester; whereto Mr. Hooker did very much incline, because of its being so near to Dedham, where he might enjoy the *labours* and *lectures* of Mr. Rogers, whom he would sometimes call, "The prince of all the preachers in England."[7]

Something went wrong, however, in negotiations with the church at Colchester, and no call issued from there. Shortly afterward, according to Mather, the church of St. Mary at Chelmsford, Essex, "wanting one to 'break the bread of life' unto them, and hearing the fame of Mr. Hooker's powerful ministry, addressed him to become their lecturer; and he accepted this offer about the year 1626."[8] It seems that he was actively preaching in Essex sometime before the end of 1626, and entered into his lectureship toward the end of that year, for his daughter Anne was baptized at Great Baddow, a village near Chelmsford, on January 5, 1627. He moved his family to Chelmsford sometime in the following year, and his daughter Sarah was baptized there on April 9, 1628.

He very quickly gained the esteem of the other Puritan ministers around Dedham and Chelmsford; there was a sort of shadow synod in that part of the county which held regular monthly meetings, and in these assemblies his voice was heard with respect. Thomas Shepard, for example, recorded the part Hooker played in directing him to his first pulpit. Shepard came to Essex from Cambridge in early 1627; he at first found no call for his services, but he stayed with Thomas Welde of Terling and "enjoyed the blessing of his and Mr. Hooker's ministry at Chelmesfoord."[9] About that time a certain Dr. Wilson had "purposed to set up a lecture, . . . and when I was among those woorthies in Essex where we had monethly fasts; they did propound it unto me; to take the lecture and to set it

<hr/>

[7] Mather, I, 334. [8] Ibid., 334–35.

[9] Thomas Shepard, "The Autobiography of Thomas Shepard," in *Publications of the Colonial Society of Massachusetts, Transactions 1927–1930* 27 (Boston, 1932), 365.

up at a great town in Essex called Cogshall." Welde was much in favor of establishing the lecture at Coggeshall, and most of the other ministers supported him until Hooker raised an objection.

> Being but yong and unexperienced and there being an old yet sly and malicious minister in the town who did seem to give way to it to have it there, Mr. Hooker did therefore say it was dangerous and uncomfortable for little birds to build under the nests of old ravens and kites.[10]

Hooker's objection changed the minds of several members of the monthly meeting, and a great debate ensued. This dispute was providentially resolved in favor of Hooker's arguments when a delegation from Earles Colne appeared, asking for the lecture to be established in their village. Although it required a seemingly providential event to bring the assembly to a "joynt consent," Hooker's opinions were influential among his peers. To change the opinions of several Puritans was the work of "an acute disputant"; to make many Puritans agree was an act of God.

One reason for Hooker's importance among his colleagues was certainly his keen and comprehensive mind, but another reason for their respect was his demonstrated effectiveness as a powerful, godly minister. Mather wrote of his preaching:

> Hereby there was a great reformation wrought, not only in the town, but in the adjacent country, from all parts whereof they came to "hear the wisdom of the Lord Jesus Christ," in his gospel, by this worthy man dispensed; and some of great quality among the rest, would often resort from far to his assembly; particularly the truly noble Earl of Warwick. . . .[11]

In addition to the moral reformation implied here by Mather, Hooker's lectures at Chelmsford persuaded many to enter upon

---

[10] Shepard, "Autobiography," 366. [11] Mather, I, 335.

the way to spiritual regeneration. Mather described several examples of remarkable transformations caused by his preaching;
although we now have no access to Mather's sources for these
anecdotes, one of them makes an important point.

> A profane person, designing therein only an ungodly diver-
> sion and merriment, said unto his companions, "Come, let us
> go hear what that bawling Hooker will say to us;" and
> thereupon, with an intention to make sport, unto Chelms-
> ford lecture they came. The man had not been long in the
> church, before the *quick and powerful word* of God, in the
> mouth of his faithful Hooker, pierced the soul of him; he
> came out with an awakened and a distressed soul, and by
> the further blessing of God upon Mr. Hooker's ministry,
> he arrived unto a true *conversion*; for which cause he would
> not afterwards leave that blessed ministry, but went a *thou-
> sand leagues* to attend it and enjoy it.[12]

After 1630 when the Laudian pressures upon nonconformists
became more intense, a large group of people from Chelmsford
and environs would emigrate to New England; although they
arrived in Massachusetts over a year before Hooker, they were
already designated as "Mr. Hooker's company."[13] Mather was
well aware of the amount of persuasion required to urge an
Englishman to exchange his comfortable Essex farm for an
American wilderness.

Hooker apparently urged other beginning ministers to

> preach over the whole *body of divinity* methodically, (even
> in the Amesian method,) which would acquaint them with
> all the more intelligible and agreeable texts of Scripture, and
> prepare them for a further acquaintance with the more dif-
> ficult, and furnish them with abilities to preach on whole

[12] Ibid., 337.
[13] John Winthrop, *Journal*, ed. James K. Hosmer (1908; rpt. New
York, Barnes and Noble, 1966), I, 90.

chapters, and all occasional subjects, which by the providence of God they might be directed to.[14]

Hooker undoubtedly began his own preaching "over the whole *body of divinity* methodically" in his capacity of catechist at Emmanuel, and he repeated the process once more in the Chelmsford pulpit. His pastoral career in England and Europe would be disrupted within a relatively short time, and when he came to reestablish himself as a pastor in New England, he would preach over these same doctrines again, reminding his parishioners of what were for him the essential facts of religion before he went on to consider their implications.

His interpretation of "the Amesian method" was not pedantic; he did not attempt sermons on each and every subject developed in Ames's *Marrow of Sacred Divinity*. He went instead to the core of Ames's systematization of Christian doctrine, expounded in Book I, Chapters xx through xxx, and preached upon "the experience of those *humiliations* and consolations, and sacred communions, which belong to the new creature."[15] For Hooker the central Christian doctrine was the notion of man's redemption through Christ, and the greater portion of his surviving works is concerned with describing the workings of redemption and exhorting men to seek after it. Mather noted, "While he was a fellow of Emmanuel-College, he entertained a special inclination to those principles of divinity which concerned *the application of redemption.*"[16] Hooker himself referred to the subject of his sermons as the application of redemption, and his last works were published posthumously under this title.

After preaching at Emmanuel on the application of redemption, "in a more scholastick way, which was most agreeable to his present station," as Mather tells us, Hooker recovered this ground "in a more popular way, at Chelmsford." Mather claims further that the product of the Chelmsford lectures "were

---

[14] Mather, I, 347.   [15] Ibid.   [16] Ibid.

those books of *preparation for Christ, contrition, humiliation, vocation, union with Christ, and communion,* and the rest, which go under his name."[17] He is referring to a series of books which appeared between 1632 and 1638 with titles such as *The Soules Preparation for Christ, The Soules Humiliation,* etc. These books taken as an ordered series deal systematically with the whole process of the application of redemption, and judging both from internal evidence and from publication dates, they were all delivered originally as sermons in England. If they are studied sequentially, they provide an understanding of Hooker's theological center.[18] We can best understand his practice of preaching by following his own expository methods up to a point; if we "open" the phrase "application of redemption" after the manner of a Puritan preacher opening his sermon text, we find two things worthy of consideration: first, what is meant by redemption; second, what is meant by application.

II

An account of redemption must begin in the Beginning, for it was Adam's adventure with the lady and the snake in Eden that began the history of human sorrow. Any young New England Puritan would discover at the head of his primer the fatal rhyme, "In Adam's fall/We sinned all." No Puritan finally doubted that "all mankinde was in *Adam* his loynes, and *Adam* in innocencie represented all mankinde, he stood (as a Parliament man doth for the whole country) for all that should be born of him; so that look what *Adam* did, all his posterity

---

[17] Ibid.

[18] Quotations from these books will be identified parenthetically in the text of this chapter with the following letter code:

The Soules Preparation = SP.
The Soules Humiliation = SH.
The Soules Vocation = SV.
The Soules Exaltation (London, 1638) = SE.
The Soules Implantation = SI.

did."[19] Not only was man cast out of Eden, the harmoniously ordered garden of nature, into the wilderness, but also his own nature became a wilderness of sin and death. Adam's experience was a universal experience, Hooker explained, for as Adam fell, so

> a poore sinner having fallen from God, and departed from him, he goes away from God and all goodnesse at that one stroake; he that goes away from God, the God of all strength, must needs be weake; and he that goes from the God of wisdome, folly must needs possesse him, because God is the God of all wisdome, and all wisdome must be from him; and hee that goes from God, goes from life and happinesse, therefore death and cursednesse must needs seize upon him: now hee that hath gone from God, hath gone from all these, and therefore he is full of nothing but wants, miseries, and troubles, and vexations, that are come in upon him, and overwhelme him. (*SV*, 315)

The inexorable logic of the fall had made the life of natural man nasty, brutish, and short, and Thomas Hobbes to the contrary, the Puritan held that man could not recover the Edenic order through civil means.

The aboriginal human tragedy was compounded by the inability of Adam and his descendants to restore the divine and perfect order from whence they fell. Natural man still had an immortal soul and a vision of an impossible perfection and happiness—"For a man to be able, and to have a power and principle of life, to performe duties of himselfe, and to please God of himselfe, it was once possible in the time of mans innocency; Adam had it" (*SH*, 13)—but Adam's children lacked the abilities to realize the vision of order. Man's only hope after the fall was his knowledge that he had been originally created by a loving God; unable to right his own wrong, man had to

---

[19] Hooker, *The Saints Dignitie and Dutie* (London, 1651), 28.

look beyond himself to a principle of love which might restore his corrupted heart.

While God was indeed Love, the Puritans saw that He was also Justice, and this attribute made the working out of the tragedy's happy ending considerably more difficult. When Adam broke covenant with God, he incurred a debt which he was unable to pay. Adam's debt to God was handed on to his children, and Hooker's frequently used metaphor of the sinner as a bankrupt in debtor's prison described the natural human condition. Before man could be restored to the exercise of Christian liberty, the power to choose good which Adam lost, he had to be bought out of prison, to be redeemed. "Redemption is the buying of man into freedome, from the bondage of sinne, and the devill, by the payment of an equall price."[20] Natural man's insoluble problem was his inability to come up with "an equall price" for the original sin; a debt to God could only be paid in divine currency, and the just God of the Puritans insisted upon payment before he would restore man. The loving God, however, devised an ingenious solution by which the debt could be paid: "Seeing it could not be paid by man, the helpe of a Mediator was necessary, who should come betweene God and man, making a perfect reconciliation betweene them."[21] God himself, in the person of his Son, became man in the form of Jesus Christ and paid Adam's outstanding charges. Christ's redemption was not a right, however, but a gift, and it had to be given, or "applied," to men. Redemption, according to Puritan theologians, was given to man through a new covenant; God contracted anew with man and drew him back to Himself with a new agreement. "The way of application," said Ames, "is called in the Scriptures a new covenant."[22]

All men shared a common humanity with Christ, but this was not sufficient grounds for participation in the new cove-

---

[20] Ames, *Marrow*, 70.　　　　[21] Ibid.
[22] Ibid., 101.

nant, for Judas and Pontius Pilate were also men. Puritan divines said nothing new when they held that the one way man could participate with Christ in the new covenant was through saving faith. "Now faith is appointed as that onely meanes whereby the soul may bee succoured, and heart furnished anew," Hooker claimed (*SV*, 316). Man's saving connection with Christ was not natural, as was the connection with Adam, but "our implantation into Christ, is the worke of the Spirit, whereby the humbled sinner stands possessed of Christ, and is made partaker of the Spirituall good things in him."[23] Nor was the new covenant universal or national as it was for Noah and Abraham, but personal, experienced by man as God's election of himself alone.

The faith required by God for participation in the new covenant was not the natural man's rational, notional consent to divine truth but a spiritual, experiential assent of the soul to the grace it perceived in the heart. "It is one thing to believe, that there is a God, and another to believe into God," said Hooker (*SV*, 317). While God elected to distribute this grace only in accordance with His own mysterious will, man had to be willing to be saved in order to experience this participation in God through faith. Hooker, more than most of his Puritan colleagues, stressed the nature of faith as voluntary experience; he warned his Chelmsford congregation, "If you have not grace, it is because you will not have it, and therefore if you perish thanke your selves, for you would not bee saved."[24] He developed this doctrine of the covenant only incidentally in his sermons in order to show why conversion, a spiritual change from nature to grace, was necessary for men. Hooker's major intent in his preaching was to detail "after what manner, and by what meanes" God worked saving grace and faith in the hearts of men. A major concern of his preaching would

[23] Hooker, *The Soules Ingrafting Into Christ* (London, 1638), 3.
[24] Hooker, *Unbeleevers*, 65.

be to explain how man, God willing, could will his conversion, or to be more accurate, could experience his conversion as an act of will.

St. Paul's miraculous conversion was not typical of the regenerating experience as observed and described by many of the Puritan divines; although God could and did work by miraculous intervention in human affairs, He apparently preferred to work through second causes. God foresaw the fall of Adam in the garden and the coming of Christ into the wilderness, and He implanted into the universe at its creation principles which would work themselves out in history. God's guidance and governance of man did not usually manifest itself as miraculous intervention but as history, the detailed pattern of all events proceeding from the divine first cause. Although God did not force His presence upon men, His care over them was nevertheless sure; Hooker told his congregation, "Our Savior hath a special care for those that shal beleeve on him, even in the worst condition of their Unbeleef."[25]

When God gave man the saving faith necessary to enter into the covenant, His dealings were articulated in time; Hooker frequently cautioned sinners awaiting conversion, "God will bestow what he hath promised, yet hee reserves the time to himselfe."[26] This warning implied that there would be an interval between the extension of the promise and the actual gift of saving grace; in this interim man could only wait upon God and hearken to His will. God's will, according to Hooker, demanded sinners in the way of regeneration to use the means appointed by Him for seeking grace. "God . . . useth meanes, not for want of power," explained Ames, "but through the abundance of his goodnesse: that namely he might communicate a certaine dignity of working to his Creatures also, and

[25] Hooker, *A Comment on Christs Last Prayer in the Seventeenth of John* (London, 1656), 22.
[26] Hooker, *Doubting Christian*, 363.

in them might make his efficiency more perceivable."[27] Man's efforts in behalf of his own salvation had no intrinsic merit, since he lacked Christian liberty, but they seemed indispensable to Hooker in the ordinary course of spiritual transformation. Before man received saving grace, he must have preparation— "a fitting and enabling of the soule for Christ" (*SH*, 1). This concept of preparation was not original with Hooker, but his formulation of it is central to what later became orthodox theology in New England.[28]

Hooker informed his congregation, "A preparation there must be, for a sinner naturally as he hath no grace, so hee is not naturally capable to receive grace."[29] Preparation, as expounded by Hooker and his colleagues, was both God's preparation of man and man's preparation of himself to receive grace: "On Gods part, he breakes the cursed Combination betwixt Sinne and the Soule, hee drawes us from Sinne to himselfe. Something on our part touching the disposition of our hearts: and that in two workes. 1. Contribution, 2. Humiliation."[30] Although Hooker usually defined preparation in this way as including both contrition and humiliation, in his second book, *The Soules Preparation for Christ*, he discussed it as contrition only. "This contrition," said Hooker, "is nothing else but namely when a sinner by the sight of sinne, and vilenesse of it, and the punishment due the same, is made sensible of sinne, and is made to hate it, and hath his heart separated from the same" (*SP*, 2). In his larger development of the nature of contrition, Hooker divided it into three major parts; gaining a sight of sin, finding a sound sorrow for sin, and being separated from its corruption. The method of *The Soules Preparation*, like that of *The Poore Doubting Christian*, was both descrip-

---

[27] Ames, *Marrow*, 40.

[28] See Pettit, 88–101. In the first chapters of this book he ably develops the English and continental backgrounds of preparationist theology.

[29] Hooker, *Ingrafting*, 1.   [30] Ibid., 2.

tive and prescriptive; he analyzed the work of God in the soul of the man in preparation and urged all reprobates in the congregation to attempt their share of this work.

He began by reminding the natural man in his audience both of the danger of his present condition and of the difficult course before him: "A little mercy will not serve thy turne, thou that hast been an old weather-beaten sinner," he says, therefore, "expect it with much difficulty and harnesse in thy selfe" (*SP*, 10). He followed this warning with a description of a "true sight of sinne": "It is not every sight of sinne will serve the turne, nor every apprehension of a mans vilenesse; but it must have these two properties in it, First, he must see sinne clearly; Second, convictingly" (*SP*, 12–13). The distinction drawn here between true and misleading sights of sin is similar to that made above between believing in God and believing into God; a true sight of sin prepared the way for a spiritual transformation, and a false view merely added one more notional bit of self-damning knowledge to the mind. In order to obtain a contrition which could effect a change in the soul, man's clear sight of sin must comprehend both the nature of sin and its results for the sinner; when a man got a clear sight of sin, he must realize both that "there is nothing so contrary and opposite against the Lord," and that "it is sinne that doth procure all plagues and punishments to the damned" (*SP*, 16–17).

Mrs. Drake's agonies were in part caused by her fallacious view of reality, and in a similar way a natural man's torments would result from his failure to perceive the real nature of the creation. Men viewed sin not in the context of the spiritual reality which gave being and life to the universe but in terms of the material world, "in regard of the profit that is therein, or the pleasure that we expect therefrom" (*SP*, 20). To see sin clearly was thus to see it ideally as the opposite of life and goodness; to see it convictingly, man had to see his own particular sins which estranged him from God. The clear sight of sin which was to be first obtained Hooker described as a correction of man's understanding; the convicting sight of sin subsequently brought general knowledge to bear in a practical fashion upon the heart. "I would have you perceive your own particular sinnes and follow them to your hearts, and make hue and cry after your sinnes, and dragge your hearts before the Lord" (*SP*, 25). The purpose of conversion was to effect a change for the good in the heart of man, and conviction of sin was the first step toward a renewed heart.

Earlier preachers of the doctrine of preparation had, upon theological grounds, stressed terror of the divine Law as the first stage of conversion. Hooker's substitution of a right knowledge and conviction of one's own sinful state for less particular "legal terrors" was based upon his conception of human psychology. Hooker's theological preceptors agreed that the center of human corruption was the will; in natural man, said Ames, the will "is neither by itselfe, nor by reason sufficiently determined to good actions, and so it hath need of its owne and internall disposition to worke aright."[31] Hooker explained in terms of faculty psychology the rationale behind God's demand for conviction of personal sin:

> The reason why, and how it comes to passe, that God deales thus with poore sinners, is taken from the office which the Lord hath placed between the heart and the man, the ground lies thus.
>
> There are two things in the soule, First, you conceive and understand a thing. Secondly, you wil and choose it. The

[31] Ames, *Marrow*, 198. Concerning the relationship between will and intellect, Ames and Hooker were both voluntarists, i.e., they held that the will was not necessarily determined by reason. Education, or in a more restricted sense, preparation, could regulate intellect but could not restore the fallen will which could be recreated only by grace. Thus Hooker could teach preparation without infringing upon divine sovereignty or falling into Arminian rationalism. See Norman S. Fiering, "Will and Intellect in the New England Mind," *William and Mary Quarterly* 29 (1972), 515–58.

first is the inlet of the heart, so that no thing can affect the heart, but so farre as reason conceiveth it, and ushers it home to the soule; the understanding saith, this or that is good, and then the will saith, let me have it.   (*SP*, 30)

Unable to cause action of itself, the understanding was thus the normal means of influencing the will, for "nothing commeth to the heart to be affected but onely by the head and understanding" (*SV*, 110). To the limited extent in which a man could give his will "its owne and internall disposition to worke aright," he must approach it through the understanding. Although God in conversion worked directly upon the heart, man must prepare the heart indirectly through right reason. The dead heart of reprobate man was enlivened as it was "made sensible of sinne," but a "sight of sinne" must precede the quickening of the sensibility.

To help reason direct the heart, Hooker first reminded his congregation, "An ignorant heart is a naughty heart," and he then developed an elaborate method for bringing home a conviction of sin to the heart. He detailed three means to obtain a conviction of sin, three "shifts whereby the soule labours to beate back the power of word" (*SP*, 40), and three motives to obtain conviction. This method of proceeding is much like that of *The Poore Doubting Christian*, especially in that he describes the three "shifts" as "lets that may hinder a man" from convicting himself of sin (*SP*, 36). There was one important reversal: Mrs. Drake was encouraged to judge herself by God's work in order to discover her condition was not so bad as supposed, but the reprobates were enjoined to "looke your selves in this glasse of the Word, . . . if you could but see the filthinesse of your hearts, you would be out of love with your selves for ever" (*SP*, 37). Conviction of sin required careful management, for there could be too little as well as too much, and the preacher shaped his exhortations to the souls of his listeners. Preaching was in effect a kind of public pastoral care, and Hooker saw the method used in *The Poor Doubting Christian* as equally adaptable to the conditions of natural men at large.

Hooker developed out of his text a further argument to enforce conviction for sin, and once more it is familiar to readers of his first treatise: "Serious meditation of our sinnes by the word of God is a speciall meanes to breake our hearts for our sinnes" (*SP*, 81). The difference of condition between the doubting Christian and the preparing sinner was again acknowledged, but the procedure in dealing with both types of case was similar, for the desired effect of a spiritual change of heart was the same in both cases. The doubting Christian was advised to meditate upon the promises, the good news of the Bible, but the natural man was to consider the condemnation of reprobates. Hooker's discussion of meditation was here both more explicit and more detailed than in the earlier book, but its general outlines were the same. The natural man in the way of preparation was urged to consider his own wickedness and God's justice, but like the doubting Christian, he was also advised, "Labour to see the mercy, goodnesse, and patience of God" (*SP*, 100). He was warned, "Take heed that the heart doth not flie off and shake off the yoke . . . meditation brings all those sins and miseries, and vilenesse, all are brought home to the heart, and the soule is made sensible by this meanes" (*SP*, 112). If meditation succeeded, it would not only enforce the conviction of sin, it would introduce the soul dead in sin to a first taste of a new life. The taste was bitter, but Hooker held that any sign of life or sensibility was encouraging.

The object of meditation, as Hooker defined it, was the same, no matter what the state of the meditator's soul; the doubting Christian was urged to see a greater good in Christ's promise than anywhere else, and the preparing sinner was told, "So farre see thy sinnes, so farre be affected with them, . . . that they may make thee see the absolute necessity of a Christ" (*SP*, 115). An important part of the pastoral instruction given to the natural man was this distinction between ends and means; the soul in way of preparation must keep its attention upon the divine end of its aspirations in order to progress through the ordered pattern of means. The clear and convicting sight of sin, while essential for any effective restructuring of the soul, was only a means to regeneration; reprobate man must next use this newly acquired knowledge of his sin in order to arrive at the next way station of preparation. The clear sight of sin has corrected the natural man's understanding, but a reformation of the will, "the proper principle of life, and of morall and spirituall actions,"[32] is requisite for regeneration. Hooker termed the affective aspect of contrition "sound sorrow," and the greater portion of *The Soules Preparation* was concerned with its description and with the means of receiving it.

Hooker reminded the natural man that he "is yet to be conceived as in the way of preparation for Christ; not to have any formall worke of grace whereby hee is able to doe anything for himselfe" (*SP*, 167). Sound sorrow was worked upon the passive soul by God and often came after "the hammer of Gods Law layeth a sudden blow upon the heart, and thus discovers the vile nature of sinne" (*SP*, 136). After he received this sound sorrow, the reprobate became a "broken hearted sinner," and as his heart was broken, it was liberated from bondage to sin. One of the necessities for a clear sight of sin was a recognition of the divine good lost through human corruption; sound sorrow translated this knowledge into the language of the heart, so that a man in the way of preparation was both intellectually and emotionally repelled by sin. The first step toward the good was the rejection of evil, the bondage of Adam's natural children, "so that the union between sin and the soule is now broken and room is prepared and way is made for the Lord Jesus to come into the soule" (*SP*, 161).

Since conversion happened in history and not in the eternal moment, Hooker warned his congregation that in every part of

[32] Ames, *Marrow*, 198.

their regenerating experience they must take great pains in examining the state of their souls. Although sound sorrow often came after a "sudden blow upon the heart" that "discovers the vile nature of sinne," the actual breaking of the heart, the working of godly sorrow, was not usually done in a day. The hammer blow might be complete, as in Paul's case, but in the ordinary course of regeneration men must not "thinke the Lord never workes grace but in this extraordinary manner" (*SP*, 178). Sinners must not deceive themselves that a pang of remorse was indeed sound sorrow, for, as

> when men goe into a farre Countrey for merchandize, they will not take rattles and such toyes for their money; but such commodities as they may get something by; so when the Lord comes for broken hearts, you must not thinke to put the Lord off with a little painted sorrow: No, no, it is a broken heart that the Lord will not despise.
>
> (*SP*, 186–87)

Presumption, the confidence that "a little painted sorrow" was the genuine emotion, was one of the main causes of hypocrisy. The hypocrite would be condemned not for his deceit of Christ, an impossibility, but for his failure to reject his own corruptions, his self-deceit. Since hearts were more often melted into sound sorrow than hammered into it, men might overlook the grace given to them and despair of their condition: "When God works gently with Christians, they hardly perceive the work, though wise Christians may approve that which is done" (*SP*, 182). Presumption and despair are the Scylla and Charybdis of the Christian voyager, and he must carefully chart his affections in order to avoid these great hindrances to salvation.

If a sinner attained sound sorrow for his sins, he should be able to enjoy the three fruits of contrition: the secret hope of mercy by which God supports broken-hearted sinners, a willingness to make free and open confession of his sins, and a thorough detestation of sin. All these fruits were evidences of a "new heart" in the sinner, the beginning of a new structure of value and behavior, but, unfortunately, they did not always occur. The sinner often deprived himself of his own happiness by not carrying godly sorrow to its logical and spiritual conclusions; in Hooker's second book in the Chelmsford series on redemption, *The Soules Humiliation*, he described the means by which the soul in preparation could complete the process of separation from sin.

The source of the poor doubting Christian's difficulties was pride, and the same pride, whether manifested overtly as presumption or inversely as despair, kept carnal men from attaining regeneration. "Pride . . . is opposite to the covenant of grace" (*SH*, 198), and in natural man "there are mountaines of pride and untoward stoutnesse of heart, and many windings and turnings, and devices which the heart hath, by reason of many lusts that are in it." This "knotty knarlinesse of the heart, and that pride, and all such cursed corruptions" must be removed so that "the doore may be set open, and the heart made ready that the king of glory may come in" (*SH*, 2). If fallen man was to escape the death and misery inherited from the old Adam, he must voluntarily reject the whole inheritance of sin. It was not only his intellectual attitude to the world which must be changed by the divine Word, but his emotional response to it. For Hooker and his Puritan brethren, conversion was concurrent with the birth of an entire new range of affections, the awakening of a new sensitivity to life: "All the old things are done away, and become new, he is new in heart and life" (*SH*, 3).

After a sinner felt the necessity for a new life in order to escape from his bondage to sin and death, he "naturally . . . seekes for succour (not from God nor from Christ) but from himselfe and from his owne abilities" (*SH*, 7). It seemed logically absurd, however, that an imperfect being could repair the ruin wrought by his first parents through his own imperfect actions, and the aim of humiliation as Hooker preached it was that man should lay aside his natural powers in order to receive a spiritual power from Christ.

> For the covenant of grace is this, Beleeve and live. The condition on our part is faith, and beleeving. Now faith is nothing else, but a going out of the Soule, to fetch all from another, as having nothing of it selfe, and therefore this resting in our selves, will not stand with the nature of this covenant.
> (*SH*, 127)

Humiliation was this "going out of the Soule," a rejection of the natural self, in order to attain a union with the divine source of all power and excellency. Sound sorrow led to a detestation of sin, but sin had so infected the natural self that it in its turn must be rejected in favor of a "new heart."

The Soules Humiliation exposed all those "windings and turnings, and devices which the heart hath" to evade God's will, and just as Hooker left Mrs. Drake waiting for a "full gaile of spirituall winde," so here the sinner in the way of preparation is on the threshold. He is

> pared and fitted for Christ, as a graft for the stocke. He is come to the very quicke, and is as little as may be. All his swelling sufficiency is pared away: For, he is not onely brought to renounce his sinne, but even his sufficiency, and all his parts and abilities; which *Adam* needed not have done, if he had stood in his innocency. In a word, hee is wholly pluckt from the first *Adam*, (for here is the maine lift) so that now the second *Adam* Christ Jesus, may take possession of him, and *be all in all in him*.   (*SH*, 132)

True humiliation attained, the soul's preparation was complete; the separation from sin begun with contrition has been taken as far as natural man can go. With humiliation, the part of redemption which consists of "something on our part" was finished, and the soul waited now for the direct application of Christ's merits. Although preparation had been made possible by the divine gift of grace, God's part in the redemption of man is consummately the lifting him out of his natural estate into a state of sanctifying grace.

"A man's life and conversation must be at Gods disposing" to complete his preparation for redemption (*SH*, 163), but man himself could go far to prepare himself. Hooker preached the doctrine of preparation not to a limited group of potential saints but to all men who would listen; while strict Calvinist theology emphasized that only a few men would be saved, Hooker preached that all men might be saved if they would only submit themselves to God. "It is possible for any Soule present (for ought I know or that he knowes) to get an humble heart" (*SH*, 209). Although he did not deny there were limits to the number of men God would save—indeed, He hardened the hearts of those He would not redeem—Hooker proclaimed the possibility for all men to find salvation. Contrition and humiliation were gifts from the living God to the inert soul, but men must themselves attempt sorrow and humility in order to discover if this grace had been given to them.

In the years when Richard Sibbes was counseling the lawyers of Grays Inn, "A sincere heart will offer itself to trial," Hooker was urging Chelmsford's reprobates, "Let every man try his owne heart, whether ever God hath given him this gracious disposition of Soule or no?"[33] If the sinner carefully used Hooker's various "tryalls" and discovered humility in himself, then it was an almost certain sign that God had graciously humbled his heart. As Sibbes put it, "If we choose him, we may conclude he hath chosen us first."[34] No matter how dead in sin a man might seem to himself, Hooker advised him to embark upon the way of preparation, for how else was he to know that he may not already have been offered saving grace? To find evidence of a new quickening spirit in the heart, there must first be an action, even though a spiritually good act merely proved the prior existence of grace in the soul.

[33] Sibbes, *Soul's Conflict*, 165.   [34] Ibid., 268.

Hooker described God's gift of saving grace to men in terms of the Pauline metaphor of ingrafting, and this trope provided the controlling image for his description of the latter steps of conversion. The divine gardener pared and fitted fallen man for ingrafting into the root of spiritual life and truth, but man had to cooperate with God in cutting away his own "swelling sufficiency." Hooker saw no inconsistency here, for the way in which he developed the metaphor of the soul as a graft into Christ included the sense both of man's passivity and of his activity; the sinner was possessed by Christ, and he possessed Christ simultaneously. The description of the mutual possession of Christ and the humbled sinner as implantation could explain to natural men both the inevitability of conversion for the elect and sufficiency of Christ. If the natural man's sin was cut off and his pride pared away, he could be immediately opened to the divine good; if the old Adam was removed, only the new Adam remained as possibility. Essex farmers knew well that an expert would immediately insert a prepared scion into the stock—"The Lord will not delay to come into an humbled soule" (*SI*, 10)—and they would also realize that a graft flourishes not of itself but because of the vital juices of the stock into which it is implanted. "As in ingrafting naturally, so of implanting spiritually of the soule into Christ, when the soul is brought unto this, then a sinner comes to be partaker of all the spirituall benefits, all shall be communicated to us" (*SV*, 33). Not only was the Lord certain to come into a truly humbled heart, He would provide it with all the necessary grace to achieve salvation.

Just as Hooker divided preparation into contrition and humiliation, so he divided ingrafting into the several parts of vocation, justification, adoption, and sanctification. Vocation was the formal offer of salvation to the soul "when the soule is brought out of the world of sinne, . . . and this hath two particular passages in it; partly the call on Gods part, partly the answer on ours" (*SV*, 33). God called all men to Him through the medium of the Gospel, but this was a common and outward call, made to the understandings of men and not to their hearts. Vocation was the revelation to a humbled soul of the particular applicability of the Gospel promise to himself; it came "when the Lord by the cal of his Gosspell doth so cleerly reveale the fulnesse of mercy, and certifies to the soule by the worke of his spirit" (*SV*, 33–34). "The cal of his Gosspell" was the "call on Gods part" to come and receive mercy, and it was identical to those parts of Scripture which Hooker entitled "the promises." The divine call to the soul contained in these promises was the offer to man of a new covenant, and in vocation a man was enabled to accept God's terms.

Hooker maintained that "there is a spirit of Wisdom and revelation, that is put forth" in the preaching of the Word, "but its . . . true that this Spirit goes along with this word, and works in this word, as seems good to the good pleasure and wil of Christ."[35] This "spirit of Wisdom" was the third person of the Trinity, and it enabled the prepared heart to perceive directly the promised divine good. "The Spirit doth forcibly soke in the rellish of . . . grace into the heart, and by the overpiercing worke, doth leave some dint of supernaturall and spirituall vertue on the heart" (*SV*, 45). The Spirit in the Word preceded Christ as an antitype of John the Baptist, who announced the birth of the Messiah to all men, and it certified the promise to the soul. The humbled heart thus was enabled to perceive the divine call in the promise, because it had been changed by the presence of the divine spirit: "As the Sun is seen by his own Light, It must be the wisdom from above, that must enable us to see the things that are above."[36]

The soul was enabled by the presence of the Spirit to respond to the call from God: "The Lord . . . by the worke of his Spirit hee doth bring all the riches of his grace into the soule truly humbled, so that the heart cannot but receive the

[35] Hooker, *Comment*, 449.   [36] Ibid., 444.

94

same, and give answer thereto, and give an eccho of the subjection of itselfe to be governed thereby" (*SV*, 34). The condition upon man's part of entering into the covenant was faith, and the soul could now respond to God's call as an echo to its source. Man's action became a mirror image of God's initiatory action, and the act of faith became an act of a renewed will. Faith, however, was not the end of the regenerative process, but a means to it; faith was "a spirituall instrument and engine, whereby the soule goes to God to fetch a soule, whereby he may live" (*SV*, 320–21). After a soul responded to the call of God it was justified, adopted, and sanctified, as a result of its saving faith.

> In Justification, Christ layes down a price, . . . and the soule is freed from the guilt and punishment of sinne; . . . In Adoption, Christ not onely cals a sinner, and justifies him, but adopts him, and makes him of a sinner a sonne, there is a nearer possession, and he hath the priviledges of a sonne; . . . In Sanctification, the Lord Christ, by the power of his Spirit, leaves a stampe of his Image, grace for grace, he is marked for his owne, this is the further possession; he is freed from the power of corruption. (*SI*, 4)

These three steps completed the soul's redemption, at least in as much as it would be completed in this world.

After vocation, the soul was a faithful follower of Christ: since "every true beleever is joyned unto Christ" (*SE*, 3), he shared in the spiritual attributes of the divine stock. Because Christ atoned for the sin of Adam and sins of all men, believers received mercy from the Father and remission of their sins when they were joined to Christ. Justification gave the soul a fresh start, unencumbered by guilt for his past deeds; this new righteousness was not sufficient for redemption in itself, however, for Adam had it, and he fell in spite of it. Christ kept his believers from returning to the bondage of sin by adopting them into himself; by adoption Christ preserved and quickened the grace already given to the faithful heart. "There is a kinde of conveyance of the vertue of his merits, and power of his grace unto the soules of those that beleeve in him, and are knit unto him by a true and lively faith" (*SE*, 58).

Justification, in terms of the ingrafting metaphor, was the purging of the old spirit from the scion, and adoption was the transfusion into it of a new life from the stock. Sanctification, the last part of redemption experienced in this life, was the bringing forth of flowers and fruit. The sanctified soul possessed the Christian liberty lost by Adam, and he was henceforth able to perform good acts, to offer what Hooker called a "new obedience" to God.[37] "Even thus it is with most Christians, the Lord hath possesst us of libertie, and yet he requireth that we should work out the remainders of iniquitie."[38] Sanctification restored the image of God in man by enabling him to perform Godlike acts; as Sibbes reasoned, "God himself is pure act, always in acting; and everything, the nearer it comes to God, the more it hath its perfection in working."[39] Agreeing with Sibbes, Hooker argued the end of regeneration to be the return of the power of significant action to the soul.

> Where ever there is faith, it is working. Faith it is not an idle grace, it is not a fancie or an opinion that Christ hath died for us, and there is an end, but it is a working grace, where there is faith, there is work, and what work is it? it is a work of love.[40]

Propelled by sin and terror after the fall, man is at last through the process of redemption, drawn by Love; he is converted from a self-destructive existence to a life full of the possibilities of creation, "a work of Love."

The ultimate evidence of redemption was this ability to perform sanctifying works, but as Hooker and his colleagues were

---

[37] Hooker, *Chief Lessons*, 270.   [38] Hooker, *Saints Dignitie*, 39.
[39] Sibbes, *Soul's Conflict*, 199.   [40] Hooker, *Saints Dignitie*, 5.

careful to establish, salvation was not procured by man's works but by God's love alone. The work of love which is sanctification was done by man, but it was a result of the divine love for him; as in vocation, man's action was only a reaction to the divine stimulus. "The ball must first fall to the ground, before it rebound backe againe; so the Lord Jesus must first dart in his love into the soule, before the soule can rebound in love and joy to him againe" (*Sl*, 208). Sanctification was not the cause of redemption but only the sign that saving grace had a prior existence in the soul.

Thus was man restored to his original happiness; he began as a natural man, laboring under fear and misery, and he ends as a child of God, living in love and joy. He escaped his bondage to sin and the vicissitudes of the material world in order to return to the living God.

> Wherever there is faith, there is a victorie over the world, before there is faith, there the soul is a slave to the world, but if once there be faith, he is more than a conqueror, he is not the worlds slave, but the world is his, the world is trampled under his feet, and is a dead flower to him, that hath neither beauty nor sweetnesse in it.[41]

Although the believer gained a victory over the world, it was not a victory in the terms of the world; he merely realized what had always been true since the fall, the world is a "dead flower." The possibilities of life were expanded for the faithful heart, but his mansion was a spiritual one and not an earthly palace. History was not reversed for the Christian soul: he did not revert to the condition of Adam before the fall, but he progressed to the happiness that Adam might have enjoyed in time, had he not sinned. The new covenant was not a mere reenactment of the old but the offer to man of a new basis for life. The old garden was irrevocably turned into wilderness by Adam's sin, and the new garden existed outside the fallen

[41] Ibid., 7.

world: "I know there is a wilde kinde of love and joy in the world, counterfeit coyne," said Hooker, "but this is not the love and joy we meane, we will have garden love and joy, of the Lords owne setting and planting" (SV, 205).

This was the scheme of redemption as Thomas Hooker preached it to the men and women of Chelmsford, and with slightly different emphases he preached the same doctrine ten years later to the pioneers of the Connecticut Valley. So much for the matter of his sermons, what then of his manner of making them effectual in the hearts of his listeners?

III

During the process of conversion, God had earthly servants in applying Christ's merits to the elect. "All things which are necessary to salvation are contained in the Scriptures," said William Ames.[42] Since this was true, argued Hooker, then "a powerfull ministry is the onely ordinary meanes which GOD hath appointed soundly to prepare the heart of a poore sinner for the receiving of the Lord Jesus" (SI, 68). The Scriptures were the Word of God, and the minister therefore preached not his own words but God's Word: "Whatsoever it is that the Scriptures make known to us, God from heaven hath spoken it, even as truly, and as really, as though he had spoken it immediately. . . . Whatsoever any faithfull Minister shall speake out of the Word, that is also the voice of Christ."[43]

This lofty conception of the preacher's duty placed a heavy burden both upon the minister and upon his congregation. The preacher had to be a "faithfull Minister" who could exercise a "powerfull ministry," expounding only God's truth and never losing sight of the end of preaching: "An unbeliever comming into the congregation of the faithfull he ought to be affected, and as it were digged through with the very hearing

[42] Ames, Marrow, 150.   [43] Hooker, Saints Dignitie, 135.

of the Word, that he may give glory to God."[44] Preachers must strive to make their sermons moving expositions of the Word, but they must never let their listeners forget that all life-giving grace came from God and not from the human means. If the preacher were faithful to his mission to struggle with the hearts of men, then his listeners rejected his message at their peril. As Hooker warned his congregation,

> My brethren, it is all one, if hearing the Minister speak unto you the word of God, and bring home to you the re-proofes, and admonitions, and counsels thereof, you kick his Word from you, and happily take up armes against him; it is all one (I say) as if you take up armes against God and despised him.[45]

If the minister preached only to please the fancies of his congregation or of his patron, he forfeited God's pleasure and gained nothing. If the people rejected a faithful minister, they rejected God and His truth. The end of preaching was not to procure material gain or public approval but to return lost souls to God and to gather the elect into a divine unanimity.

Puritans held that their ministers were the spiritual descendants of the Hebrew prophets, and in their preaching they were in fact prophesying, making "a publique and solemne speech . . . pertaining to the worship of God, and to the salvation of our neighbours."[46] The Puritan definition of prophet included all of the Old Testament figures who in any way spoke the will of God—Enoch and Noah as well as Isaiah and Daniel; unlike their Old Testament types who were called directly by God, the Puritan prophets were singled out by

[44] Ames, *Marrow*, 159.　　　[45] Hooker, *Saints Dignitie*, 198.

[46] William Perkins, *The Arte of Prophecying*, trans. Thomas Tuke (London, 1607), 1. The Puritan term "prophet" was applied to any person who spoke the will of God as the Puritans understood it, regardless of Old or New Testament distinctions; a prophet was not necessarily miraculously inspired.

the church. They enjoyed, however, powers similar to their scriptural models, for "so you must conceive of Gods Ministers, though they bee poore soules, yet Gods Spirit labours through them, and when they strive with the soules of men, and labour to plucke them out of their sinnes, then Gods Spirit strives."[47] While the Old Testament prophets were extraordinary ministers to the people of Israel, Puritan prophets were ordinary ministers who preached the truth mediately out of the Scriptures, thus performing the same function to the people of the world. The difference between the practice of Isaiah and that of Hooker arose from their different ways of knowing God's will and not from any difference in their worldly missions. The Spirit which spoke through Enoch and Isaiah was the same divine "spirit of Wisdom" which "doth ever accompany the Word and the Ministry thereof."[48]

The Old Testament prophets enjoyed several advantages denied to the ordinary Puritan minister; Enoch and Isaiah were immediately advised by God, but the ordinary minister must learn God's will through a careful study of Scripture. Perkins described two parts of preaching, preparation and promulgation; the Bible prophets needed no preparation, but seventeenth-century prophets needed all the resources of a Cambridge education in order to discover the will of God. Before a minister could preach upon his selected text, he must find out what truth that text contained by "using a grammaticall, rhetoricall, and logicall analysis."[49] Although "the Scripture doth not explaine the will of God by universall, and scientificall rules, but by narrations, examples, precepts, exhortations, admonitions, and promises," said Ames, explication of the truth was possible because "there is only one sence to one place of Scripture." An educated minister thus had the tools necessary

[47] Hooker, *Unbeleevers*, 93.
[48] Hooker, *The Saints Guide*, in *Three Treatises* (London, 1645), 13.
[49] Perkins, *Arte*, 26.

to uncover God's will, for "the Scriptures are understood by the same meanes that other humane writings are, many by the skill, and use of *Logick, Rhetoric, Grammar*, and those tongues in which they are expressed."[50]

A well-trained preacher could understand the will of God by careful preparation almost as well as the Old Testament prophets did by inspiration. But just as the prophets of old had an epistemological advantage over their seventeenth-century heirs, so they had a rhetorical advantage: the Spirit which taught them God's will also gave them the words with which to promulgate it. Since the Scriptures were often records of the prophets' preaching, however, the modern prophets had ready to hand a rhetorical text as well as a theological guide. "That Rhetorike which we finde in Scripture to be used by the Prophets and Apostles, hath great use in Preaching if it be used with the like prudence."[51] Bible rhetoric had been framed by the "spirit of Wisdom," and it had been proved effective in the hearts of men; explanation of the divine will by means of "narratives, examples, precepts," etc. was used in Scripture "because that manner doth make most for the common use of all kinde of men, and also most to affect the will, and stirre up godly motions, which is the chief scope of Divinity."[52]

Hooker's sermons were based upon Scripture truth and couched in Scripture rhetoric, but they were also shaped by his knowledge of the human mind. Several stages of intellectual activity in the hearer's mind went between the preacher's enunciation of the sermon and the words' affecting of the listener's will. Hooker defined these perceptual stages as he instructed his congregation in the proper method of hearkening to the pulpit message:

By hearkening, briefly you must understand these several particulars. The first is, a hearing with the ear. The second is,

[50] Ames, *Marrow*, 152.   [51] Ames, *Conscience*, IV, 78.
[52] Ames, *Marrow*, 151.

a closing with the truth, by the understanding of that we hear, for look as the ear receiveth the sound, so the mind and undertsanding must apprehend the sense, and assent to the truth of what is delivered. Thirdly, the memorie must retain and hold, that which the understanding hath received. The last and principall thing is the stooping of the soul, and subjection of the heart, to that which is understood and remembered.[53]

As one might gather from our discussion of his doctrine of preparation for Christ, this progressive schooling of the mind is analogous to the steps of regeneration, and the preacher similarly addressed each faculty of the mind in its turn until the heart was affected. When Hooker described the working of faith in psychological terms, he portrayed the Spirit operating upon each faculty in a way peculiar to that faculty, and he showed the Spirit following the same order of movement from the understanding to the will.[54]

The first test of a sermon's effective promulgation was obvious; the preacher's voice must be loud enough to be heard throughout the church, and his enunciation and delivery must be distinct and well-paced. While it was no great problem to make a sermon audible, it was a greater difficulty to phrase it so that "the mind and understanding must apprehend the sense." Although the sermon's content had to be clear to Chelmsford's illiterate artisans and farmers, it also had to have sufficient intellectual complexity and interest to involve the Earl of Warwick and other educated gentlemen who might be present. Hooker and the other Puritan preachers achieved this balance of simple clarity and intellectual comprehensiveness by using

[53] Hooker, *Saints Dignitie*, 124–25.

[54] It is characteristic of Hooker's theology in general that he adapts it to his model of mind. The central fact of all experience, whether natural or regenerate, was for him the process of mind (which was also the process of soul). All pastoral or prophetic acts had to face up to this divinely ordained pattern of human knowledge and action.

an established form for their sermons and by carefully modulating the rhetorical effects possible within this form.

Hooker always cast his sermons into the traditional mold of doctrine, reason, and use, although he varied the proportions of any given sermon to fit the occasion. He would first state the text upon which the sermon would be based, usually a whole verse of Scripture, and he would then "open" the text. Opening the text meant explaining those places that were "Crypticall and dark," as well as delineating the various truths referred to in the text.[55] The Puritan prophet respected beyond all earthly possessions the language of Scripture, and it must be understood correctly in order to discover the unseen truth behind the material fact. The only means to achieve this comprehension of reality was through a painstakingly acquired knowledge of the Word containing the will of God and the Spirit of salvation. When Hooker opened a text, he revealed intricacies of meaning which were previously unrealized by his congregation.

Having opened the text, Hooker next proceeded to state his doctrine. This was the particular truth of Scripture which he wished to teach his congregation, the subject, as it were, of his sermon. The doctrine might be readily apparent in the text itself, in which case the opening was usually brief, but more frequently the doctrine would be inferred from the text, and the opening would supply the basis for the inference. As an example, in a sermon on Proverbs 8:32, "Now therefore hearken unto me, O ye children . . . ," Hooker found as his doctrine, "The voice of the Lord Jesus Christ ought only to be attended to, and must be obeyed of all his faithfull servants."[56] It is easy to see how this could be drawn from the Scripture text, but in order to establish the authenticity of the doctrine, the preacher had first to expatiate upon the key phrases "hearken," "unto me," and "children." The opening of the text justified the doctrine as an authentic divine truth.

[55] Perkins, *Arte*, 132.   [56] Hooker, *Saints Dignitie*, 126.

Hooker customarily reinforced the statement of the doctrine with a set of reasons which proved the theological and intellectual validity of his teaching. The reasons explained what the doctrine actually meant in human terms, and they supported it with corroborating Scripture. The proofs of a doctrine's reasonableness were thus drawn from both sources of knowledge available to man, from right reason, presenting the truths learned through experience, and from truth revealed by God.

The final part of the sermon was the application, or uses, and it was the most important in the eyes of the Puritan prophet. The application aimed directly at affecting men's hearts, the main end of preaching, and it attempted to do this by showing the doctrine's usefulness to particular kinds of men. When a preacher framed the uses of his doctrine, he needed not only a sound knowledge of Christian teaching but also an intimate familiarity with the spiritual condition of his flock. Perkins described seven ways of application, each one suitable to a different spiritual state; e.g., ignorant men were most in need of instruction, men not yet humbled in need of reproof and terror, and those whose hearts were broken for sin should be comforted and encouraged. Since most congregations were "a mingled people," as Perkins said, all of the various types of use could be applied in turn, "if the limitation and circumscription of the doctrine be made to those persons for whom it is convenient.'[57]

In his sermons Hooker commonly found several uses for each doctrine, and his choice of uses depended somewhat on the doctrine and somewhat on the congregation. In a sermon printed in *The Unbeleevers Preparing* (London, 1638), with a doctrine claiming "No man of himselfe by nature can will to receive Christ" and drawn from 1 Corinthians 2:14, he found four uses. The first was to "condemne that sottish and foolish conceit that harbours in the minde of many silly poore ig-

[57] Perkins, *Arte*, 121.

norant soules" who believed that faith might come any other way than by hearing the Word (105). The second application was "an use of examination" by which "every soule that heareth the word this day . . . may understand what their condition is" (110). The third was "an use of terrour" to those men who were unwilling to be saved by Christ (113), and the last use was one of exhortation, urging men to use the God-given means of salvation (119).

This sermon was aimed at men not yet humbled; in the later sermons of this volume explaining the more advanced steps of the regenerative process, the "use of terrour" was almost completely discarded in favor of uses of comfort and consolation. Even in this series of applications, the use of terror has been followed by a more encouraging and positive application of the doctrine. Hooker did not want to leave his listeners in a state of panic; some men needed a healthy fear of God's wrath, but only terror directed to a good end could help a natural man. Hell-fire preaching, expounding on the rigors of the law, had a place in Hooker's course of lectures on salvation, but it was always in the context of the divine promises and Christ's atonement. The uses of the sermon were fitted to the needs of all sorts of men, for the ministers "are the Stewards of the Lords house, and give to every one their portion, terrour to whom terrour belongs, and comfort to whom comfort belongs" (SP, 76).

Hooker organized his sermons into this conventional structure of doctrine, reason, and use for several reasons. First of all, it provided an adequate intellectual machinery for displaying the divine truths embedded in Scripture; the formal demands of the structure forced the preacher into making both a clear definition of the truth and a particular application of it to the audience. The use of an established and familiar sermon form thus enabled the less intellectually gifted members of the audience to apprehend the truth. If they could anticipate the whole rational shape of the sermon, they could attend more closely to the detailed explanation within it. Just as men seeing a play for the second time gained new insights because they already knew the ending, so the men of Chelmsford could follow the doctrine's reasons more intently, knowing that particular applications of these truths would be given to them. Because the preacher always used the same form, his listeners need never worry about where his argument was leading.

The familiarity of structure was also an aid to the hearer's retention of the truths unfolded in the sermon; committing the good news of the Gospel to the memory was an important part of hearkening to the Word. Ames objected to those ministers

> who invert and confound those parts, doe not provide for the memory of their hearers, and doe not a little hinder their edification: because they cannot commit the chiefe head of the Sermon to memory, that they may afterward repeat it privatly in their families, without which exercise the greatest part of that fruit doth perish which would by Sermons redound unto the Church of God.[58]

In addition to preserving the proper order of the sermon, Hooker usually emphasized the heading of each part. Before and after stating the doctrine, he would speak to the effect that "this is our doctrine," or "this is the point to be made." The uses and the reasons were distinctly enumerated; the "firstly's" and "secondly's" in Puritan preaching were not mere rhetorical tics but important elements in the sermons psychological strategy. The memories and understandings of the hearers must be edified before the human mind could bring the truth to bear on the heart.

The formal structure of the sermon kept the preacher to the point of discourse, but, paradoxically, it also allowed for a very complex exposition within the seemingly stark limits of the form. A clear sight of truth could only be obtained by

[58] Ames, *Marrow*, 156.

concentrating upon God's revelation, and at the same time this concentration could unfold the intricacy and richness of the truth. Hooker's sermons were particularly complex—in fact he strained the conventional form—because of his passion for application. He would often introduce applications (uses) after each of the reasons to a doctrine and then include another set of applications of the doctrine in the usual position. He was clearly maintaining the order of the parts of the sermon—no use before a reason—but many a listener must have had to push his attention to the limit to remember the whole sermon without notes.[59] John Donne, Lancelot Andrewes, and Jeremy Taylor attracted listeners by the nearness of their sermons to poetry; Hooker attracted a different sort of listener by means of the logical intricacy of his preaching. This must have been one of the features of his lectures which appealed to men like the Earl of Warwick. Despising mere rhetorical ornament, Hooker created an intellectual and emotional density in his sermons by his careful explication of the complexities of the Word. A successful sermon involved the preacher and the listeners in a common spiritual quest, and Hooker's ability to reveal the intellectual complexity of Scripture was one means to involve the understandings of his more intelligent listeners.

The proper use of this conventionalized form was the first part of promulgation, and every well-trained Puritan prophet could adapt it equally well to his own sermons. Not all preachers were as successful as Thomas Hooker in leading men to conversion, however, since preaching was as much a matter of talent as it was of training. Puritan prophets might be taught the discipline of framing sermons after the approved model, and they might learn the art of rhetoric, but the ability to practice the rhetorical art in an affecting manner was the gift of God.

[59] See Alfred Habegger, "Preparing the Soul for Christ: The Contrasting Sermon Forms of John Cotton and Thomas Hooker," *American Literature* 41 (1969), 342–354.

The preacher's first step in preparing a sermon, said Perkins, was to "diligentlie imprint in his mind . . . the severall doctrines of the place he meanes to handle, the severall proofes and applications of the doctrines, the illustrations of the doctrines, the illustrations of the applications, and the order of them all." The intellectual form and content of the sermon were of paramount importance, and the preacher should be "in the meane time nothing carefull for the words, *Which* (as Horace speaketh) *will not unwillingly follow the matter that is premeditated.*"[60] A hard student could master the required preparation of the sermon, and the Spirit would provide fitting words for the sermon.

Many men nevertheless misused their rhetorical gifts, and the Puritan prophets emphasized the importance of restraining human linguistic cleverness. The preacher's duty was to glorify God and struggle with the hearts of men, not to glorify himself and tickle the depraved human fancy with rhetorical ornament. The proper language of a sermon was spiritual rhetoric, and "that speech is *spirituall*, which the holy Spirit doth teach. . . . And it is a speech both simple and perspicuous, fit both for the peoples understanding and to expresse the maiestie of the spirit." This "speech both simple and perspicuous" was the so-called plain style.[61] As the Puritans conceived it, pulpit rhetoric allowed the use of only a limited variety of rhetorical devices; the concept of plainness, far from being an absolute quality of the Puritan sermon, describes, rather, its verbal qualities relative to the golden styles of men like Donne and Andrewes. The Puritan preachers arrived at a version of plain style by the exclusion and limitation of several rhetorical techniques used by the High Church preachers.

Quotations from Greek and Latin and from humane authors were frowned upon both because they obscured the glory of God's Word and because they hindered an effectual under-

[60] Perkins, *Arte*, 131. [61] Ibid., 134–35.

standing of the preacher's argument. Quotations from the classical languages were considered to be fashionable in some circles, but Hooker commented:

> I have sometime admired at this: why a company of Gentlemen, yeomen, and poore women, that are scarcely able to know their A.B.C. Yet they have a minister to speake Latine, Greeke, and Hebrew, and to use the Fathers, when it is certaine, they know nothing at all. The reason is, because all this stings not, they may sit and sleep in their sinnes, and go to hell hoodwinckt. (*SP*, 69)

Greek, Latin, and Hebrew could only confuse the farmers and merchants of Chelmsford as well as lead the minister into a show of sinful and useless pride. When Hooker had recourse in his popular sermons to the original tongues of Scripture, he always translated it anew and never quoted the original.

Strange quotations also tended to distract listeners from close attention to God's Word. Although Perkins advised the preacher to "privatly use at his libertie the artes, philosophie and varietie of reading, whilst he is in framing his sermon," he reminded his students that effective promulgation of the sermon required "the hiding of humane wisdome." Increase Mather recollected that his father, Richard, "would often use that saying, *Artis est Celare Artem*"—art is to conceal art.[62] God intended that men should be saved by the "spirit of Wisdome and revelation" in the Word and not by the authority of Justin Martyr or Gregory. Hooker occasionally referred to humane authors, but he prefaced his own paraphrase of their statement with only a generalized attribution, "the fathers say," etc. His wide study and reading were completely integrated into the style of his sermons, for a Puritan sermon was intended as a unified whole of logic and rhetoric. The sermon was definitely not a vehicle to be ornamented by lumps of quotation.

[62] Ibid., 132–33. Increase Mather, *The Life*, 85.

The Puritan plain style linked with the conception of the preacher as a prophet demanded that rhetoric be used as a means of furthering only the will of God. The plain style was equated with spiritual speech; commenting on Scripture rhetoric, Ames noticed that there were some forms of human rhetoric not allowed by this model:

> Now in Scripture there is great use of Tropes and Figures of sentences; but for Figures of Words, which consists in likenesse of sounds, measures and repetition, very few examples of them are to be found.[63]

"Tropes and Figures of sentences" included the various sorts of imagery, such as simile and metaphor, as well as stylistic features like synechdoche, metonymy, and dialogue. All of these figures might occur in normal speech, and since they involved the logical manipulation of large blocks of language, they could be useful in clarifying meaning and edifying congregations. "Figures of Words" were rhetorical techniques like alliteration and assonance, rhythmical prose, rhyme, and the repetition of a statement for tonal effect. They were sensual manipulations of individual words or clauses, independent of the rules of logic. These figures tended to be consciously applied tricks of a poet or orator, and while they had some use as aids to memory, all too often they evaded a rational development of the argument and impeded understanding. If one word was sufficient to show the truth, it only destroyed the simplicity and perspicuity of the statement to add a second word for sensual effect. This is not to say that the Puritans repudiated the importance of the senses; the senses were necessary epistemological tools, and sensuous language was to be used as a means to understanding but not as an end in itself.

Hooker agreed with Ames in rejecting the "witty" style of preaching which made heavy use of figures of the word: "A powerfull ministry," he said,

[63] Ames, *Conscience*, IV, 78.

consisteth not in words only, not in a company of fine gilded sentences, where there is nothing but a jingling and tinkling, nothing but a sound of words; there is no kingdome all this while, no power all this while in such a kind of preaching: this will not worke effectually in the hearts and consciences of men. (SI, 76)

In practice Hooker did not reject all "Figures of Words" out of hand; for example, he occasionally used alliteration as a mnemonic aid, and in this very quotation he uses a variety of *repetitio*, although he extends the meaning of the total statement with each new phrase. Although his sense of rhythm was well developed, he did not lull the congregation with mellifluous parallelisms but varied his periods to hammer home the truth.

Hooker spoke to his audience not as to a group come to partake of a sensual feast, but as individual men and women in search of salvation, and his sermons emphasized the sovereignty and immediacy of God. Hooker's audiences were participants with him in one of God's ordinances, for all those who truly "hearkened" to the minister's words were acting their allotted roles in a rite prescribed by God. In a powerful ministry, "the Lord knocks at the doore of the soule, findes him out behinde the Pillor, awakens him asleep in his Pue";[64] when Hooker was in the pulpit, the people of Chelmsford were led to see the truth and eternal presence of the Word as well as its beauty. During the course of the sermon, God was with listeners in their pews under the special form of the "spirit of Wisdome and revelation," and Hooker intended his pulpit rhetoric to struggle with men's hearts by revealing the presence of a merciful God.

Hooker used the rhetorical techniques of the prophets both to explicate God's ways to men and to involve men in the redemptive process. A very limited use of "Figures of the

[64] Hooker, *Saints Guide*, 29.

Word" could aid the memory, but he demonstrated the immediacy of God and the clarity of His truth most powerfully with "Tropes and Figures of sentences." Tropes were identical to the "narrations" and "examples" with which Scripture explained the will of God, and they were thus the most fitting rhetorical figures for the sermons of a Puritan prophet. He used a trope, for instance, to explain why Christ did not always give assurance of His love to the elect:

> I have seene the father deale so with the child, when the father is going on in his journey, if the child will not goe on, but stands gaping upon vanity, and when the father calls he comes not, the onely way is this, the father steps aside behind a bush, and then the child runs and cries, and if he gets his father againe, he forsakes all his trifles, and walkes on more faster and more cheerefully with his father than ever. So when the Lord Jesus Christ sometimes makes knowne himselfe to us, and would carry us on in a Christian course cheerefully, we are playing with trifles, and grow carelesse, and cold, and worldly, and remisse in prayer, and dead hearted; the onely way to quicken us up is to hide himselfe, and to make us give up ourselves for lost; and then they that could scarcely pray once a weeke now will pray three or foure times a day. (*SI*, 152–53)

Perkins in his treatise on *The Arte of Prophecying* gave a lengthy description of several tropes useful in sermon rhetoric, and this trope of Hooker's is an example of what he called "Anthro-pathia . . . a sacred Metaphor, whereby those things, that are properly spoken of man, are by a similitude attributed unto God."[65] Hooker used the trope to clarify a difficult question of theology; if Christ brought life and happiness to His faithful, and if this happiness was caused by assurance of His love, then why did He not always give this assurance to the faithful? Hooker had already explained to his congregation

[65] Perkins, *Arte*, 54.

that one sign of faith was the holding of Christ above all trifles and vanities of the world; when Christ concealed Himself from His followers, He was thus acting not to punish but to preserve them in their faith. Christ taught His faithful the facts of spiritual life just as an earthly father instructed his child in the dangers of the world.

The preacher could explain this point of divinity abstractly, but if he did, he would run the risk of making Christ seem rather cold and punctilious. The trope edified men by explaining Christ's motives, and it moved men in a fashion peculiar to the human heart by describing God's motions in terms of correspondent human emotions. Although the diction and the rhythm of the trope carefully excluded sentimentality, the trope drew upon a reservoir of sentiment in the hearts of men. The people of Chelmsford might well have acted as the metaphoric father did in teaching his child, and for most people his actions would certainly seem reasonable and loving. The trope thus mirrored the divine love for man in the more readily comprehensible image of human love, and it inspired a response of childlike trust and affection to the divine Father.

The trope also contained dramatic interest; in a very few words, it outlined a story with a beginning, a middle, and an exciting and satisfying conclusion. The few concrete details assisted the listeners to create an image in their own minds of the situation described by the preacher, and at the same time these details joined with the syntax of the trope to illuminate the emotional interplay between the father and the child. The situation built comparatively slowly, and when the father "steps aside behind a bush," the short period gave the congregation a sense both of the abruptness of the father's disappearance and of the child's resulting panic. Because the father is a loving parent, he has not ignored the child, but has stopped his journey in order to correct his waywardness; he conceals himself behind the bush not only to edify the child but also to be in a position where he can watch over him. The sudden reunion of the father and the running and crying child gives way to the almost cinematic conclusion of the two of them walking off together toward their common goals.

Hooker's tropes often had all the interest of a short story or of a play, but there was no danger that people would go to the church of St. Mary only to hear the preacher tell anecdotes about men hiding behind bushes. The trope in point is introduced by a more or less abstract discussion of the theological principles involved, all proved with citations from Scripture, and the human similitude of the father and child is quickly resolved into the portrayal of Christ as spiritual father to His faithful. The sense of satisfaction and well-being aroused in the audience by the satisfactory completion of the first part of the trope is carried over to the moral explication of the metaphor; the moral thus gains an additional constructive emotional force. The dramatic interest in the portrayal of the first part of the trope lures the hearts of the congregation into fastening themselves upon the divine truth revealed in the latter part of the trope. The bare, stylized presentation of the first part prevents the metaphor from being separated from its moral.

Hooker seems to have realized the affecting possibilities of the dramatic interest created by well-worded tropes; he often heightens this interest by using other "Figures of sentences." For example, in a use exhorting natural men and those in the way of preparation to use the ordinance of God, he introduced dialogue into an anthropathic trope:

Let us be led by all meanes into a neerer union with the Lord Christ. As a wife deales with the letters of her husband that is in a farre Country, she findes many sweet inklings of his love, and shee will reade these letters often, and daily, shee woulde talke with her husband a farre off, and see him in the letters, Oh (saith shee) thus and thus he thought when he writ these lines, and then shee thinkes hee speakes to her againe; shee reads these letters onely, because shee would be with her husband a little, and have a little parlee with him in his pen, though not in his presence; so these ordinances are but the Lords love-letters, and wee are the Ambassadors of Christ; and though wee are poore sottish ignorant men, yet wee bring mervailous good newes that Christ can save all poore broken hearted sinners in the world. (*SH*, 73–74)

The wife's expression of her love for the absent husband is cunningly placed at the rhythmic balance point of the whole passage; the building speed of the first part of the trope climaxes with her words, and the listener's attention and affection are led into an account of the "Lords love-letters." The slower rhythm of the second part of the trope provides emphasis for the minister's argument and allows sufficient time for the truth to sink into the hearts of the congregation. When the "spirit of Wisdome" spoke in Hooker's sermons to a sinner by means of such affecting imagery and forceful rhythms, it surely found him out "behind the Pillor," awakened him "asleep in his Pue."

The use of dialogue, or "interrogation" as Perkins called it, effectively implicated the listener into Hooker's sermons. Tropes using dialogue made affecting narrations and examples by providing speaking parts with which the hearers could identify themselves. Hooker's imagery was drawn from scenes familiar to his audiences, and when he portrayed a metaphoric situation, they would be able to recognize themselves in it. Fathers and wives were portrayed in the tropes with enough detail to seem real to the listeners, but at the same time with sufficient generality for them to see themselves in the position of the trope's characters. Dialogue carried the congregation still further into the rhetorical texture of the sermon by giving speech to their imaginations.

Hooker's use of dialogue was often quite extensive, as when he described the condition of a sinner similar to Mrs. Drake:

Come to a contrite Soule, and say to him why walkest thou so uncomfortably, seeing thou hast now a title to mercy and salvation in Christ: See what he replies, I a title to mercy? . . . I have beene a vile wretch and enemy to God and his glory; what I a title to mercy? We reply againe; God gives grace to the unworthy, hee justifies the ungodly, and not the godly, and if hee will give you mercy too, what then? Hee replies againe, What mercy to me? Nay it is prepared for those that are fitted for it; . . . Wee replie againe, . . . you deprive your selves of mercy; you have a child's part, and a good portion too, if your proud hearts would suffer you to see it. Then the Soule saith, I would have the Lord say to my Soule, bee of good comfort, I am thy Salvation; if the Lord would witnesse this to mee by his Spirit, then I could believe it. Content then, onely let us agree upon the manner how it must be done, and how God shall speake it. Will you then yield it? Yes. Then know this, What the Word saith, the Spirit saith, for the hand and the sword, the Word and the Spirit goe together . . . The Word saith, *Every one that is weary shall be refreshed.*[66]

This rhetorical figure invited men to see their own condition mirrored in that of the contrite soul, and as the congregation listened to the preacher's figure, it was drawn into the dialogue. The preacher retained within the figure his external role of ambassador from Christ, and the listeners were almost imperceptibly fitted into the opposing part of the soul seeking salvation. The shift from the second person singular to the second person plural in the midst of the figure was not grammatical carelessness but a careful use of rhetoric to involve the hearers. Most interesting is the strategy of the preacher in the last speech; he removes himself from the figure, quotes Scripture to the contrite soul, and the congregation and the Word are left speaking the one to the other.

[66] Hooker, *Humiliation*, 174–76. In this excerpt I have slightly modernized the punctuation and capitalization in order to emphasize the dialectic interchange.

Not all people in the congregation would be contrite or distressed souls, and they would certainly not all be drawn into the figure in the same way. To some men the preacher's figure showed their own souls, to others the figure showed the souls of their friends and neighbors. Hooker's rhetoric revealed the listeners to themselves, but it also revealed the nature of man to men. The sermon was a means of personal revelation, but it was also able to strengthen the social bonds of the congregation. The trope quoted in the previous paragraph was a comfort to certain distressed souls, those most able to make a simple and direct identification with the figural soul; it showed natural men the ease with which grace might be obtained if they would only put themselves in the way of preparation; finally, it reminded the saints, who were secure in their faith, of the spiritual storms they had weathered and of the probable misery and unhappiness of their contrite brethren. The rhetoric worked upon those latter two types of men by involving them in the figure in a manner slightly different from the involvement of distressed souls. Natural men would be drawn into the controversy between the soul and the minister, and they would end by giving a tentative acceptance to his doctrines. The saints would become involved and end by giving sympathy to those people who were in reality like the metaphoric contrite soul.

I V

Hooker's sermons tended to make the Chelmsford congregation a particular godly community within the encompassing worldly community. Chelmsford men knew the political and geographical bounds of their shire and of their country; Hooker taught them from the pulpit the spiritual bounds of the world they should inhabit as Christ's faithful. The rhetoric he used in his sermons on redemption defined the internal concerns which brought the Christian community together, and the same rhetorical technique could define the community's spiritual boundaries in time and space. Effectual, powerful preaching of the doctrines of preparation and application of redemption turned a group of Essex people into "Mr. Hooker's company."

Not all of God's creation was as placid and prosperous as Chelmsford, and since the spiritual community was distinguished by the degree of grace with which God favored it, it was important to see how Chelmsford stood in the world. Hooker occasionally surveyed mankind with extensive view in order to reveal dangers to Christian hearts at home.

> When the fire of Gods fury hath flamed and consumed all the country round about us; Bohemia, and the *Palatinate*, and *Denmarke*, when the fire hath thus burnt up all, yet this little Cottage, this little *England*, this Spanne of ground, that this should not be searched, nay when the sword hath ruinated and overcome all the other parts of Christendome, where the name of the Lord Jesus is professed, we sit under our Vines and Figtrees, there is not complaining in our streets, our wives are not husbandlesse, our children are not fatherlesse: marke the reason and ground of all, is nothing else but Gods mercy towards us, . . . notwithstanding our unthankefulnesse and carelesnesse.[67]

"God is the Author of the deliverance of his Servants," said Hooker, and the reason why one nation among many had been preserved was the presence therein of the faithful.[68] This national security existed at the divine pleasure, however, and if His servants rejected Him, He should surely desert them: "The estate of Gods Church may be such, that he may lend no further succour and deliverance unto it."[69] If the national community was to stand amid the wilderness of the world, the

---

[67] Hooker, *Foure Learned and Godly Treatises* (London, 1638), 115–16.

[68] Ibid., 104. [69] Ibid., 133.

spiritual community must strengthen itself and remain righteous before the Lord.

Hooker's description of God's favor to England must have touched the love of country in the men of Chelmsford, just as the patriotic Londoners of a generation before had responded to the deathbed speech of John of Gaunt in *The Tragedy of Richard the Second*. The minister obviously shared their affection for "this little *England*," but his figure was not mere jingoism, for it led the congregation to consider the proper source of patriotism. The countries of Europe had once a prosperity and power comparable to England's, and that was poor security. National pride was justified only when it was a result of divine mercy to a faithful people, and a nation's greatest treasure was its saints. A people's preservation was in fact less cause for patriotism than it was for thanks to God and a careful obedience of His will. If "the fire of Gods fury" could rain down on other parts of creation, it was time for good Englishmen to make sure their own hearts were in order.

The spiritual community existed in time as well as space, and just as the preachers were the successors of the prophets, so the community had its spiritual antecedents. God's truth was timeless, and wherever in time faithful men believed the divine truth, there Christians found their home. The congregation of Chelmsford was set apart from "all the other parts of Christendome" by the favor of God, and Essex Christians found their real nation in history. Hooker's description of Paul on the road to Damascus revealed the bonds between the primitive church and the Christian community in England. "See that of *Saul* when he was running to Damascus, ah (saith he) I will take these Puritaines in their Conventicles; a light shined suddenly from Heaven and almost tumbled him downe into Hell."[70] The Saul of Hooker's figure was the Saul of Acts, but the preacher's choice of diction revealed a kinship between

[70] Hooker, *Saints Guide*, 28.

the persecutor of the primitive church and the pursuivants of Bishop Laud. The image of Saul was a type, a foreshadowing in Scripture of persons who would occur later in history as antitypes; Saul, "running to Damascus," prefigured for Hooker the episcopal inquisition of the godly in Essex. The typical image revealed the chronological boundaries of the community of God's faithful, for the invisible church of the saints was one through all time, and Scripture truth was modern truth.

Hooker used this figure in order to evoke a response from his listeners to the antitypes of Saul in their own time. All was not in order in the England of the late sixteen-twenties: Sauls were beginning to make serious depredations in the ranks of the Puritan prophets, and many faithful ministers faced the choice of flight or imprisonment. The silencing of godly ministers was a threatening sign that God was about to desert even "this little *England*." The presence of God was "the particular favour of God expressed in his ordinances, and all the good and sweet that followeth there. The purity of Gods word and worship, is that which God reveales himselfe in."[71] The bishops' party was seeking to prevent men from preaching redemption, and preaching was the chief of the divine ordinances for the purification of the hearts of men. If the bishops had their way, God's worship would be no longer pure, and the resulting punishment of England would be worse than that of other nations. "Thou England which was lifted up to heaven with meanes shalt be abased and brought downe to hell; for if the mighty works which have been done in thee had been done in India or Turkey, they would have repented ere *this*; . . . and marke what I say, the poore native Turks and Infidels shall have a cooler summer parlour in hell than you; for we stand at a high rate, we were highly exalted, therefore shall our torments be the more to beare."[72]

[71] Hooker, *Danger*, 8.   [72] Ibid., 20.

FOUR

The Netherlands Experiment

THOMAS HOOKER'S sermons from the pulpit of St. Mary's Church led many of the people of Chelmsford and Essex to discover their salvation; after his death, years later in New England, men looked back to realize that Hooker's preaching had been a high point of the English Reformation as they had witnessed it. John Fuller, for example, "having mentioned that Name of pretious memory, worthy Mr. Hooker, now at rest with the Lord (Saint *Hooker*, I may call him as *Latimer*, Saint *Bilney*)," went on to "acknowledge with all hearty Thankfulnesse to God in Christ, . . . that great mercy and unspeakable blessing, which Essex Chelmsford, . . . my self, and many others then enjoyed, in the labours of that Powerfull, Soul-saving, Heart-searching Minister of Jesus Christ."[1] Fuller was only one of many to be stirred by the powerful ministry, for as Cotton Mather recorded years later, "The light of his ministry shone through the whole county of Essex."[2] The testimonials to Hooker's affecting and effectual ministry which speak loudest in the pages of history are not, however, these encomiums tucked away in the prefaces of forgotten books; in 1629 he was honored with the displeasure of Bishop William Laud, and in this period Laud was singling out the most influential and effective Puritan ministers by silencing and imprisonment.

Laud, just entering upon his career as the most vigorous defender of the prerogative powers of the English Church, had

---

[1] John Fuller, "Epistle Dedicatory," in John Beadle, *The Journal or Diary of a Thankful Christian* (London, 1656), sig. A6r.
[2] Mather, I, 335.

been translated to the see of London in 1628, and both as Bishop of London and later as Archbishop of Canterbury he exerted all of his energies toward subjecting the English Church to a strong central government. Laud was a chief demon in his Puritan opponents' cabinet of political and religious horrors, but, while he seems to have been occasionally tactless and was aggressive in defending episcopal and royal power, he has been much maligned. Laud worked as sincerely as Hooker did to establish an English spiritual community which would worship God in accordance with His truth, but the Puritan and episcopal conceptions of the spiritual community were at odds with each other on critical issues. Hooker, Ames, and their friends felt the backbone of the English Church to be preaching ministers in their congregations; Laud and King Charles conceived of the church as a body held together and legitimized by the episcopacy. Since there could be only one truth, there was no possibility for toleration of unorthodox opinion or practice in the spiritual community, and since the English Church was a national church, all Englishmen had to agree to a common definition of the truth.

Shortly after coming to the English throne, King James I analyzed the religious situation in his new kingdom:

At my first coming, although I found but one religion, and that which by myself is professed, publicly allowed and by the law maintained, yet found I another sort of religion, besides a private sect, lurking within the bowels of this nation. The first is the true religion, which by me is professed and by the law is established: the second is the falsely called Catholics, but truly Papists: the third, which I call a sect rather than a religion, is the Puritans and Novelists, who do not so far differ from us in points of religion as in their confused form of policy and parity; being ever discontented with the present government and impatient to suffer any superiority, which maketh their sect unable to be suffered in any well-governed commonwealth.[3]

Hooker, his fellow ministers in the Essex monthly meeting, and hundreds of men like them throughout England were creating by means of their preaching a Puritan community within the larger English community; their hope was to expand the community of the saints so that it would become identical to the English nation. They claimed to pose no threat to the political order of the state, but the later events of the Civil War might seem to some observers to justify James's anxiety over "Novelists." The Puritan ministers were further defining religious truth by refusing to conform to those church practices which they regarded as idolatrous; in their view the greatest threat to England was not disorder caused by church reformers but the danger of an incompletely reformed church lapsing into papistry. The episcopal party had been on the defensive since the Elizabethan Settlement; for them the church and the order of worship had been defined in accordance with Scripture and tradition, and their problem was now to maintain the established truth. Nonconformist ministers must be made to wear surplices while performing religious services; lecturers were to wear gowns instead of ordinary cloaks while preaching, and they were to be restrained from preaching on the baffling doctrines of election. Above all, they must put away their itch for extempore sermons and spontaneous prayer; the formal liturgy must be observed.

In 1622, four years before Thomas Hooker entered the pulpit at Chelmsford, King James attempted to inhibit the lecturers—who were almost all of a Puritan inclination—by forbidding them "to preach in any popular auditory on the deep points of predestination, elections, reprobation, or of the uni-

---

[3] Quoted by Ralph Barton Perry, *Puritanism and Democracy* (1944; rpt. New York, Harper, 1964), 69.

versality, efficacy, resistibility, or irresistibility of God's grace."[4] Sunday afternoon sermons, which were usually preached by the lecturer where there was one, were to be limited to discussion of the "Catechism, Creed, or Ten Commandments." By this time the lecturers were too well entrenched for mere proclamation to have much effect upon their activities, and in June 1626 James's successor, Charles, made a similar attempt to restrict the lecturers with no more success than his father.

James had made sporadic attempts at suppressing the more vociferous Puritans, but in general he failed to make much headway against them. One reason for James's lack of success was the reluctance of George Abbott, the Archbishop of Canterbury, to follow up any systematic scheme of eradicating or restricting the lecturers. Abbott's sympathies had been shaped by the Elizabethan reformers, and his greatest antipathy was for the papists. In 1627 Charles had the see of Canterbury sequestered to a commission, and Abbott was eliminated as an influence in Church affairs. One of the commissioners appointed to supervise the archdiocesan business was Laud, then Bishop of Bath and Wells; in 1628 the London bishopric became vacant, and Charles moved to bring Laud into the immediate circle of his court. On July 2 of that year he sent a *congé d'élire* to the Dean and Chapter of St. Paul's, ordering them to elect a new bishop for London, and on the same day he followed this formal order with an instruction to elect Laud as their bishop.[5]

By the spring of 1629 Laud was receiving intelligence on the activities of nonconformists throughout his diocese, and it became obvious that severer restrictions on the Puritan ministers were needed. In February, Parliament had presented to the King the Heads of Articles which protested against, among other things, "the bold and unwarrantable introducing . . . of

---

[4] Quoted by G. L. Walker, *Hooker*, 40–41.
[5] *Calendar of State Papers, Domestic Series, Charles I,* 1628–29 (London, 1859), 189.

sundry new ceremonies and laying of injunctions upon men."[6] Charles promptly adjourned the Parliament, and Laud began suspending Puritan ministers and lecturers in earnest. One of the first men to be affected was Hooker's friend and mentor, John Rogers of Dedham, and by late spring of 1629 Laud was interested in the activities of Thomas Hooker himself. On May 20 Samuel Collins, Vicar of Braintree, wrote to Dr. Arthur Duck, Laud's chancellor, urging the bishop to "connive at Mr. Hookers departure."[7]

Collins recognized that in the few years Hooker had been preaching in the Chelmsford pulpit, he had managed to secure the loyalties of a considerable number of men, among both clergy and laity. As we have already seen, Hooker was accorded a more than usual respect by his associates, even in the first years of his residence in Essex, and by 1629 he had advised many younger preachers, men like Thomas Shepard, helping them to become powerful and faithful ministers in their own pulpits. "His private conference . . . hath already more impeached the peace of our church than his publique ministry," said Collins, "there be divers young ministers about us, . . . that spend their time in conference with him, . . . and return home . . . and preach what he hath brewed. . . . Our people's pallats grow so out of tast, that noe food contents them but of Mr. Hooker's dressing."

Hooker seems to have refrained from direct attacks upon the episcopacy, but he was sharply critical of "those which are enemies to Gods faithful Ministers, [which] are the greatest adversaries that the Church or State hath."[8] He attacked the persecutors of the "Ministers of Grace" from neighboring pul-

---

[6] Quoted by Thomas W. Davids, *Annals of Evangelical Nonconformity in the County of Essex* (London, 1863), 143.

[7] All quotations from this letter are from Davids, 150–51.

[8] Hooker, *Spirituall Munition: A Funerall Sermon* (London, 1638), 31. Quoted by Sargent Bush, Jr., "Four New Works by Thomas Hooker: Identity and Significance," *Resources for American Literary Study* 4 (1974), 10. This sermon was delivered in June 1626.

pits as well as from his own in Chelmsford, and while he confined himself to generalized descriptions, most listeners must have recognized the objects of his attacks. If Hooker did not name names, others were less hesitant to identify "enemies to Gods faithful Ministers," and Collins was alarmed by the outspokenness of Hooker's friends: "All men's eares are now filled with the obstreperous clamour of his followers against my Lord . . . as a man endeavoring to suppress good preaching and advance Popery." As Collins measured the situation, Hooker's influence and popularity were so great that he should be treated with exceptional circumspection. "All would be here very calme and quiet if he might quietly departe . . . If these jealousies . . . be increased by a rigorous proceeding against him, the country may prove very dangerous." Collins himself was frightened of the risk he took by coming between the people of Essex and the Bishop of London; he closed his letter by pleading, "And now I humbly crave your silence, and that when your worship hath read my letter none may see it, for if that some in the world should have the least inkling thereof, my creditt and fortune were utterly ruined."

Shortly after May 20 Hooker was called before Laud's High Commission to answer for his preaching and his nonconformity. Collins wrote again to Dr. Duck on June 3, 1629, stating that he had gone to Chelmsford to speak with Hooker; he apparently wished to urge once more Hooker's quiet departure from the diocese, but the Puritan had already left for London, by way of Leicestershire. Hooker might well have entertained fears of imprisonment at the hands of Laud; English prisons were not the healthiest lodgings, and he may have wished to make for the last time his annual visit to family and friends in his native county.

According to Collins, the news of Hooker's call to appear before the bishop was causing a great stir across the countryside, and even Cambridge disputed it *"pro et con."* "All men's heads, tongues, eyes, and ears are in London, and all the counties about London taken up with plotting, talking, and expecting what will be the conclusion of Mr. Hooker's business. . . . It drowns the noise of the greate question of Tonnage and Poundage."[9] Collins was now even more frightened by the public outcry over Laud's proceeding, for he complained, "I dare not say halfe of that I heare; paper walls are easily broken open." He once again urged Duck to warn the bishop of the dangers in dealing rashly with Hooker: "Let him be as cautelous as he will, yet in his present course the humour of our people will undoe him." The timid Collins did see, more than a decade before the Civil War, that spiritual repression might lead to civil disorders. In mid-1629 religious problems had managed to displace for a time even the pressing economic issues attendant upon a period of depression.

The danger Laud foresaw was not public, civil revolution but an internal seizure of power by Puritans who were slowly coming to control a large number of the parish clergy. Laud agreed with Collins on the importance of silencing Hooker, for "if he be once quietly gone, my Lord hath overcome the greatest difficulty in governing this part of his diocese." The Bishop also probably agreed with Collins' presentation of the Hooker affair as an important test of strength between the establishment and the nonconformists. "This will prove a leading case," said Collins, "and the issue thereof will either much incourage or else discourage the regular clergie." Laud was quite capable of proceeding with a high hand against his ecclesiastical inferiors; eighteen months later when he confronted Thomas Shepard, "falling into a Fit of Rage, . . . he look'd as tho' Blood would have gush'd out of his Face, and did shake as if he had been haunted with an Ague Fit, to my Apprehension by Reason of his extream Malice and secret Venom."[10] Hooker seems to have irritated Laud less than Shepard did—it was said of the Chelmsford lecturer, "He was a person who, while doing his

[9] Davids, 152.
[10] Shepard, "Autobiography," 369n.

Master's work, would put a king in his pocket"[11]—and rather than peremptorily to send Hooker out of the diocese with threats to preach no more, he simply suspended him from his lectureship and required him to post a bond guaranteeing his reappearance upon demand. A Mr. Nash, tenant of the Earl of Warwick and resident of Much Waltham, paid this bond of £50, and the preacher was suffered to return home to Essex.

At this time Hooker was living at Cuckoos Farm in Little Baddow, a hamlet near Chelmsford, with his wife and children —he had three daughters and an infant son, named after his brother John. He kept a grammar school there, probably opened after his suspension from preaching, and employed as his usher John Eliot, later to achieve fame as the Apostle to the Indians in New England. As a schoolmaster Hooker could work almost as effectively as when he was actively preaching; both lecturers and schoolmasters were teachers, and one could teach God's truths in a classroom as well as from a pulpit. During this brief interlude of peace in the Hooker household, a further trial was laid upon the family: Sarah Hooker, aged sixteen months, died in August 1629.

Hooker was apparently not content to limit his activities to teaching grammar school. He was able to go on counseling the young ministers of the neighborhood, and since he had been silenced as much for the activities of his followers as for his own nonconformity, he was sure to have further trouble with Laud. On November 3, 1629, a Mr. John Browning, rector of Rawreth, complained to the Bishop of London that "one Mr. Hooker, lately in question before your honour . . . doth even still, to this present, . . . continue his former practices."[12] John Michaelson, the rector of Chelmsford, was sympathetic to the cause of church reform, and he may have permitted his lecturer to preach in defiance of Laud's orders. More likely, Hooker preached in the homes of various laymen who sup-

[11] Mather, I, 345.   [12] Davids, 152–53.

ported him, and his meetings were among those "conventicles" which the episcopal Saul was attempting to overthrow. Browning complained that "some of the people hereabouts" were "overmuch addicted to hearing the Word (as they call it) even to the neglect of God's holy and divine service and worship." Men like Browning must have found themselves facing depleted congregations on a Sabbath day, when many of their parishioners would take themselves off to hear a powerful ministry.

News of Browning's complaint must have gotten out rather quickly, for just one week later, on November 10, a petition was sent to Laud by forty-nine ministers of Essex who supported Hooker:

> Whereas we have heard that your honour hath been informed against Mr. Thomas Hooker, preacher at Chelmsford, that the conformable ministers of these parts desire his removal from the place, we, whose names are hereunder written, being ministers in the partes adjoining, all beneficed men, and obedient to His Majesty's ecclesiastical laws, doe humbly give your lordship to understand that we all esteeme and knowe the said Mr. Thomas Hooker to be, for doctryne, orthodox, and life and conversation honest, and for his disposition peaceable, no wayes turbulent or factious, and so not doubting but he will contynue that good course, commending him and his lawfull suite to your lordship's honourable favor, and entreating the continuance of his libertye and paines there, we humbly take our leave, and remaine your honour's humbly at command.[13]

Among the signers were Michaelson, Thomas Welde, and Nathaniel Ward; the latter two would become prominent figures in the Massachusetts Bay Colony. Curiously enough, the Reverend Mr. Collins, so terrified of the popular wrath, also subscribed the petition.

[13] Davids, 153.

By the time another week had passed, Laud had a counter petition in hand, sent in by forty-one "of the conformable part of the cleargy of his lordships diocese."[14] This petition, the canvassing for which probably inspired the plea of Hooker's supporters, bewailed "licentious irregularities" which seemed about to force the "said conformitants . . . eyther with non-conformitants to runne the same way against lawe and conscience, or else to loose . . . the credite of our ministerie." The Puritans were a menace to the consciences of good churchmen as well as a danger to the "peace and welfare" of the diocese. Church peace could be obtained only by "that generall uniformitie so much to be desired," for unless all men could agree upon the same version of divine truth, faction would destroy English spiritual life. The receipt of two contradicting petitions, both heavily subscribed, would be sufficient proof of factionalism, even if the bishop lacked other evidence of it.

Laud was now forced to act in order to preserve order in his own diocese, especially since the Hooker case had drawn such great attention from all parts of the English Church. Given the nature of the two petitions, there was little doubt which would find favor in the bishop's eyes. The second petition offered four compelling reasons for acting in favor of the conformitants:

> That hereby God Almighty be most glorified, the church better edified, your Lordship's owne self most honoured, and we the poore ministers of your diocese better encouraged, for which we shall bee ever bound to pray for your lordship's long and happie government of this sea.

All these were better reasons for action than a mere recommendation of Mr. Hooker's goodness. The signers of the second petition added testimonials of their loyalty to the established form of worship and the church hierarchy; men like the pastor of Colchester were ready to enforce all of the Laudian

[14] Davids, 158.

reforms over the protests of Puritan nonconformists.[15] The bishop could not afford to refuse support to his most ardent friends, and in July 1630 Hooker was ordered to reappear before Laud's High Commission. He would probably have been called in sooner in the year, had Laud not been very ill in the latter part of 1629.

Hooker chose not to appear before Laud a second time; he could hardly expect to be let off so easily as he had been before. Cotton Mather said that Hooker "could not now attend because of an ague then upon him," but a more important reason for failing to appear was that "Mr. Hooker's friends advised him to forfeit his bonds, rather than to throw him self any further into the hands of his enemies."[16] To defy Laud's summons was to ask for exile, since a man of Hooker's stature and fame could not be hidden for long by sympathizing friends. Indeed, pursuivants were becoming daily more zealous and efficient in tracking down nonconforming ministers. Two years later the pressure was such that a less well-known man like Thomas Shepard found great difficulty in preserving his freedom, even after he had fled to the north of England. Although it must have seemed certain that Hooker would soon have to

[15] Some years later an anonymous parish wit protested Mr. Roberts' zeal in introducing in the name of conformity what seemed to be popish customs:

> The complaint which I have in hand
> Is of our parech teutore,
> Because with honner he is turned
> To be a persicutor.
> The reson whi is onlie this—
> His parech would not yeld
> That he a foolech rayle mayt not
> About the tabell build.
> And now all those that will not paie
> To building of the same,
> Then unto Dockter Ailett's cort,
> He will return ther name.

(Quoted by Davids, 159n.)
[16] Mather, I, 338.

leave his people in Chelmsford, it was no light matter to desert them.

Hooker had once preached to his people the doctrine, "The followers of Jesus Christ cheerefully undergoe what ever afflictions are allotted to them."[17] Later in that sermon he made an application of this doctrine to men in the ministerial calling which was now particularly relevant to his own situation: "If a Minister hazard the good of his Congregation by flying, woe to him. . . . all afflictions that lie betwixt me and duty, undergoe them, though hell gates were open."[18] Hooker had no intention of offering himself for a senseless martyrdom, however; in the balance between affliction and duty, one was required to bear afflictions only while performing duties commanded by God. Death or imprisonment kept faithful ministers from preaching and caring for their congregations, and they were therefore bound in conscience to avoid these obstructions to the performance of their calling. God could, of course, desire His servants to witness to the truth by their martyrdom, but more often He sent afflictions such as persecution to prove the constancy of the faithful.

If the choice were between exile and prison, a preacher could legitimately accept exile, for there at least he could further the work of God among men, and exile might be God's way of calling him to another place. It was a difficult case of conscience to determine at exactly what moment the only remaining alternatives were flight or prison or worse. Richard Mather drew up for himself a long list of arguments showing the reasonableness of his removal to America, and when John Cotton was forced to consider exile, he sought the advice of the venerable John Dod. Hooker almost certainly conferred with his friends, with men like John Rogers and Thomas Welde, before he decided upon a course of action. He may also have consulted with Richard Sibbes, who had been one of the counselors of Mrs. Drake; one of the fruits of the Chelmsford years had been

[17] Hooker, *Chief Lessons*, 68.   [18] Ibid., 74.

a draft of *The Poore Doubting Christian*, published in 1629 along with a collection of Sibbes's sermons. In July of that year he met at the Earl of Lincoln's estate at Sempringham with the gentlemen of the New England Company. His business with Winthrop and his associates at this time is unclear; he rode up to Lincoln in company with John Cotton and Roger Williams, and they all may have been invited to come over to New England.[19]

In addition to his *Poore Doubting Christian*, Hooker wrote a preface to John Rogers' *The Doctrine of Faith*, also published in 1629. Rogers' request for a preface was an especial sign of honor on the part of the older man; his book had already gone through two editions, and the presence of a preface by Hooker in the third edition testified to his standing as an expert upon the stirrings of faith in the souls of the repentant. Rogers also invited him to preach before his congregation at Dedham, and Hooker delivered a sermon later printed as *The Faithful Covenanter*. By far his most useful friend and patron at this time was Robert Rich, the Earl of Warwick; Lord Robert, who had probably used Mr. Nash of Much Waltham as a front in putting up Hooker's bond the previous summer, hid the refugee minister in 1630 for a short time at Old Park in Great Waltham. After Laud's second summons, Hooker was a wanted man, and he could not simply take any ship to escape from England and episcopal persecution. Some time in the spring of 1631 the arrangements for escape were completed, and Hooker and his family secretly took ship for the Netherlands.[20]

[19] See Roger Williams' note of this journey in his *The Bloody Tenent Yet More Bloody*, ed. Samuel J. Caldwell, *Publications of the Narragansett Club*, IV (Providence, 1870), 65. The Company had already sent Francis Higginson to New England. Higginson, who had been counseled during his conversion by Hooker and who was a former minister in Leicester, may have introduced Hooker to the Company, but Hooker's own fame would have been sufficient grounds for an invitation to Sempringham.

[20] Alice Clare Carter transcribes the register of the Amsterdam English Church to report, "In January 1631 Mr. Thomas Hooker preacher

A recurring feature of New England Puritan hagiographies was the relation of marvelous providences which delivered the escaping saints from the perils of the sea and the pursuivants. Later generations liked to think that the Lord saved their ancestors just as He had saved the Apostles on the Sea of Galilee, and another favorite image was that of Laud's agents as eternally frustrated Egyptians in pursuit of Israel. Mather recorded Hooker's deliverance thus:

> In his passage thither, he quickly had occasion to discover himself, when they were in eminent hazard of shipwreck upon a shelf of sand, whereon they ran in the night; but Mr. Hooker, like Paul, with a remarkable confidence, assured them that they should be preserved; and they had as remarkable a deliverance. I have also heard that when he fled from the pursevants, to take his passage for the Low-Countries, at his last parting with some of his friends, one of them said, "Sir, what if the wind should not be fair, when you come to the vessel?" Whereto he instantly replied, "Brother, let us leave that with Him who keeps the wind in the hollow of his hand:" and it was observed that, although the wind was cross until he came aboard, yet it immediately then came about fair and fresh, and he was no sooner under sail, but the officer arrived at the sea-side, happily too late now to come at him.[21]

In the context of similar accounts, the anecdote becomes myth, but the point is clear—escape from Laud's pursuivants was a touch-and-go affair for a man in Hooker's position.

---

came into these countries," *The English Reformed Church in Amsterdam in the Seventeenth Century* (Amsterdam, 1964), 192. Keith L. Sprunger, however, corrects this to read "in Junij 1631," "The Dutch Career of Thomas Hooker," *New England Quarterly* 46 (1973), 18. Hooker was preaching by the summer of 1631 and his invitation seems to have come after Thomas Potts' death in April.

21 Mather, I, 338.

There were several probable reasons why Hooker chose to go to the Netherlands rather than to join the company of English Puritans who had begun the settlement of Massachusetts in the previous summer. First, if obliged to leave in a hurry with the pursuivants hot on his heels, Hooker would have found it much easier and quicker to arrange for transportation to Holland than to New England, especially in the winter months, for the trans-Atlantic ships left later in the spring. Furthermore, there were fewer ships leaving for America in 1631 than in 1630; the main party of the Bay Company colonists had gone over only in the preceding summer, and in 1631 men were waiting to hear of the colonists' success before leaving England. He had probably not given up yet on the possibilities of reform in the English Church; if his case could arouse so much support in 1629, perhaps the Puritan party was nearly able to control the church. In addition to these reasons for hesitation, the religious conditions of the New World were still uncertain, despite what he may have learned in his conference with the Winthrop group of 1629. The religious structure of the New England settlement was still largely unknown in the mother country, and there was an active classis of English churches in Holland which were known to be governing themselves as nonseparating congregationalist churches.[22]

This English Classis in the Dutch Netherlands was founded in 1621 under the leadership of John Forbes, minister to the Merchant Adventurers' church in Delft (and one more of the ministers who had interested himself in Mrs. Drake). Forbes and a majority of the English ministers in Holland had petitioned both King James and the States General of the Netherlands for permission to establish an independent classis similar to those of the French and Walloon ministers exiled in Holland. The petitioners represented themselves to James as being

[22] See William Hubbard, *A General History of New England From the Discovery to MDCLXXX* (Boston, 1878), 167 for comment on scarcity of ships in 1631.

free in their soules and consciences from any disrespect, censure, prejudice, or condemnation of the churches of his Majesties dominions, reserving unto them all due reverence and acknowledgement as to the true Churches of Christ, equally precious in the sight of God (through the same most precious faith) with themselves; resolving still to hold communion with them notwithstanding any difference of externall order.[23]

The petitioners were vague about the sort of "externall order" they intended to establish in their churches, and James and his Privy Council probably assumed they were going to erect a Presbyterian classis similar in organization to the classes of the Dutch Reformed Church.[24] Having gained the approval of the English government to establish their classis, the ministers applied to the States General for its permission. The States General readily consented, believing the English classis would bring order to the rag-tag assortment of dissenting churches which was constantly raising internal squabbles and threatening diplomatic relations with England. The States General must have assumed much the same intentions on the part of the English ministers as the Privy Council had; the French and Walloon classes were supposedly precedents for the English organization, and they were modeled after the Dutch example.

Forbes and his friends, however, set up a classis which was unlike anything the Reformed Churches had yet seen. The reformed model of church discipline gave synods and classes power over individual churches in order to preserve the uniform purity of ordinances and doctrine. The new English classis denied that it had any disciplinary power over individual congregations; the classis was intended as an association of ministers for the purposes of mutual advice and encouragement. If a particular church erred and would not respond to

[23] Quoted in Stearns, *Congregationalism*, 85.
[24] Ibid., 9.

classical admonishments, the other members of the classis could withdraw the "right hand of fellowship," but they could not interfere with the internal business of the congregation unless invited. In this respect the English classis was not so much designed after the classical form of the Dutch Reformed Church as it was after the form of something like the Essex ministerial meeting. Forbes and his associates were in 1621 the first men to follow in practice the ideas of the so-called nonseparating congregational Puritans.[25] The English classis did not advertise its differences with the Dutch Reformed discipline, and for almost ten years these first congregationalists were able to conceal their heterodoxy.

While he was in England, Hooker never espoused a church organization at variance with the established model, and he avoided direct attack upon the bishops. He had, nevertheless, come to agree with the disciplinary model of the nonseparating congregationalists formulated by William Ames, Henry Jacob, and others. As we shall see, a few months after his arrival in Holland he wrote a brief defense of several leading congregationalist principles, and the friends he sought out in the Low Countries were those ministers of the English classis who were most vigorous in their defense of congregationalism.

When Hooker arrived in the Netherlands, he went first to stay with the Reverend Hugh Peter, pastor of the English church in Rotterdam. Peter was an aggressive and outspoken young preacher who had been forced to seek refuge after a short, clamorous career in England. Peter seems to have been rather rash and hasty by temperament, and in 1660 he would pay for his overzealousness by sharing the fate of the regicides. The immediate cause of his flight to Holland was the prayer he delivered in Christ Church, London, on St. Andrew's Day, 1626. After his sermon, he requested that God would remove from

[25] The major account of the background and consequences of nonseparating congregational Puritanism is Perry Miller, *Orthodoxy in Massachusetts, 1630–1650* (Cambridge, Mass., Harvard Univ. Press, 1933).

Queen Henrietta, Charles's Roman Catholic wife, "the Idols of her father's House, and that she would forsake the Idolatry and superstition wherein she was and must needes perish if she continued in the same."[26] It took all the policy and influence of Peter's mentor, the Earl of Warwick, to smooth over the resulting scandal. The Bishop of London now had his eye on Peter, however, and in August 1627 the young Puritan was called in for further interrogation about his orthodoxy and conformity. Peter prefaced his defense upon this occasion by commenting, "I having consulted with Antiquity, and with our modern *Hooker*, and others, humbly desire your Lordship to accept the satisfaction following."[27] The succeeding document, a typically Puritan bit of special pleading, did not impress the bishop, for Peter was suspended by the end of 1627, and he went to the Netherlands shortly thereafter.

Although Hooker's and Peter's careers at Cambridge overlapped by a few years, they undoubtedly became friends in Essex. From 1623 to mid-1626 Peter was the curate of Rayleigh, a village less than fifteen miles from Chelmsford. Peter and Hooker would have met at the monthly assembly of ministers, and Peter was one of those "divers young ministers" who spent "their time in conference" with Mr. Hooker and so worried Samuel Collins. A further bond between the two Puritans was their friendship with the Earl of Warwick; Lord Robert had advanced Peter's career and gotten him out of several scrapes with the authorities, and he had also sheltered Hooker and probably arranged for him to go to Peter.

In all likelihood Hooker and Peter exchanged correspondence before Hooker left England, and they may have seen each other during the course of Peter's two visits to London and Essex in 1628 and 1630. One final reason for Hooker's removal to Holland may have been Peter's suggestion of a possible clerical post there. The English church at Amsterdam had as

---

[26] Stearns, *Strenuous Puritan*, 41.   [27] Ibid., 41–42.

its minister John Paget, who had proclaimed his allegiance to the Dutch Reformed Church in 1605 and had been pastor of the Amsterdam church since its inception. Paget was assisted by Thomas Potts, who fell ill in 1628; his illness turned out to be debilitating and chronic, and Paget and the church elders began searching for a replacement in 1629. Several members of the congregation requested that Peter, by then a proctor at Franeker University in Friesland, be invited "to ease the minister and to have a man ready if Mr. Potts might die."[28] Several reasons, one of the most important being that Potts was not yet dead, prevented Peter's installation as a minister of the Amsterdam church. Peter subsequently accepted a call from the church in Rotterdam, where Hooker found him and he became a member of the classis of English ministers.

Peter may well have informed Hooker of the expected death of Potts, who did indeed pass away in April 1631. There was now officially a vacancy in the ministry of the Amsterdam church, and Hooker as the most eminent unattached English preacher in the Netherlands was the logical candidate to receive the call to the position. There was one difficulty, however, which Hooker may not have known when he left England, but which he almost certainly would have learned from Peter in Rotterdam. When the English classis was formed in 1621, several English ministers had refused to join, either out of separatist principles or because they insisted upon conforming to the Church of England. Thomas Paget, who had himself been forced to leave England for nonconformity, joined the Dutch classis and refused to participate in Forbes's congregationalist organization. Paget's dissent from the established English discipline was in favor of the presbyterian system as practiced in Scotland and the Dutch Netherlands, and he was unwilling to move further to the left with Forbes's group into congregationalism.

[28] Carter, 74.

The actual reason for Paget's rejection of Hugh Peter as an assistant was Peter's maintenance of congregationalist principles of church discipline. If he would be willing to accept Hooker as an assistant, the Amsterdam church might be drawn into the English classis. The presence in the Netherlands of English ministers who refused to associate themselves with Forbes's classis was a continuing danger to the classis' existence. The States General had authorized the classis in the belief that all the English churches would join, and thus if there were dissension and controversy in any English church, the classis would be blamed, whether or not the troublesome church actually was a member.

Paget resisted the English classis because his own conception of the proper form of church government followed that of the Dutch Reformed Church. He had been a notable opponent earlier in his career of the separatists, or Brownists, who had disturbed Amsterdam with their wranglings. His position as pastor of the Amsterdam church in the decade of the 1620s was difficult just because of his previous successes against the Brownists; a large minority of his congregation were ex-separatists, and they now leaned toward the principles of the nonseparating congregationalists such as Forbes and Peter. Paget, like most reformed Protestants at this time, failed to grasp the rather subtle distinction between the congregationalists and the Brownists, and it must have seemed to him that a large part of his congregation was about to backslide into old heresies. This vocal minority was capable of extensive campaigning among the rest of the congregation in order to achieve its aims, which often contradicted the principles of John Paget as well as those of the Dutch Church. Paget several times had to struggle to preserve order in his own church. His basic defense against schism in the Amsterdam church was to keep out ministers with differing ideas of church polity; men like Peter, Hooker, and, later, John Davenport were possible rallying points for a subversive minority in the church.

When the affairs of the English classis later came under the scrutiny of the ecclesiastical authorities at home, an informant wrote to Sir William Boswell, the Ambassador to The Hague,

> Stephen Oswood, an Inn Keeper dwelling neer the Old Church at Amsterdam, wrote a Letter to Mr. Hooker presently upon the death of Mr. Potts. Mr. Hooker, upon his Invitation, promised to come, But must be *Caled*; he would but come first to Rotterdam, expecting the Call from hence.[29]

Hooker must have left England in May or early June, "presently upon the death of Mr. Potts" in April, and he stayed with Peter in Rotterdam, waiting for a regular call. He might have profited from information about the turbulent state of affairs in Amsterdam, but there is no evidence that Peter was aware of either the incipient revolt in the congregation there or the real depth of Paget's objections to congregational principles. Peter's involvement with the Amsterdam church had been somewhat brief and vague; since Paget did not have to explain his disapproval of Peter's congregational principles when rejecting him as Potts's successor, Peter may not have been aware of the intricacies of the situation in Amsterdam. Hooker might thus have been poorly informed about the state of the Amsterdam church, or, judging from the tenor of Oswood's letter, he might either have assumed the church was organized upon congregational principles or have seriously overestimated the strength of the congregationalist minority.

Several members of the church's consistory, the ruling body of lay elders and ministers, held congregationalist opinions, and upon several occasions in the ensuing controversy they acted on their own in defiance of Paget, the ex-officio president of the consistory. Upon this occasion they so far prevailed over Paget as to issue a letter on July 2, 1631, inviting Hooker to "exercise his gifts" before the church. Hooker preached on a

[29] Stearns, *Congregationalism*, 116.

141

trial basis for a short time after this, and he then left Amsterdam for The Hague in order to get medical advice. This visit was possibly necessitated by a recurrence of the sickness with which he had been afflicted in England. While he was at The Hague, two elders of the church came to him with a second letter, requesting "a more perfect trial" of his preaching.[30] Paget was a clever politician, and he probably agreed to these probationary requests by the consistory until he could collect direct evidence supporting his objections against Hooker. The letters did not constitute a formal call, requests for trial preaching being customary in both the Dutch and English churches. Paget could give in to the consistory's wishes without crossing his own principles, and at the same time he could attempt to persuade the other members of the consistory of Hooker's unfitness to serve as his assistant. While all this maneuvering was going on, he was committing himself to nothing.

Paget was unable to buy enough time to convince the church's ruling body not to issue a call to Hooker, and he must have realized that he could not put off this candidate as easily as he had Peter. Relations between Hooker and Paget became more tense after Hooker's return from The Hague; in one of his sermons Hooker used a trope involving a wooden horse, and this figure was apparently understood by Paget to conceal an attack upon himself.[31] Hooker was defended by a minority of the congregation, led by Oswood, an ex-separatist, and the internal wrangling and dissension, which Paget had hoped to prevent, began to manifest itself. The consistory saw no objection to Hooker, in spite of Paget's disapproval, and in the late summer or early autumn of 1631 they attempted to give him a formal call.

This call would have been irregular, since the Amsterdam church was bound to observe the procedure adopted by the Dutch Church for calling ministers. According to Paget,

[30] Carter, 76.   [31] Carter, 77.

> The synods of these Reformed Churches, describing the Order to be observed in the Calling of Ministers, do require a choice to be made by the Elders and Deacons; approbation by the Magistrates; allowance of the Classis; and, in the last place, consent of the Congregation.[32]

The consistory, with the encouragement of a significant part of the congregation, was about to ignore this order by proceeding with the call without gaining the approval of either the Amsterdam magistrates or the classis. If they succeeded in their efforts, they would turn the Amsterdam church into a congregationalist organization in one stroke. Paget was faced with a revolution in his own church, but if he had gone to the classis for help at this point, he would have risked receiving a censure himself for failing to control his congregation.

Paget had one last arrow in his quiver; he demanded that Hooker answer before the consistory certain questions designed to test his orthodoxy. The consistory objected to this trial, for it was the classis' duty to determine a ministerial candidate's orthodoxy, but they could hardly afford to stand upon the principle of due process, since their whole proceeding had ignored the usual forms. Hooker desired Paget to put his questions in writing, and Paget drew up a set of twenty propositions. Hooker returned written answers, and the consistory felt his answers revealed no just reasons to prevent a call. Paget quickly translated the questions and answers into Latin, and he bypassed the consistory by delivering them to the Dutch classis of Amsterdam for consideration and advice. He also informed the classis of the consistory's actions and requested an opinion on their propriety. On October 6, 1631, the Amsterdam classis debated the issue, and they decided that Hooker "could not with edification be allowed hereafter to preach to the English Church in this city."[33] This decision was understandable in view of Hooker's answers to the twenty propositions; Paget

---

[32] Stearns, *Congregationalism*, 28n. [33] Ibid., 28.

had cleverly set them forth to reveal the difference of opinion between the Dutch and English ministers over church discipline, and Hooker's honest but impolitic responses revealed the distance between the two men. Hooker's set of answers to Paget's twenty propositions is his first known public statement concerning his beliefs about church discipline; presumably he must have spoken his mind to friends and parishioners in Essex, but this document defined his position forever in the spectrum of the Reformation. Fifteen years later he would elaborate his position at great length in the *Survey of the Summe of Church Discipline*, but the ideas of that book are the ideas of the answers to Paget's twenty propositions more fully explained and grounded.

Several of the questions reflected Paget's fears of schism in his own church, and they were designed to screen out any minister who might encourage the contentions of the ex-separatists in the Amsterdam church. The first three questions, for example, pertained to the proper relationship between the church and members of Brownist congregations; they asked whether it was lawful for men to participate in the separatists' church services, whether church members who also worshiped with separatists were to be tolerated or censured, and whether "Brownists as have not renounced their Separation from the Church of England . . . may lawfully be received for members of our Church."[34] The answers must have been rather frustrating for Paget; Hooker agreed with Paget:

> To separate from the faithful assemblies and Churches in England as no true Churches is an error in judgement, and a sin in practice, held and maintained by the Brownists, and therefore to communicate with them, either in their opinion or practice, is sinful and utterly unlawful.

[34] All quotations from Hooker's answers to the twenty propositions are from Ms. Carter's transcription of the text (193–200) as written into the register of the Amsterdam church.

If Hooker had stopped there, Paget might have been a bit easier in his mind about his prospective colleague, but Hooker went on to say that if a man rejected the Brownists' opinions, it was not absolutely unlawful "to communicate with them in the part of God's worship." He admitted that the practice "may prove occasionally offensive," but "if these occasions of offence may be removed, . . . then it is not a sin to hear there occasionally." Hooker's admission of extenuating circumstances in the latter half of the answer effectually negated, in Paget's eyes, the condemnation of separatism made in the first half.

In answer to the second question, Hooker admitted by implication that censure was a possible alternative in dealing with church members who went to hear the Brownists, but he also undercut this concession to Paget by maintaining that "before they be convinced of their sin they ought rather to be tolerated than censured." His reminder that "the same degree of pains for convincing is not so sufficient in one disposition as in another" probably further irritated Paget, for the older man had known from long experience the difficulties involved in convincing Brownists of the evils of separation. Hooker's statement seems almost callow, as if he refused to credit Paget's former controversies with Parker and Ainsworth. When Hooker came to deal with dissenters in New England, however, he always tolerated before he censured, and he took the same "degree of pains in convincing" as he had done earlier with Mrs. Drake. On the other hand, Paget had more than enough trouble with Stephen Oswood and his friends, and he could hardly wish to tolerate them further.

Hooker's answer to the third question was equally unsatisfactory, and it must have been one which the Dutch classis viewed with great displeasure. Hooker claimed that refusal to renounce separation from the Church of England did not unfit a man for church membership, and the reasons he advanced for this opinion pointed up the confusion between the positions of the separating Brownists and the nonseparating congregationalists. Hooker denied that separatism was a heresy, but he admitted it was an erroneous opinion. Since the separatists were not heretics, as the anabaptists were, he was willing to coexist with them, as he did in the Lyford case of 1626, without taking part in their error. Hooker argued against Paget that to reject a separatist "for an erroneous opinion or practice . . . is to confirm the Brownists in that insupportable and absurd censure, which now they maintain touching those who hold the Church of England to be true Churches." Hooker and his congregationalist colleagues held that the English Church was composed of true churches in its congregations, although they were contaminated by papist superstition in their ceremonies and hierarchy; the errors in the English Church were in "things indifferent" and did not constitute just grounds for separation. To make an erroneous but not heretical opinion a bar to church membership was to apply to the Brownists their own mistaken principle of separating over things indifferent.

This answer would have confirmed Paget's worst suspicions; he required ex-separatists to renounce, however equivocally, their former errors and to refrain from attending the services of separatist assemblies. Hooker's positive standards for admission to the church were, on the other hand, no more acceptable to Paget than the admission of non-recanting separatists. Hooker believed that fit men for church members were "visible Christians," those "being in . . . judgement and life other ways altogether unblameable . . . in the judgement of charity . . . accounted a member of Christ and so a saint." The presence of a new heart, a regenerate spirit, fitted man for the church, and not his opinions on church discipline, as long as they were not heretical. This meant that only those men who were demonstrably among the elect could be admitted to the church. A candidate for Paget's church was not required to prove his election before he was received into the membership; he had to believe in Christ, but he was not required to have believed into Christ. Hooker conceived of the church as a particular congregation composed of those who were "in the judgement of charity" accounted among the elect, and at this point the disagreement between Hooker and Paget over church polity became in fact a disagreement over doctrine.

Because he required evidence of election prior to admission to the church, the overwhelming majority of Hooker's published sermons aimed at leading men to seek Christ rather than instructing them in the proper forms of worship and church government. The frame of church discipline was a matter of concern, but it was only a means toward encouraging men to strive for a spiritual renewal. Both Paget and Hooker believed that the church in its broadest definition was a body of faithful Christians brought together to worship God and to enjoy His renewing and strengthening graces, and both men believed God found pleasing only the worship offered to Him by these faithful Christians. The root of the disagreement was over the definition of a faithful Christian and, hence, over the requirements for church membership and even the nature of the church in its social context. Hooker's answer to the nineteenth question, one on doctrine rather than discipline, emphasized the distance between the two ministers. He there stated in brief his doctrine of preparation and the double repentance described by himself and John Rogers. Paget had not subscribed to this latest refinement of the Calvinist scheme, and he held that a Christian experienced only one repentance after receiving faith and that there was no such thing as a preparatory repentance. His standards for acceptable faith were as a result less strict than Hooker's, for he accepted as faith the historical belief in Christ as Savior that Hooker had rejected in favor of the spiritual believing of a regenerate heart.

Questions four through ten, concerning various church practices, were of lesser importance; Paget included them because they had been matters of contention with the separatists, and Hooker's brief and equivocal answers indicate that he failed to see their relevance in the present situation. The eleventh questions, however, brought into the open the whole political question at issue between Paget and his own consistory and between Paget and the English classis. Here Paget asked Hooker whether a particular congregation had power to call a minister without the approbation of the classis. Paget's recurrence to the Dutch classis in order to rule his own consistory had made the issue of Hooker's call a public and political concern, and this eleventh proposition was preeminently a political question. Paget refused to deviate from the procedure established by the Dutch Church for calling ministers, and this procedure gave the classis a veto on the particular church's choice. Hooker directly contradicted the accepted procedure by stating that, "a particular congregation hath complete power by Christ's institution to give a complete call unto a Minister without any derived power from a Classis." He argued that there were particular churches before there were classes; hence, the power which rested first in Christ was derived next to the congregation and only afterwards to a classis. If a church had entered freely into a classis, Hooker held that it could seek classical approval of a ministerial choice, but "if the Classis should not approve they may lawfully and without sin choose without or against the approbation of the Classis if they saw good reason." As Paget saw it, Hooker's position here was in full agreement with the central plank of the separatist platform and nothing more than a defense of ecclesiastical anarchy.

Propositions twelve through eighteen concerned other limits of a particular congregation's power, and the last two questions were of a doctrinal nature, concerning the nature of justification. Hooker's answers were again somewhat equivocal, but it was easy enough to read his disagreement with Paget between the lines of his answers. The differences of opinion between the two men which had been revealed in most of these questions might have been successfully compromised; Hooker's stand on the first three questions and upon the eleventh question made any compromise impossible. The first three answers seemed to reveal that Hooker was soft on Brownism, and his answer to the crucial eleventh proposition made both Paget and the Dutch classis realize that his opinions tended to undermine their authority and the church order which they had established. Hooker was not a combative man over differences of opinion such as these, although he would not retreat from what he saw as truth, but he had been thrust into the role of revolutionary by his answer to the eleventh proposition. He was certainly not the first man to announce these opinions about church government—Ames and Jacob had expressed them years before—nor was he the first to practice them— Forbes and his associates had been operating their classis in the congregationalist way for the last ten years. Hooker was, however, the first preacher with congregationalist principles to come into open conflict with the Dutch Church; for the first ten years of the English classis' existence both the Dutch and English ministers avoided any embarrassing investigations into differences of discipline. In 1631 the Dutch Church was forced to take notice at last of the heterodox organization of the English classis, and their first step, taken by the Amsterdam classis, was to prohibit Hooker from preaching in that city.

The consistory apparently attempted once more to defy the classis and their own pastor; they laid aside the idea of giving Hooker a call, but in the latter part of October, after the decision of the classis had been announced, they decided to give Hooker permission to preach in their church. This maneuver got them nowhere, for they were required to revoke their invitation, and they received a classical censure for having recorded it in the church register.[35] Hooker probably would not have accepted this offer anyway, for in the meantime he had removed to Delft to become Forbes's assistant.

Paget's questions had been pressed upon Hooker rather suddenly, and he was rushed in writing out his answers. As he was answering the propositions, however, he realized that there

[35] Carter, 79.

was little chance of compromise with Paget and that the real point of the questions was to lure him into making an actionable statement. He noted of the fourth proposition, for instance, "Why it should be questioned I see not, unless men desire to find differences of opinion." Hooker had little desire to raise disturbances over things indifferent, and after his last answer he wrote what was in effect a resignation of any claim to the ministry of the Amsterdam church:

> And because I do apprehend your opinion and affections to be so far settled that you apprehend there cannot be a peaceable concurrence in such distances of judgement to deliver you from all fear either of any molestations that might come unto your spirit or division to your congregation I am resolved contentedly to sit down and suddenly as I see my opportunity to depart wishing that the God of Peace would provide so comfortable Assistance as might suit with you in all truth and godliness for your mutual comfort and the building up of the body of Christ.

Hooker wished at least as strongly as Paget wished to avoid wounding the body of Christ, the church, and he saw in October 1631 that the only way to secure peace was to remove himself from the false position in which he had been placed. When the Amsterdam classis forbade him to preach in the city, he had already given up any intention of so doing.

Hooker had left England because he was no longer permitted to preach in peace. His first attempt at finding a haven in the Netherlands had ended in dissension and a public brouhaha. His next attempt was not to fare much better, although he would be able to avoid entangling himself in the church's quarrels. Forbes's congregation at Delft was the church of the Merchant Adventurers, and in the fall of 1631 a contention had arisen there between Forbes and his elders on one side and the Merchant Adventurers' Deputy, Edward Misselden, on the other. In October, Forbes and his elders decided the spiritual qualifications of "divers handicraftsmen and others unfree of this fellowship" of the Adventurers entitled them "to have their voices with the brethren of the Companie" in the election of the elders and deacons of the church. Misselden complained that extension of voting rights to all members of the church tended "to the prejudice of the priviledges granted to this fellowship."[36] Hooker had left Amsterdam to avoid the unseemly quarrel with Paget, and he arrived in Delft only to land in the middle of one more church disorder.

The quarrel was kept within the church during the autumn of 1631, but in the following year the matter got out of hand; Forbes appealed against Misselden to the States General and to the main court of the Merchant Adventurers at Hamburg, and Misselden countered with an appeal to the English Privy Council later in 1632. On October 29 Misselden appeared before the Privy Council in London and submitted to them a list of "The Abuses" of the "English Churches in the Lowe Countries." By this time Misselden had gone beyond attacking Forbes alone, and he accused all the ministers of the English classis of "Corrupting our Nation; Writing scandalous books; holding Continuall Correspondence with the Refractories of England."[37] Deputy Misselden thus managed to give the Council a somewhat prejudicial view of the dispute; the argument was originally over the control of the local church organization —whether only the fellows of the Company or all the saints, regardless of their membership in the Company, had the power to elect elders and deacons—but Misselden convinced the Privy Council that he had been "affronted in his government by some factions of the Company for his desire to conform them to the divine service of the Church of England."[38] The issue of a congregational church order was indeed at the heart of the dissension between Misselden and Forbes, but prior to his appearance before the Privy Council, the deputy had not

[36] Stearns, *Congregationalism*, 31–32.
[37] Ibid., 33–34.　　　　　[38] Ibid., 124.

shown any exemplary zeal for the "divine services of the Church of England."

The Privy Council responded to the deputy's complaint by ordering the Merchant Adventurers' London Commissioners to return with him to Delft and to settle the differences which had arisen in the church. Within a month Misselden and the commissioners were in Delft, but they discovered that Forbes had left the city in the middle of the preceding summer to visit the army of Gustavus Adolphus somewhere in Germany. Hooker had been left behind in Delft to maintain the ministry of the church, and it was Hooker who inherited Forbes's quarrel. Hooker and the elders were consequently forced to confront the commissioners by themselves, which might have been just as well, since Forbes's aggressiveness was in large part responsible for aggravating the quarrel with Misselden.

Hooker, the elders, and the members of the Delft congregation did all they could to appease Misselden and the commissioners without committing themselves to any changes in the established congregational order of the church. Seventeen members of the church stole a march on Misselden by informing Sir William Boswell that "they were ready to take the oaths of supremacy and allegiance whenever required and to conform to all the laws of England when they came to live therein." In the meantime they would abide by the laws of the United Provinces and by the church order of the English classis as it was established "by the joint authority of our State as well as of this State."[39] When the commissioners subsequently held their court on December 4, 1632, they reduced the Delft church "to a conditional conformity," and they obtained a subscription to four propositions apparently supporting this conformity. The propositions were in fact almost meaningless because their wording was extremely ambiguous and noncommittal. They promised that God's Word was truly

[39] Ibid., 36.

preached at Delft, that the discipline used there was according to the Word, that the congregation submitted to be ruled by their pastor and elders, and that anyone not submitting to this rule would be held as a heathen and publican.[40] This document in no way compromised the previous stand of Forbes and the elders. Laud, to whom it was presented in England, undoubtedly saw its hollowness. The propositions did, however, satisfy the commissioners, and if the church could have mollified Deputy Misselden, in spite of having implicitly called him a heathen, the whole affair might have been passed over.

Forbes was inclined to fight for all of his principles with little regard for their intrinsic practical or theological importance. Late in 1631, for example, he had embarrassed Hooker by appointing himself as his champion before the Amsterdam classis; Hooker had already left Amsterdam, but Forbes demanded that the Dutch classis present reasons for not accepting Hooker as Paget's assistant. Unsatisfied by the reasons, the pugnacious Forbes "writt an Expostulatory letter to the classis which they tooke very unkindly; and sent him back a sharpe answer reprehending his medling in things above his place, and plainly blaming the arrogancy of his spirit and though to blame Bishops [was] himself more than Episcopall."[41] Because of Forbes's interference in the Hooker-Paget dispute, the case was not settled until September 7, 1632, when the South Holland Synod concurred with the Amsterdam classis. Forbes's scheming had only made Hooker's position in the Delft church more uncomfortable; the Dutch churchmen were disturbed by the English church's acceptance of a minister already found unacceptable by them. Furthermore, the Delft church affair had called attention once more to Hooker and his involvement in nonconformist dissent.

The English classis had survived in the Netherlands for over a decade because Forbes and his friends had cleverly played

[40] Ibid., 37.   [41] Ibid., 117.

the Dutch authorities off against the English. By calling the attention of the South Holland Synod, which had sponsored the English classis in the first place, to irregularities and disorders within the English churches, Forbes went far toward alienating one of his most effective supports. After he returned to Delft in January 1633, he proceeded to goad the English authorities into taking repressive action by appearng before the Privy Council in London with a counterpetition to Misselden's appeal of the year before. The Archbishop of Canterbury sat on the Council, and Laud was by this time the archbishop; his experience in dealing with nonconformists enabled him to see through the ambiguous dodges of Forbes's rhetoric. Since Laud was now on the Privy Council, Forbes's appearance was highly impolitic; it was a fatal error to call the archbishop's attention to the disorders in the English churches in the Netherlands. The Council, subsequent to Forbes's petition, ordered William Boswell to end the nonconformity of the English classis.

Boswell immediately took steps to secure the cooperation of the Dutch civil and ecclesiastical authorities, and he was thus able to prevent Forbes and his associates from their usual game of invoking Dutch protection against English threats, and vice versa. Hooker apparently realized in early 1633 that the Delft church and the English classis were facing dissolution, and, although Forbes and the other congregationalist ministers of the Netherlands had involved him in a succession of ecclesiastic quarrels, he remained loyal to them. Misselden wrote Boswell in March of 1633 that Hooker was giving Forbes "diligent advice" to stand firm in the congregational way. The younger minister was, however, doubtful of the immediate outcome to the current struggle against the forces of episcopacy; he also apparently advised Forbes that it might be necessary "to go for New England."[42]

Hooker had come to the Low Countries in order to find an opportunity to preach the gospel in peace and harmony. Two

[42] *Ibid.*, 45.

years had passed in the search, and two attempts at finding a pulpit had only involved him more deeply in contention and disorder. He had inadvertently walked into two explosive situations, and although he was able to escape with integrity, he had little to show for his efforts. His prospects in Holland were unpromising, and after his involvement in the messy affairs at Amsterdam and Delft had made his name notorious among English authorities, he could no longer return to his home country. In all this, however, he was not a mere victim of circumstances, but a witness to his conception of the truth.

If Hooker had wanted only security and peace, he could have found it in Amsterdam by disguising his true sympathies, but God's truth, once clearly perceived, weighed more than man's comfort, and he answered Paget's propositions in the knowledge that his answers would force his removal from Amsterdam. Although he inherited seemingly by accident Forbes's quarrel with Deputy Misselden and the Privy Council, Hooker was by no means innocent of the "Abuses" with which Misselden had charged the members of the English classis. He was guilty of "Corrupting our Nation" by catalyzing the ex-separatists' disorders in the Amsterdam church; he undoubtedly held "Continuall Correspondence with the Refractories of England," and, perhaps worst of all in Laud's view, he too had written "scandalous books." It was probably during his first year in the Netherlands that he wrote out from his sermon notes the text of *The Soules Preparation for Christ*, first published in 1632.

In the eyes of the English establishment the most scandalous piece of writing which Hooker had worked on in Holland was his preface to William Ames's *A Fresh Suit Against Human Ceremonies in Gods Worship*, published in 1633 and smuggled into England through the offices of that perennial troublemaker, Stephen Oswood. The title of the book sufficiently explains the object of Ames's comprehensive attack; in his preface Hooker was engaged in defending nonconformity against the strictures of Doctor John Burgess, Ames's father-in-law. Burgess had charged that nonconformity to the rites of the church led to separation, profaneness, and civil war, and Hooker refuted each of these accusations in detail. At the end of the preface he noted the price that had to be paid by the saints for the liberty to follow the dictates of their consciences:

> What do not men loose by unconformity? Even all their liberty, not only of providing for themselves, and their families; but even of breathing in any ayre, saving only that, which may be drawn out of stinking prisons. Nay somtyme all the Commodity of their Country, or Nationall habitation; being forced to flye even unto the Indians for safety, to say nothing of their losse of life itselfe, by cruell imprisonments.[43]

In the years from 1629 to 1633 Hooker had faced the serious possibility of receiving many of these rewards for nonconformity, and now he was about to test one of them, "being forced to flye even unto the Indians for safety."

The English classis in the Netherlands had attempted to discard the Erastian forms of the English national church in favor of a pragmatically developed organization designed to encourage men to experience Christ in their lives. For a while Hooker had hoped that the English church reforms would create institutions able to support experimental religion, but in the process of working out their new model of church government, the English ministers called down on themselves the very repression they had sought to escape by fleeing to Holland. In the latter part of his stay in the Low Countries, Hooker wrote to John Cotton, complaining,

> The state of these provinces to my weak eye, seems wonderfully ticklish and miserable. For the better part, heart re-

[43] Hooker, "The Preface" to William Ames, *A Fresh Suit Against Human Ceremonies in Gods Worship* (Amsterdam, 1633), sigs. 14^r, K^v.

ligion, they content themselves with very forms, though much blemished; but the power of godliness, for ought I can see or hear, they know not; and if it were thoroughly pressed, I fear least it will be fiercely opposed.[44]

The results of the Misselden controversy were to prove him right on the last count, and the last remaining haven in the English-speaking world for the practice of the power of godliness and heart religion seemed to be the new settlements in New England.

In addition to his general dissatisfaction with the religious situation in the Netherlands and his unhappiness at becoming a pawn in various distasteful church quarrels, Hooker had a more personal reason for wishing to leave the Low Countries; he informed Cotton,

> My ague yet holds me; the ways of Gods providence, wherein he has walked towards me, in this long time of my sickness, and wherein I have drawn forth many wearyish hours, under his Almighty hand (blessed be his name) together with pursuits and banishment, which have waited upon me, as one wave follows another, have driven me to an amazement; his paths being too secret and past finding out by such an ignorant, worthless worm as myself.[45]

The cold and damp climate of the Netherlands was no place for a sufferer from ague, as Hooker had been for the last several years, and the combined weight of his difficulties finally led him to see the direction pointed out by the Almighty hand.

When John Winthrop and his companions left England in 1630 to institute the Massachusetts Bay Colony, John Cotton preached a farewell sermon; Cotton found his text from 2 Samuel 7:10, "Moreover I will appoint a place for my people Israell, and I will plant them, that they may dwell in a place

[44] Mather, I, 340.   [45] Ibid.

of their owne, and move no more," and his doctrine was "the placing of a people in this or that Countrey is from the appointment of the Lord."[46] So many obstacles had arisen to prevent Hooker from following his calling that it became apparent that God's will had not destined Holland to be his resting place. He faced only "stinking prisons" in England, and now that Laud's arm was about to reach across the North Sea, there remained only one refuge. A large group of his old Chelmsford parishioners and friends had gone to New England and begun a new town on the banks of the Charles River. No correspondence between Hooker and his "company" has survived, but it is almost certain that sometime in 1632 the embattled minister in the Netherlands was urged by his friends to emigrate to America. Sometime in the spring of 1633 Thomas Hooker left Delft for England, there to take ship, looking once more for a place of his own.[47]

[46] John Cotton, *Gods Promise to His Plantations*, in Old South Leaflets, No. 53 (Boston, n.d.), 5.

[47] Some evidence exists to indicate that Hooker had agreed to migrate to New England before he left Essex. The meeting with Winthrop in 1629 and the appearance of "Mr. Hooker's company" in 1632 point this way. It also seems likely that he may have intended the Delft ministry as only a temporary position during the period of Forbes's absence in Germany. However, in December of 1629 he had not yet decided to come to New England; the meeting with Winthrop had been indecisive. See Winthrop's letter of December 17, 1629, in *Winthrop Papers*, II (Boston, M.H.S., 1931), 178.

FIVE

Massachusetts

AFTER Thomas Hooker had definitely decided to rejoin his former parishioners as their pastor, he attempted to find another minister to assist him in New England. According to Cotton Mather, he advised the people of Newtown in the Bay Colony to obtain John Cotton, if he would agree to come. Cotton declined, and in his stead were considered three younger ministers: Thomas Shepard; John Norton, chaplain to Sir William Masham of High Lever, Essex; and Samuel Stone, lecturer at Towcester in Northamptonshire. The choice fell upon Stone, and when Hooker returned to England a hunted man, Stone sheltered his old Essex colleague and his family in Towcester. Mather recorded one narrow escape from the authorities in which Stone played a principal part; when the pursuivants knocked "at the door of that very chamber where he was now discoursing with Mr. Stone,"

> . . . He [Stone] stepped unto the door, with his pipe in his mouth, and such an air of speech and look, as gave him some credit with the officer. The officer demanded, Whether Mr. Hooker was not there? Mr. Stone replied with a braving sort of confidence, "What Hooker? Do you mean Hooker that lived once at Chelmsford!" The officer answered, "Yes, he!" Mr. Stone immediately, with a diversion like that which once helped Athanasius, made this true answer, "If it be he you look for, I saw him about an hour ago, at such an house in the town; you had best hasten thither after him." The officer took this for a sufficient account, and went his way.[1]

[1] Mather, I, 340–41.

Linguistic evasion like Stone's was a means of Puritan survival in a world of Oaths of Supremacy and subscriptions of orthodoxy to archbishops, and in this case, at least, Hooker owed his freedom to the ready wit of his friend and associate.

By the middle of 1633 Cotton had also found it impossible to remain any longer in England, and when the ship *Griffin* left the Downs in early July 1633, she carried Cotton, Hooker, and Stone. Pursuivants had been alerted to detain both Cotton and Hooker, and for the first few days out of England they and their families used assumed names. After Cotton and Hooker revealed themselves, the ship's crew and passengers were treated to a feast of prophesying. Mather reported, "By one or other of these three *divines* in the ship, there was a sermon preached every day, all the while they were aboard; yea they had three sermons, or expositions, for the most part every day: Mr. Cotton in the morning, Mr. Hooker in the afternoon, Mr. Stone after supper in the evening." Hooker and Cotton were the first two ministers to come to New England who had been famous in their own right in the old country; after the *Griffin* docked, the Bay colonists noted with a pious pun that God supplied their three great necessities—they had "*Cotton* for their *clothing, Hooker* for their *fishing*, and *Stone* for their *building*."[2] In addition to this distinguished clutch of ministers, the *Griffin* carried John Haynes, later to become the first governor of Connecticut, and Atherton Hough, a prosperous merchant and a follower of Cotton who would become involved in the colony's first great heresy trial.

Hooker's earlier sea voyages had been passages of the frequently stormy North Sea while enroute to and from the Netherlands, and he probably expected little good from the much longer and more tedious Atlantic crossing. The *Griffin* left comparatively late in the year, and by the time she neared the American coast, she might well have expected to run head

[2] Ibid., 265.

into a hurricane. The daily course of three sermons seems to have proved efficacious, for when they arrived at Boston on September 4, 1633, John Winthrop noted that they had lost only four persons, "whereof one was drowned two days before, as he was casting forth a line to take mackerel."[3] Hooker's health was apparently not endangered, and he does not seem to have been particularly bothered by his ague for the next decade. The voyage was even more propitious for Cotton, since in the midst of it his wife delivered their first son, "whom he called *Sea-born*, in the remembrance of the never-to-be-forgotten blessings which he thus enjoyed upon the seas."[4]

After the arrival of the *Griffin*, "Mr. Hooker and Mr. Stone went presently to Newtown, where they were to be entertained [by Thomas Dudley, the Deputy Governor of the Colony], and Mr. Cotton stayed in Boston."[5] Hooker's and Stone's calls to the pulpit of the Newtown church had been issued before they left England, and there was never any doubt about where they intended to settle. It is not clear from the available records that there was an established church at this time in Newtown; a meetinghouse, complete with the luxury of a bell, had been built approximately a year before Hooker's arrival—on December 24, 1632, it was decided that voters would "meet every first Monday in every month, within the meeting-house in the afternoon, within half an hour after the ringing of the bell."[6] There is, however, no record of when the church was formally gathered, and organizing the new church would have been Hooker's first concern had it not been already accomplished. It seems unlikely that the prospective church would have gone very far without the guiding presence of their ministers, although some sort of tentative organization might have been established. At the same time as he was beginning to gather his church formally, Hooker would have taken stock of his new

[3] Winthrop, I, 105.   [4] Mather, I, 265.   [5] Winthrop, I, 106–7.
[6] Lucius R. Paige, *History of Cambridge, Massachusetts* (Boston, Houghton, 1877), 247.

surroundings and proceeded to settle his family in for the winter; he and Susannah now had three daughters and two sons, and they received a third son, Samuel, probably in the fall or winter of 1633.[7]

Hooker would have found himself in a small, compact community only belatedly taking shape as a town. Newtown was in theory first settled in 1630, the same year as Boston, Charlestown, Roxbury, and Watertown, but comparatively few families chose to set down there. Watertown to the west and Charlestown to the east were previously established, and Newtown was composed of a slim stretch of land between these two plantations. The very existence of Newtown was a touchy political issue in the first few years of the Bay Colony, for it served as a geographic reminder of the first disagreement among the civil leadership of the young colony. When the Winthrop party arrived in 1630, they found Salem, the first settlement, too small for their numbers, and they explored the bay formed by the conjunction of the Mystic and Charles Rivers in order to discover a new site. The first parties of discovery found a site on the Mystic River, now the town of Medford, which Governor Winthrop felt was the best location for the colony's new chief plantation. Deputy Governor Dudley, however, urged that a second exploring party be sent out, and this party discovered an alternate location "three leagues up Charles

---

[7] The composition of Hooker's family on his arrival in America is uncertain. The three daughters, Joanna, Mary, and Sarah, who grew to adulthood, and his older son John were definitely there. John Winthrop reports the death by smallpox of "Mr. Hookers younge sonne" in a letter dated December 12, 1634, *Winthrop Papers*, III (Boston, M.H.S., 1943), 177. It is not clear whether or not this son was born in America. Also, tradition alone supports Samuel's birth in Newtown; he died on November 6, 1697, supposedly aged 64, but there is no reliable authority for his age at death. If he were indeed 64 by November 6, 1697, chances are somewhat more likely that he was born in England and came over on the Griffin as an infant. The son who died in 1634 may have been born in Newtown.

River."[8] Dudley advocated this site for the new settlement, and after a week a compromise was worked out whereby the new settlers were to build at Charlestown, halfway between the other two sites.

By the end of 1630 the Charlestown group had splintered into seven towns, and the colony leaders began to confer about establishing a central, fortified town. At Watertown on December 21, 1630, they determined on "a place a mile beneath the town," the site originally desired by Dudley.[9] In order to persuade settlers in the other towns to relocate in the projected capital, the magistrates agreed to build their own houses in the following spring. Dudley subsequently resided there, as did his son-in-law, Simon Bradstreet; Winthrop began to erect a house, but took down the frame and removed it to Boston, leaving behind an indignant Dudley. None of the other magistrates attempted to move from their original towns to Newtown, and the design of making it the colony's central town fell through.

By the middle of 1632, Dudley began to raise objections in the General Court to Winthrop's administration of colony affairs. Winthrop, a shrewd politician, sensed the cause of his deputy's irritability and looked about for means to pacify him. One mollifying device was easily contrived; in that year the group of planters known as "Mr. Hooker's company" had begun to settle about Mount Wollaston, south of Boston. By order of the General Court which met in August, these people removed to Newtown and revivified Dudley's languishing town. The quarrel was further smoothed over when the "ministers afterward, for an end of the difference between the governor and deputy, ordered, that the governor should procure them a minister at Newtown, and contribute somewhat

[8] Darrett B. Rutman, *Winthrop's Boston, Portrait of a Puritan Town, 1630–1649* (Chapel Hill, Univ. of North Carolina Press, 1965), 25.
[9] Winthrop, I, 54.

towards his maintenance for a time."[10] Hooker's arrival a year later removed a considerable burden from Winthrop, for suitable ministers were difficult to obtain in the first years of the Bay Colony.

Dudley had already built a large and handsome house before Hooker's old parishioners arrived in Newtown, and some progress had been made in laying out the town. After the arrival of the new settlers, the process of creating a town in the wilderness was speeded up: the new meeting-house was erected; acreage in the common fields was allotted; laws were passed regulating the construction of private dwellings. By mid-August 1633, William Wood was able to write in his *New Englands Prospect*:

> This is one of the neatest and best compacted Townes in *New England*, having many faire structures with many handsome contrived streets. The inhabitants most of them are very rich, and well stored with cattell of all sorts; having many hundred Acres of ground paled in with one generall fence, which is about a mile and a halfe long, which secures all the weaker Cattle from the wilde beasts.[11]

Wood's brief account of Newtown revealed two facts central to later developments in the community. First, the Newtowners, after the arrival of Hooker's company, had an extraordinary sense of community. The town was "compacted" partly for safety from Indians and from wild beasts, but early laws passed in the monthly meetings show concern for urban aesthetics and for the involvement of all the town's individual planters in a single social entity. At the first town meeting held in the new meeting-house, the voting inhabitants

[10] Ibid., 92.
[11] William Wood, *New Englands Prospect*, Publications of the Prince Society, No. 3 (Boston, 1865), 43–44.

ordered, that no person whatever [shall set] up any house in the bounds of this town [without] leave from the major part.

Further, it is agreed, by a joint consent [that the] town shall not be enlarged until all [the vacant] places be filled with houses.

Further, it is agreed, that all the houses [within] the bounds of the town shall be covered [with] slate or board, and not with thatch.

Further, it is ordered, that all [the houses] shall range even, and stand just six [feet on each man's] own ground from the street.[12]

The Newtown planters were apparently rich enough to forego the short-run economy of thatch roofs, and their ambitious extent of paled cattle-common also indicates that they had no objection to becoming even richer, for in the early days of the Bay, cattle-raising was the most profitable industry. Ambitious was the best word to describe the community Hooker found; not content with gradually duplicating the familiar villages of Essex, they tried to legislate one into existence immediately. Frustrated at not becoming the political center of the colony, Newtown could still become its most imposing town.

II

Hooker probably did not know what sort of rough quarters to expect upon his arrival in the land of the Indians, and the attractive situation of Newtown would have been a welcome sight. Even more welcome, however, would have been the sight of so many of his old friends and parishioners; according to Mather,

[12] Paige, 18.

Inexpressible now was the joy of Mr. Hooker, to find himself surrounded with his friends, who were come over the year before, to prepare for his reception; with open arms he embraced them, and uttered these words, "Now I live, if you stand fast in the Lord."[13]

Hooker's first pastoral concern after returning to his erstwhile flock would have been to determine if they did indeed "stand fast in the Lord." It is likely that at this time Hooker reviewed any steps previously taken to form a church and called upon his practical knowledge of church government gained in the Netherlands. His Chelmsford church had been a national, parish church, open to all residents of the town; in Newtown he would have proceeded to discover which of the settlers were the saints, believers into Christ, and he would have established his church according to the most approved congregational model.

The first planters of the Bay Colony, said William Hubbard, a second-generation historian,

by some kind of covenant soon moulded themselves into a church in every Plantation, where they took up their abode, until Mr. Cotton and Mr. Hooker came over . . . . who did clear up the order and method of church government, according as they apprehended was most consonant to the word of God.[14]

The first architects of the New England Way were undecided about the exact nature of their new church polity. Hubbard singled out George Phillips of Watertown, for example, as being the most knowledgeable about the true principles of congregational organization, but Phillips lacked support for his ideas until Cotton and Hooker arrived. Apart from the immediate respect they commanded from the other New England

[13] Mather, I, 342.   [14] Hubbard, 181.

ministers, Cotton and Hooker were uniquely qualified to direct the establishment of a new ecclesiastical policy.

Cotton was famous in both Englands as a scholar, and in the course of a long career as a dissenting minister he had been in a limited way smuggling congregational principles of organization into his parish in the old Boston. He remembered that "there were some scores of godly persons in Boston in Lincolnshire, (whereof some are there still, and some here, and some are fallen asleep) who can witness, that we entered into a covenant with the Lord, and with one another, to follow after the purity of his worship."[15] Hooker's scholarship had been approved by no less a man than William Ames, and, most importantly, he was the first man to arrive in New England with prior experience in administering a congregational church. He had assisted Forbes in Delft, and he had observed Hugh Peter's heralded reorganization of the Rotterdam church into a covenanted community of visible saints. Peter's substitution of the covenanted group of visible saints for the more inclusive but spiritually less pure community of the parish was for Hooker one more step toward the final reformation of the Christian church. "For these are the times drawing on, wherein Prophecies are to attain their performances,"[16] and Hooker was at last able to bring the prophecy of the primitive church into actuality as the performance of the New England Way.

Twelve years after his arrival in Boston Harbor, Hooker defined in his *Survey of the Summe of Church Discipline* the principles of congregationalism as they had been developed in New England; there he maintained that "mutuall covenanting and confoederation of the Saints in the fellowship of the faith according to the order of the Gospel, is that which gives con-

---

[15] Cotton, *The Way of Congregational Churches Cleared*, in Larzer Ziff, ed., *John Cotton on the Churches of New England* (Cambridge, Mass., Harvard Univ. Press, 1968), 198.

[16] Hooker, *A Survey of the Summe of Church Discipline* (London, 1648), Sig. a^r.

MASSACHUSETTS

stitution and being to a visible church."[17] In Hooker's explication even the churches of England, which were true churches in spite of their corruption by human ceremonies, were characterized by a covenant, although it was often only an implicit covenant shown by the practice of the covenanters without a verbal profession. An explicit covenant, however, in which the saints made open profession to an agreement to follow the will of God was a more perfect way of constituting a church. The explicit covenant, such as that of Peter's Rotterdam church or those of the already constituted Bay churches, was better able to inform and convince the members' judgments concerning their duties as Christians; it kept them from "cavilling and starting aside from the tenure and terms of the covenant," and it made "their hearts stand under a stronger tye and [be] more quickened."[18]

In order to bring the hearts of Newtown "under a stronger tye," Hooker probably spent some time acquainting himself directly with prospective members of the church; not all of the residents were known to him, and he had not seen the people he did know for nearly three years. Out of his discussions with his people he would have gathered evidence of assuming them to be among the saved and thus qualified for church membership. In later years the churches of the Bay Colony required for admission a public confession of faith by the candidate, which displayed convincing evidence of his possession of saving grace. The introduction of the experiential test as a prerequisite for church membership seems to have been most notably effected by John Cotton.[19] Hooker's standards for admission seem to have been more lenient than Cotton's, and in the years to come serious differences of opinion

[17] Ibid., 1, 46. The *Survey* is in four parts, each separately paginated.
[18] Ibid., 49.
[19] See Edmund S. Morgan, *Visible Saints: The History of a Puritan Idea* (New York, New York Univ. Press, 1963), 95–105.

over this and related issues would divide the two foremost New England divines.

In the years immediately following his arrival in New England, Cotton was preaching that the church must receive proof of "the sincerity of the regeneration of such who are to be received (especially in the first gathering and plantation of a church)"; new members had to demonstrate "certain and infallible signs of their regeneration."[20] In 1633 these requirements do not seem to have been as rigorously pressed as they were in later years, when both the Boston church and other churches in the Bay raised several notches higher the spiritual hurdles to church membership. During the same years in which Cotton was demanding "certain and infallible signs" of sainthood, Hooker taught that the visible saints who were to be members of the church should be determined by *"rationall charity* directed by rule from the word, . . . (leaving *secret things* to God)."[21] While Cotton was attempting to realize an ideal coincidence of covenanted church members with God's elect, Hooker proceeded upon the assumption that "people may be said to be *within the covenant* two waies. Either, *Externally* in the judgement of *charity: Internally* and spiritually, according to the judgement of *verity* and truth."[22] There was thus no need to determine infallibly a man's spiritual state, one of God's "secret things," for it was impossible to make both the internal and external covenants, the invisible and visible churches, coincide.

Even hypocrites could join Thomas Hooker's church, if they could give satisfactory evidence "in the judgement of charity" that they might belong to the external covenant. There are many long passages in Hooker's sermons which display what seems to be an almost obsessive concern for hy-

[20] Quoted by Pettit, 134. [21] Hooker, *Survey*, I, 14–15.
[22] Ibid., 36. Also, cf. Hooker, *The Faithful Covenanter* (London, 1644), 10–11.

pocrisy; he was not, however, addressing himself simply to hordes of sinful frauds who were clamoring for admission to the covenant but those people already in the church who were not in fact the saints they took themselves for. "Rationall charity can go no further than to hopefull fruits," said Hooker.

Externally those are within the covenant, who expressing their repentance, with their profession of the truth, ingage themselves to walk in the waies of God, and in the truth of his worship, though they have not for the present that sound work of Faith in their hearts, and may be shall never have it wrought by Gods spirit in them.[23]

The important tests for fitness as a church member were thus an expression of repentance for sin, "orderly walking" in a course of life which was free from gross or habitual sin, and a willingness to subscribe to the church covenant and submit to church discipline.

Hooker came to his people in New England less as a judge of their spirituality than as their pastor in the wilderness, their guide both to moral conduct, walking "in the waies of God, and in the truth of his worship," and to the intricate process of salvation. He would have encouraged the prospective church members to continue seeking for a clear, powerful, and permanent assurance of their redemption, but he was more immediately concerned with their behavior, the "hopefull fruits" indicating that they stood fast with the Lord. Those citizens of Newtown who were of "Mr. Hooker's company" may have been already gathered into a covenanted group, since it was not altogether uncommon for Puritan ministers in England to enter into covenant with the godly members of their parishes. Cotton, we have previously noted, had covenanted with "some godly persons in Boston in Lincolnshire," and Hooker's mentor and friend, John Rogers of Dedham, had also covenanted with some of his parishioners. Hooker's dis-

[23] Hooker, *Survey*, I, 11, 36–37.

covery that his friends stood fast in the Lord would thus mean that they had been faithful to their original covenant. The first members of the Newtown church may have merely renewed their old covenant and simultaneously admitted several new members, such as Samuel Stone, who were not among the original Chelmsford group.

There is unfortunately no way of knowing the exact wording and terms of the covenant which brought the Newtowners under a stronger tie. It may have been an almost unimpressively brief statement; the covenant adopted in 1629 by the Salem church of Samuel Skelton and Hooker's friend, Francis Higginson, was only one sentence long:

> We Covenant with the Lord, and one with another and doe bynd ourselves in this presence of God to walke together in all his waies, according as he is pleased to reveale himself to us in his Blessed word of truth.[24]

Later covenants of other churches usually used more words, but their meaning and intention were identical to that of the Salem agreement. One clue to the wording and nature of the Newtown covenant of 1633 does exist. In 1670 the church, transplanted to Hartford, Connecticut, split over certain doctrinal differences (mainly the Half-Way Covenant issue), and the seceders claimed to be following the ecclesiastical pattern "formerly settled, professed, and practiced under the guidance of the first leaders of this Church of Hartford."[25] The historian of the First Church of Hartford suggests that it seems more than likely that "the first Covenant of the old Church may be preserved to us through the new."[26] This covenant of 1670 reads:

[24] Quoted by Ola Elizabeth Winslow, *Meetinghouse Hill: 1630–1873* (New York, Macmillan, 1952), 22.

[25] G. L. Walker, ed., *Historical Catalogue of the First Church in Hartford, 1633–1885* (Hartford, 1885), xii.

[26] Ibid., xiii.

171

Since it hath pleased God, in his infinite mercy, to manifest himself willing to take unworthy sinners near unto himself, even into covenant relation to and interest in him, to become a God to them and avouch them to be his people, and accordingly to command and encourage them to give up themselves and their children also unto him: We do therefore this day, in the presence of God, his holy angels, and this assembly, avouch the Lord Jehovah, the true and living God, even God the Father, the Son, and the Holy Ghost, to be our God, and give up ourselves, and ours also unto him, to be his subjects and servants, promising through grace and strength in Christ (without whom we can do nothing), to walk in professed subjection to him as our only Lord and Lawgiver, yielding universal obedience to his blessed will, according to what discoveries he hath made or hereafter shall make, of the same to us: in special, that we will seek him in all his holy ordinances according to the rules of the gospel, submitting to his government in this particular Church, and walking together therein with all brotherly love and mutual watchfulness, to the building up of one another in faith and love unto his praise; all which we promise to perform, the Lord helping us through his grace in Jesus Christ.[27]

Hooker's explanation of the reasons for an explicit covenant has both a theological and a sociological force; the act of covenanting together into a church body directed both the spiritual and social aspects of the first settlers' lives from the time of their entrance into the covenant until their departure from it by death. The explicit covenant informed the members' judgments of their duties; whenever the covenant was read out in meeting in order for a new member to subscribe to it, the older members were reminded of their three most im-

[27] Ibid.

portant spiritual duties as Christians. They were expected to submit themselves to God, "yielding universal obedience"; the internal and spiritual covenant was contained within the external covenant, and if a church member had not as yet genuinely received the saving grace which enabled him to offer God the new obedience of a saint in verity, he was expected to continue to seek the Lord's mercy. In addition to giving themselves over to God, covenanted church members had agreed to "give up . . . their children also unto him." The Newtown parent covenanted for his (or her) children as well as himself, just as Abraham had covenanted for his seed of Israel. The church member parent thus took responsibility upon himself for a spiritual community, as yet unrealized in time, which would come into existence as he served as God's agent to nourish the seed of grace in his children. Finally, the external covenant encompassed a group of "unworthy sinners," and the covenanter's responsibilities were not restrained within his family's limits. He was united "with all brotherly love and mutual watchfulness" to all other members of his church, and the covenant thus created in each participant a unified spiritual concern expanding outward from his own soul to include the souls of his household and neighbors. While this so-called brotherly watch applied to the members of the church only, by implication it should be extended into the world at large, made up of countless other unworthy sinners whom God might please to take to Himself if the church made the proper evangelical overtures. The covenant is not an exclusive but an inclusive document, and as such it is open-ended; there is always room for one more repentant sinner.

The gathering of the saints into a church covenant was usually an affair of ceremony and display; when Edward Johnson's friends at Woburn joined in covenant in 1642, "messengers of divers Neighbour Churches" were present to witness the proceedings as well as representatives of the civil magistrate.[28] There is a curious silence in the records about the actual gathering of the Newtown church. Johnson merely noted that the planters "gathered the eighth Church of Christ" there in 1633 but gives no details of the gathering, and Winthrop makes no mention of it in his diary.[29] If Hooker renewed a covenant previously made with his Essex brethren, he may have seen no need to invite representatives of neighboring churches to witness it. Even if the Newtown planters framed a new covenant, Hooker might well have wished to avoid undue interference in his activities, and he could best have accomplished this by having no unnecessary witnesses when the covenant was subscribed to. He would have been especially cautious if he suspected that some other Bay ministers had different requirements for church membership than his own. He had just escaped from almost three solid years of contentions about church polity, and he must have had no great desire to begin new debates in this his last refuge.

The Newtown church seems to have followed the pattern of earlier churches in the Bay by allowing all prospective members of the covenant then residing in the town to subscribe at the same time. Later New England practice, beginning at least with Thomas Shepard's group in early 1636, called for the initial erection of seven "pillars" of the church who could show "infallible" signs of sainthood; the other members subscribed to the covenant at a later date than this spiritual elite. Under this later system one function of the witnessing messengers from the neighbor churches was to examine the seven pillars for certain evidence of their saintliness, and the examina-

[28] Edward Johnson, *The Wonder Working Providence of Sion's Savior in New England* (1910; rpt., New York, Barnes and Noble, 1959), 215.

[29] Johnson, 90. One possible reason for Winthrop's failure to mention this event is that he might not have been invited, partly because of some eminent Newtowners' antagonism towards him, partly because Hooker desired to assert the independence of his church.

tion sometimes caused difficulties. In 1636 the Dorchester church was required to postpone its gathering, and in the same year the church at Lynn was approved only with "much ado."[30] Forming the church by allowing all candidates able to pass the test of "rationall charity" to subscribe to the covenant at once rather than by beginning with the elite of the seven pillars seemed to many to be a compromise of church purity in favor of a "stronger tye" binding the hearts of the community. The tendency in the Bay Colony during its first years was to emphasize the purity of the churches; Hooker certainly abetted this trend in many ways, but he was unwilling to sacrifice the ideal of a godly community for that of a godly elite within the community. By evading neighboring ministers' interrogations of spiritual standards among his church members, Hooker could work out his own balance between church purity and the godly community by excluding the obviously unfit and by simultaneously avoiding the establishment of a spiritual elite within the church.

One aspect of the New England Puritans' attempt to create their churches as viable spiritual communities was their substitution of a mutual exercise of piety on the part of each individual member for the representative performance of human ceremonies by a minister. The New England churches had no room for parishioners who only observed the minister's performance of an act of worship; all of the church members participated with the minister in the common performance of covenant duties.[31] Once in the free air of New England, the

[30] Winthrop, I, 199.

[31] This is, of course, a Puritan's view of the differences between his reformed church and the established English church. Certainly an Anglican would hold that the people participated in the act of worship, both mediately and directly, and there were surely church members in New England who failed to involve themselves genuinely in the spiritual community. The point is that the Puritans of New England were attempting to encourage direct, personal religious experience at the expense of mediate, representative participation.

Puritans relegated some traditional rites of the church, most notably marriage, to the civil magistrate; others, such as baptism and the Lord's supper, were purged of their corrupt liturgical trappings, and some rites were completely overhauled in order to realize the goal of common participation by all of the saints. An example of this latter sort of restructuring of religious ceremony was the method of ordaining ministers.

John Winthrop noted in his journal under the date of October 10, 1633, a comparatively detailed account of Cotton's ordination as teacher of the Boston congregation; for the day following he simply noted, "A fast at Newtown, where Mr. Hooker was chosen pastor, and Mr. Stone teacher, in such a manner as before at Boston."[32] On the morning of October 11, undoubtedly many pious fathers of Newtown led their families in prayers for guidance during the day. Sometime in the morning the town bell would have given the church members a thirty-minute notice to convene at the meeting-house, and the rest of the morning was spent in prayer and prophesying led by the two prospective ministers. The afternoon session would have opened with more prayers and perhaps another sermon; only later in the afternoon, after God had been given the opportunity to make any final revelations of His will, would the actual election and installation of the ministers take place.

By this date the Newtown church members would have been assured that both Hooker and Stone had an inward call from Christ to the ministerial office, and sometime later in that day they would have formally extended the church's external call to them. This formal election proceeded by a show of hands; a representative of the congregation, perhaps William Goodwin, who might already have been elected as the church's ruling lay elder, would have proposed Hooker as pastor and then Stone as teacher for the church's visible consent. Following this popular election, the ministers would have announced

32 Winthrop, I, 111.

their acceptance of the formal call, perhaps with a short speech similar to that of Cotton on the previous day. "Demanded . . . if he did accept of that call," Cotton

> then spake to this effect: that howsoever he knew himself unworthy and unsufficient for that place; yet having observed all the passages of God's providence, (which he reckoned up in particular) in calling him to it, he could not but accept it.[33]

With the ministers' acceptance of their election, the first half of the installation rites was finished, and the second half, ordination proper which "doth depend upon the *peoples lawfull Election*," could begin.[34]

Election gave the minister the essential power to exercise his office: "Ordination is an approbation of the officer and solemn setling and confirmation of him in his office, by Prayer and laying on of hands."[35] The prayer and imposition of hands were usually performed by the presbytery of the church—at Boston, John Wilson, the pastor, and the two lay ruling elders performed the laying on of hands for John Cotton—but in a new church without an ordained minister this was done by two representatives of the congregation. Hooker's and Stone's acceptance of their calls would have been followed by more prayers, and then the two representatives of the church would have laid their hands on the pastor's head, saying, "We ordain thee Thomas Hooker to be Pastor unto this Church of Christ."[36] This simple ritual might have been amplified with a charge to the new pastor to fulfill the duties of his office in the proper spirit, or perhaps with a prayer "unto the Lord for his more especiall assistance of this his servant in his work."[37] The same ceremony would then have been per-

[33] Ibid., 110.   [34] Hooker, *Survey*, II, 40–41.
[35] Ibid., 75.
[36] Johnson, 217. Also, Winthrop, I, 110.
[37] Johnson, 217.

formed for Stone, with the slight difference that Hooker, now being pastor in fact, also laid his hands on the new teacher's head. On this ordination day ministers of the neighboring churches were probably present, and at this point they would have come forward to extend the right hand of fellowship to the new ministers. The day's services would be closed with prayer and a psalm, and the members of the Bay Colony's youngest church then returned down the "many handsome contrived streets" of Newtown to their homes, although they may have broken their fast at some sort of celebratory supper.

As the Newtown fathers led prayers in their homes that evening, they may well have had occasion to thank the Lord for bringing forth among them such an eminent display of the power of godliness, and they might have felt no little satisfaction at the day's events. Gratitude and satisfaction were, after all, the proper responses on the part of the covenant members; Christ had chosen them, had endowed them with saving grace entitling them to enter into a stronger tie with each other, and they in turn had directed their actions into a fitting practice of graciousness. The ceremonies of election and ordination emphasized every convenant member's participation in the Lord's "holy ordinances." The power to elect and ordain ministers was received by the congregation directly from Christ, and the congregation's involvement in church functions was essential for the spiritual vitality of the group and of the individual. The exercise of covenant powers strengthened covenant ties.

III

The offices which Hooker and Stone filled were equal in rank and respectability under the congregational system, but they were theoretically different in function. If Hooker always seemed more important in his church than Stone, the reasons stem from his age, experience, reputation, and personal abilities rather than from any supposed superiority of his office. Hooker's conception of the dual ministry was framed in evangelical terms, and pastor and teacher worked together to bring men to Christ. The teacher was the expounder and definer of faith and doctrine; his "aime and scope" was "to informe the judgement, and to help forward the work of illumination, in the minde and understanding, and thereby make way for the truth that it may be setled and fastned upon the heart."[38] The pastor stepped in where the teacher left off: "His labour is to lay open the loathsome nature of sinne, and to let in the terrour of the Lord upon the conscience, . . . to discover the cunning fetches of the hypocrite."[39] The people of Newtown stood in the same relation to Hooker as Mrs. Drake had fifteen years before, but even if they were less willful and self-destructive than she, the pastor's duties were no simpler, for he now had hundreds of sinners in the community in place of one.

It was characteristic of Hooker's thought that the distinctions between the pastor and teacher were cast in psychological terms; just as the teacher's aim was to direct the understanding, so the scope of the pastor's office was "to worke upon the will and affections, and by savoury, powerfull, and affectionate application of the truth delivered, to chafe it into the heart, to wooe and win the soul to the love and liking, the approbation and practice of the doctrine which is according to godlinesse."[40] The duties of the two officers obviously overlapped, for, given Hooker's psychology with its immediate connection of mind and heart, the teacher could not instruct the understanding without moving the heart, and the pastor could not move the affections except by approaching them through the understanding. Their sermons to the Newtown church would not have duplicated each other, however; when both men prophesied on the Sabbath, one in the morning and the other in the afternoon, their sermons would have been a double-barreled at-

[38] Hooker, *Survey*, II, 21.   [39] Ibid., 19–20.
[40] Ibid., 19.

tack upon carnal security and hypocrisy. Most New England churches were too small or too poor to support both pastor and teacher, but two such ministers working together constituted an effective team for awakening the whole man to his lost condition. A sinner attentive to the sermons of both Hooker and Stone would have gone home of an evening troubled in mind and heart with the sort of spiritual unrest which was the first paradoxical sign of spiritual peace.

The psychological underpinnings of Hooker's division of responsibilities between pastor and teacher reveal far more than merely the nature of his own mind. The duties of the pastor and teacher were defined in terms of their relationship to souls outside of the internal covenant; although Hooker and Stone were pastor and teacher to an externally covenanted group of visible saints, the most proper objects of their ministrations were the reprobates in the community at large and the hypocrites within the church. They were responsible to the saints, too, helping them to gain the assurance they needed of their salvation; ministers, said John Norton, were "the ordinary external means of making salvation effective in every mode, not only by the conversion of the not yet converted but also by the confirmation and edification of those who have already been converted."[41] Although "the chiefe aime and scope of our Savior (under the glory of his name,) was to provide for the speciall good of his elect," Hooker stated, he went on to enunciate the necessity of searching in the external community for the elect,

> because those his elect were mingled here with the wicked in the world, nay many an elect child proceeds of a reprobate parent, and because it is impossible for the eye of man to search into heart secrets, and inward sincerity which is

[41] John Norton, *The Answer to the Whole Set of Questions of the Celebrated Mr. William Appolonius*, trans. Douglas Horton (Cambridge, Mass., Harvard Univ. Press, 1958), 109–10.

covered there; but must judge of men according to the lawes
and limites of rationall charity.[42]

Certainly not all men would be saved, and the internal community of saints in verity would never coincide with the external world. God would, however, in every generation elect
souls outside the limits of the covenanted congregation, and
pastor and teacher together had to go out into the community
to recruit the ranks of the saints. The spiritual heart of the
community could not afford to disengage itself from its civil
context; for Hooker the church was a *point d'appui* from
which the heavenly kingdom of Christ would extend itself into
the earthly kingdoms of man, "perfecting of the [spiritual]
body, untill we all meet in the unity of the faith."[43]

The actions performed in the Newtown meeting-house on
the afternoon of October 11 strengthened the tie which bound
the faithful, and the perfection of the church simultaneously
perfected the order of the Newtown community. The church
was the spiritual core of the town, the source of righteous and
godly leaders who could realize the ideals of a Christian community, and when the church was gathered, the town was fair
on its way toward becoming a building block in the Bay Colony's New Jerusalem. The covenant relationship promoted the
honesty and zeal of public officials, and in some ways was a
more important regulation of their conduct than their oaths of
office. The oath was no more than an expression of human will,
and only a man with a new heart strengthened and quickened
in the church of Christ had the necessary stability of affection
to fulfill his oath, for "the frame of an Evangelicall heart is to
the Covenant: That is the spring of a mans practice, the first
mover, the waight that makes him strike in obedience to everie
Commandment."[44] Since unregenerate men inevitably slipped
into the visible church, means were devised to augment the

---

[42] Hooker, *Survey*, II, 2. [43] Ibid., 5.
[44] Hooker, *Faithful Covenanter*, 15.

effectiveness of church ordinances in keeping the hearts of the covenanted members up to the mark. The most important of these means was the so-called brotherly watch.

Hugh Peter, while in the Tower in 1660 awaiting his execution, made *A Dying Fathers Last Legacy to an Onely Child*, and he advised his daughter Elizabeth, "Do not therefore keep the Devils counsel; but let some able Friend *watch* you, to whom communicate your Decays or Growth. . . . But if you would go home to *New England* (which you have much reason to do) go with good Company, and trust God there: the Church are a Tender Company." Peter desired to consign his daughter to the New England churches because there her sins would be curbed by the other members of her church. Hooker maintained that Christ had "appointed each particular Brother, as a skilfull Apothecary" to correct the flaws of the rest; church members had, in fact, "*speciall power over one another*, and that by vertue of the covenant."[45] When God dispensed the outward, church covenant to men, He laid them under the duty of living according to the principles of Christian liberty, and the special power of the brotherly watch was a means to restrain hypocrites, who did not have this principle, as well as to recall erring saints to the exercise of it.

The church existed twenty-four hours a day in its covenant and not just during the times of its meeting. The ministry of Hooker and Stone provided the ordinances vitalizing the church in its convenings together, and in the rest of the week the people had also to minister to each other. "The work which is of common concernment unto all the *Members when the Assembly is dissolved*, is that WATCH which they stand engaged to expresse each to the other, for the good of the body so confederate, above or before all others."[46] On the most pri-

---

[45] Hugh Peter, *A Dying Fathers Last Legacy to an Onely Child: or Mr. Peter's Advice to His Daughter* (London, 1660), 14, 117; Hooker, *Survey*, III, 33, 2.
[46] Hooker, *Survey*, III, 1.

vate level this watch consisted of mutual exhortations and re-proofs; Hooker's sermons in the latter part of his career are full of encouragements to church members to urge their families, friends, and neighbors to seek righteousness. If the sin were too offensive or too public for private admonition, or, more important, if the sinner persisted in his errors, the case was to be referred to the elders. Hooker adopted an unusually personal tone in his *Survey of the Summe of Church Discipline* when he described the minister's responsibility for the spiritual welfare of his congregation:

> By vertue of that engagement by which I am tyed, and that *power* which I have received, I stand charged in a most peculiar manner, to prevent all taint of sin in any Member of the Society that either it may never be committed; or if committed, it may speedily be removed, and the spirituall good of the whole preserved.[47]

Hooker's ministerial function as an evangelizing prophet did not outweigh his responsibility as a pastor to the Newtown flock, and the pastoral burden was heavy in all New England churches. The minister was in the front lines of the warfare against Satan, and he often had to act with speed and confidence, at the same time proceeding always with charity and moderation, in order to prevent private sin from tainting the whole.

Shortly after Hooker's arrival in the New World, he discovered several potential sources of sinful behavior among his people, and the most immediately alarming of these was Dudley's continuing bitterness against Winthrop. Unchristian contentiousness had come to represent for Hooker one of the most serious hindrances to the practice of heart religion. He was inevitably drawn into the long-standing quarrel between Dudley and Winthrop, both because of his position as Dudley's

[47] Ibid., 2.

pastor and because he and John Haynes lived in Dudley's house all that first winter. The immediate cause of altercation between deputy and governor at that time concerned the fort then under construction on Castle Island. The General Court of the colony had decreed that the towns about Boston should supply the labor for the fort and outlying communities should later make up their share in money. All of the towns involved had sent labor forces once, and some had sent twice, although the outlying towns had as yet contributed no funds. When Newtown was summoned to complete its share of the work, "the deputy would not suffer them to come, neither did he acquaint the governor with the cause, which was, for that Salem and Saugus had not brought in money for their parts." Winthrop, upon his own account, "wrote friendly to him" in order to explain the General Court's intentions when allotting responsibilities to the various towns, and in this letter he asked Dudley to "send in his neighbors" to finish work on the fort.[48]

Dudley always found it difficult to make an outright admission of error, so instead of complying with Winthrop, he sent "Mr. Haynes and Mr. Hooker . . . to the governor to treat with him about it," and sent along "a letter full of bitterness and resolution."[49] Whether Dudley realized it or not, he was wiser in his choice of emissaries than in his course of action; Hooker was determined to avoid contention, and Haynes was a canny administrator, desirous of discreet and efficient handling of such minor breakdowns as this in the governmental machine. As for Winthrop, his greatest talent was perhaps his ability to obtain a consensus out of the most sharply contested differences among his people, and the governor and the two emissaries were able to settle the matter among themselves. Winthrop returned Dudley's letter unread, and offered the gift of a fat hog which the deputy had previ-

---

[48] Winthrop, I, 113.   [49] Ibid.

ously wished to buy. In order to avoid the appearance of offering a bribe, Winthrop made the two emissaries joint partakers of the gift, perhaps out of gratitude for their cooperation.

In a reply to Winthrop which "very lovingly concluded" the affair, Dudley wrote, "Your overcoming yourself hath overcome me. Mr. Haynes, Mr. Hooker, and myself, do most kindly accept your good will."[50] Even in his loving moments Dudley was characteristically stiff and righteous. In his linking of Haynes and Hooker with himself as men who have been aggrieved and satisfied, Dudley sounds as if he were tacitly beginning to collect an anti-Winthrop faction about himself in Newtown. His reply to the governor was obviously intended as a manner of apology and as an acceptance of peace, but at the same time, perhaps without intending it, he was claiming Hooker's and Haynes' partisanship in his concerns. Hooker and Haynes might well have been somewhat uneasy if they had recognized this implication, for, although Dudley was a townsman and fellow covenanter, they were tied by previous loyalties and fellowships to the Essex company of planters. Dudley had been first on the scene in Newtown, but he was only a comparatively late arrival into the social circle described by the church within the external community. Above all, Dudley was an empire-builder, and when his actions endangered "the unity of affection and charity," which the whole body of the saints "have one to another, and one between another," Hooker would always side with the saints.[51]

There was, however, a more serious threat than Dudley

[50] Ibid., 114.

[51] Hooker, *Comment*, 40. It is not exactly certain if or when Dudley joined the Newtown Church; on his arrival in New England he covenanted with the Boston Church, since there was no church in Newtown at the time. He left Newtown in 1635 after Hooker had decided to leave and removed to Ipswich for a short time. See Augustine Jones, *The Life and Work of Thomas Dudley, The Second Governor of Massachusetts* (Boston, Houghton, 1899).

to the harmony of the infant colony, for some time in these latter months of 1633 Roger Williams returned to Massachusetts from Plymouth. Williams had created a flurry in Boston immediately after his arrival in 1631 when he refused to join the church there "because they would not make a public declaration of their repentance for having communion with the churches of England."[52] He created further alarm among the magistrates when a few weeks later he moved to Salem and prepared to accept a call as teacher. The governor and assistants, meeting at Boston on April 12, 1631, wrote to the Salem church, requesting them to "forbear to proceed till they had conferred about it."[53] Williams subsequently removed to Plymouth, where the separatists were presumably purer than the Bay Colony congregationalists, but after two years there his "strange opinions" raised further divisions, and he returned to Salem in 1633.[54] He could not keep his opinions to himself, and about the time of his return the governor and assistants got wind of a letter in which he questioned their title to the land they occupied. Williams argued, with some force, that "claiming by the king's grant they could have no title, nor otherwise, except they compounded with the natives," for the Indians were the only owners of the lands of New England.[55] In spite of the moral force behind his objections, the letter had one serious flaw; it undermined the whole legal and civil foundation of the colony.

Williams' letter tended to subvert the Bay Colony's internal sense of legitimacy, and, more seriously, it threatened the plantation with the wrath of the King from without. In addition to the *lèse-majesté* of denying the royal title to American land, Williams charged "King James to have told a solemn public lie, because in his patent he blessed God that he was the first Christian prince that had discovered this land," and he charged "him and others with blasphemy for calling Europe

---

[52] Winthrop, 1, 62.   [53] Ibid.
[54] Bradford, 257.   [55] Winthrop, 1, 116.

Christendome, or the Christian world." This was dangerous talk, for in the preceding summer the colony was forced to employ all its influence in order to quash a petition made to the Privy Council that complained that "our ministers and people did continually rail against the state, church, and bishops."[56] The colony had many important enemies in London and in the court of Charles; if they had come into the wrong hands, Williams' statements would "have provoked our Kinge against us, and putt a sword into his hande to destroy us."[57]

This particular business was managed by the governor and assistants with the especial help of John Endicott, their man in Salem. Unfortunately for the peace of the churches and the civil state in the Bay, Williams was not yet finished with broaching strange opinions. When Samuel Skelton died in 1634, the Salem church successfully offered the office of teacher to Williams, and he now had a prominent position from which to broadcast his ideas. Under Williams' tutelage, Salem rapidly became a troublesome disseminator of seditious letters and divisive opinions. John Endicott himself, the Salem magistrate and one of the colony's most notable leaders, became infected with Williams' scruples.

At a Court of Assistants held on November 5, 1634, Richard Brown of Watertown complained that Endicott had defaced the English ensign by cutting out the cross in the belief that it was a superstitious relic of the papist Antichrist. "Much matter was made of this, as fearing it would be taken as an act of rebellion, or of like high nature, in defacing the king's colors."[58] The governor and assistants convened later in the month with some of the ministers, including Hooker, in order to map out a course of action; there was some doubt concerning "the lawful use of the cross in an ensign," but all present

[56] Ibid., 101.

[57] Winthrop's marginal notation to Williams' letter, quoted by Ola Elizabeth Winslow, *Master Roger Williams* (New York, Macmillan, 1957), 110.

[58] Winthrop, I, 137.

seemed agreed, for the moment at least, that defacing the colors "was very unlawful." A letter was sent to the colony's English agent discountenancing the act, and the question of the propriety of the cross in the ensign was referred to the ministers for further consideration. Endicott appears to have been motivated by his own scruples, but his friendship and proximity to a known troublemaker like Williams made Williams suspect as an abettor of the act. The name of Roger Williams certainly came up during the meeting:

> It was likewise informed, that Mr. Williams of Salem had broken his promise to us, in teaching publicly against the kings patent, and our great sin in claiming right thereby to this country, etc., and for usual terming the churches of England antichristian. We granted summons to him for his appearance at the next court.[59]

Williams' readiness to speak his mind was seemingly becoming infectious, for in this same meeting Hooker, Cotton, and Weld were appointed to deal with John Eliot, who "had taken occasion, in a sermon, to speak of the peace made with the Pekods, and to lay some blame upon the ministry for proceeding therein, without consent of the people."[60] If Williams' singularity were to become the model for every minister's and magistrate's conduct, the harmony of the saints would be lost in a fortnight.

Hooker was always ready to strike a blow for the Lord and for truth, but he did not go out of his path to seek quarrels. A pastor conscientious for the souls of his people had more important concerns than trading polemics with every crackbrain in the country. Nevertheless, Hooker had been in Massachusetts for only fifteen months, and already he was being drawn into an escalating series of controversies. Eliot was a pious, reasonable man, ready to hear and respond to the argu-

---

[59] Ibid., 142.   [60] Ibid.

ments of his old friend and colleague, and he was easily brought to see his errors. The contretemps between Dudley and Winthrop had been amicably settled for the moment, but there was still heat in the coals, and new differences were soon to appear. Roger Williams, unlike either Dudley or Eliot, was an exceptionally difficult case. The Bay ministers and magistrates had already demonstrated to him the errors they found in his so-called strange opinions, but he persisted in expounding them in the face of official disapproval, thus sinning against his own conscience, or so Cotton later accused him. And now Endicott was further inflaming the colony with his squeamishness over an image in a piece of cloth.

The business about the cross in the ensign was clearly the most immediate political danger to the colony, and it was also rapidly becoming a source of internal dissension. In January Winthrop summoned all of the ministers to meet at Boston to consider two questions: what to do if a governor general for New England were sent over by the mother country, and whether it were lawful to continue using the cross in the ensign. Linking these two questions together was a skillful maneuver on the part of the magistrates, since, if there were some ministerial scruples about the use of the royal colors, there was a complete agreement that the advent of a royal governor would be disastrous. Placing the two issues side by side tacitly reminded the colony's official interpreters of the divine will that defacing or discarding the banner was just the sort of gratuitous insult to the King liable to clear the way for a governor general. The meeting had little difficulty in abhorring the possibilities of a royal governor. Concerning the lawfulness of the cross, they could not conclude, but adjourned to consider it again at the General Court scheduled for the fourth day of March.

This court was held at Newtown, and Hooker preached the opening sermon. It is unfortunate that there is no transcript of this sermon, for according to Winthrop, he "showed the three great evils."[61] This may have been merely a warning against the everpresent dangers of the world, the flesh, and the devil, but it might also have been a discussion of prominent threats to the colony's welfare. In the latter case, one of these great evils would almost certainly have involved seditious speech or disrespect to the magistrates; not only was Endicott slated to appear before the court but also Israel Stoughton, a Dorchester deputy, who had questioned the power of the governor and assistants. Stoughton was barred from public office for three years, but Endicott's case was held over to the next court, "because the court could not agree about the thing . . . and the commissioners for military affairs gave order, in the mean time, that all ensigns should be laid aside."[62] The ministers had obviously not yet come to an agreement upon the issue of the cross, and until they did, it would be difficult for the civil authorities to decide what to do with Endicott.

The magistrates at the court of May 1635 discovered a way out of the impasse by leaving Endicott out of office for a year, not for defacing the flag but for rash and indiscreet behavior, "taking upon him more authority than he had, and not seeking advice of the court." Furthermore, his conduct had been uncharitable "in that he, judging the cross to be a sin, did content himself to have reformed it at Salem, not taking care that others might be brought out of it also; laying a blemish also upon the rest of the magistrates, as if they would suffer idolatry." The censure of Endicott would serve to clear the magistrates if any royal officials caught wind of the affair, but it did not quiet the controversy he had roused in the Bay. Endicott was disciplined essentially for ignoring the duties of the brotherly watch, and the magistrates accordingly invoked the responsi-

[61] Ibid., 147.

[62] Ibid. Hooker might have had some sympathy for Stoughton, for both men were disturbed by the concentration of arbitrary power in the hands of a few magistrates. Yet when Dorchester men removed to Connecticut a year later, Stoughton stayed behind.

bility of each man for his neighbor's behavior in order to quiet dissension. "Every man was to deal with his neighbors, to still their minds, who stood so stiff for the cross, until we should fully agree about it, which was expected, because the ministers had promised to take pains about it."[63]

Hooker had been exercising with the other ministers as they sought an answer to the problem raised by Endicott, and about this time he wrote a sort of theological-political brief entitled "Touching the Crosse in the Banner" as his contribution to the ministerial painstakings. "Follow the truth wee must," he wrote, but in mapping out the course of truth, he was careful not to provoke further dissension; he was almost diffident in advancing his opinions.

> Not that I am a friend to the crosse as an idoll, or to any idollatry in it; or that any carnall fear takes me asyde and makes me unwilling to give way to the evidence of the truth, because of the sad consequences that may be suspected to flowe from it. I blesse the Lord, my conscience accuseth me of no such thing; but that as yet I am not able to see the sinfulness of this banner in a civil use.[64]

Although expedience rather than principle seems to have eventually resolved the issue, Hooker's soft answer and similar efforts by others were prerequisites for any solution whatever, for men continued to hold contrary opinions about the cross.[65] The Endicott affair was intrinsically of little importance, so that Hooker in his essay could treat it as just another casuistical problem, but since Endicott's scruples threatened to expand out of all proportion into controversy, they required as much attention from Hooker as a more serious issue.

[63] Winthrop, I, 149–50.
[64] Hooker, "Touching the Crosse in the Banner," MSS, Hutchinson Papers, Mass. Archives.
[65] See Winthrop, I, 182. It seems likely that Cotton sided with Endicott and against Hooker on this issue.

The latest troubles with Roger Williams had been hanging fire while the General Court brought Endicott, the most important representative of civil government in Salem, back into line. Once Endicott had submitted to the rule of the magistrates and ministers, the Bay leaders began to proceed against Williams, the chief irritant to their peace. A first step had already been taken by the magistracy in dealing with Williams, for a few days prior to the censure of Endicott, the Salem minister had been called in to answer for preaching erroneous opinions. His present offense was in teaching that "magistrate ought not to tender an oath to an unregenerate man, for that we thereby have communion with a wicked man in the worship of God, and cause him to take the name of God in vain." Williams had an unerring instinct for discovering positions which tended to subvert the whole civil government of the colony, and this was one more of them. If oaths of allegiance or in a court could not be taken from the unregenerate, the magistrates would lose effective control over almost four-fifths of the colony's inhabitants. The ministers, including Hooker, had been requested to attend the meeting with Williams, and they "very clearly confuted" his opinions.[66] He was allowed to return to Salem in order to examine his conscience and to apply to it the lesson he had been taught.

Roger Williams had no intention of being taught by the Cottons and Hookers of the world, however, and in a short time he gave fresh cause for offense. At the same General Court which censured Endicott, the Salem men petitioned for a piece of land at Marblehead Neck, "but, because they had chosen Mr. Williams their teacher, while he stood under question of authority, and so offered contempt to the magistrates, their petition was refused." In response to what they felt was an unwarranted meddling of the magistracy in the peculiar affairs of the church, the Salem congregation, under Williams' direction, wrote to the other churches "to admonish the magis-

[66] Winthrop, I, 149.

trates of this as a heinous sin, and likewise the deputies."[67] Williams' previous teachings had tended to the subversion of the theory upon which the commonwealth was based, of the legality of the colony's existence, and of the jurisdiction of its governors, but the Salem letters endangered the actual practice of government. Massachusetts was a theocracy by courtesy, and land on Marblehead Neck was not a spiritual business; the Salem letter, by demanding church censure of the magistrates and deputies for an act within their legitimate area of concern, threatened to turn the political order of the Bay on its ear. If Williams had his way, Massachusetts would become a theocracy in law, ruled by an oligarchy of divines.

Williams was accordingly summoned before the next General Court, convening two months after the censure of Endicott, and he was confuted once more by the ministers who had been requested to attend also. The magistrates exhibited the utmost caution in moving against Williams; earlier in the spring of 1635 Israel Stoughton's objections to the magistracy's exercise of power, particularly in their use of the negative voice, a veto power over the actions of the deputies, had threatened to stir up a popular revolt to the policies of Winthrop and the assistants. He had been successful enough in his protests to have the voters fail to return Winthrop or any other of the original group of assistants to the governorship. In dealing with Williams, the magistrates had to ensure that a majority of the voters were convinced of his guilt and of the threat he bore to the public security. Although the Bay Colony's legal philosophy demanded that Williams be allowed his day in court, the elaborate process of court appearances and theological confutations was less an act of reverence to the principle of due process than it was a political maneuver to forestall popular outcry on Williams' behalf. The General Court accordingly endorsed the judgment of the Court of Assistants, declaring Williams' opinions "to be erroneous, and very dangerous, and the calling him to office . . . was judged a great contempt of authority. So in fine, time was given to him and the church of Salem to consider of these things until the next General Court, and then either to give satisfaction to the court, or else to expect the sentence."[68]

This decision, as well as the rejection of the Salem petition for Marblehead Neck, was designed to drive a wedge between Williams and his own congregation, and in the next few months the Salem teacher was effectively isolated. The success of this policy in large part was owing to Williams' own intransigence; he demanded that his church "not communicate with the churches in the bay; neither would he communicate with them; except they would refuse communion with the rest."[69] This was separation *reductio ad absurdum*, and the men of Salem, when forced to choose between their teacher and their neighbors, overwhelmingly deserted Williams. When the General Court met in October 1635 they had Williams exactly where they wanted him.

Hooker had been one of the ministers previously called by the court to confute Williams' errors, and he was at this time singled out to deliver the final blow. Hooker's reputation as an acute disputant had followed him all the way from Esher, and he joined to it here in Massachusetts a reputation as one of the colony's most perspicacious theologians. The climax of Williams' trial was his debate at this court with Hooker, the champion of orthodoxy, and it was almost a reenactment of scenes from their old days in Essex, where Williams had first revealed his disputatious nature. The stakes in this argument before the court were, however, much higher than they had been in the dispute the two men had carried on as they rode to Sempringham six years before. Hooker was endeavoring to protect the unity of the saints, and Williams was fighting for his career and for his integrity.

The debate turned out to be not climax but anticlimax; John

[68] Ibid., 154.   [69] Ibid., 157.

Cotton, in the midst of his long controversy with Williams, later quoted a brief interchange which leads one to suspect that the afternoon of October 8, 1635, was spent in elevated quibbles. Williams and his congregational opponents agreed in principle for the most part, but Hooker and his self-proclaimed orthodox colleagues were attempting to find a means to put their principles into practice while Williams was unwilling to compromise his purity with any merely political expedient. In a sense Williams was calling the Bay Colony ministers' bluff, trying to force them into an explicit avowal of their beliefs, but the ministers would not be called. Hooker and Williams seem to have avoided debating first principles as they skirmished over the peripheral accidentals of their opinions. Although Hooker confirmed his reputation among the Bay ministers as a polemicist with his supposed refutation of Williams, he was in fact unable to reduce his opponent from any of his positions. The Salem minister was sentenced to depart from the Bay within six weeks, but his arguments were not silenced by the force of logic and rhetoric.

In the brief span of two years Thomas Hooker had thus been drawn out of his pastoral duties to intercede in a series of disputes which tended to become more portentous and more engrossing. The petty disputes between Winthrop and Dudley were easily resolved since Dudley was well-intentioned and Winthrop added sagacity to saintliness, but the business of John Endicott's scruples and that of Williams' errors required an unusual amount of trouble and study. The paper which Hooker produced on the cross in the banner was a scholarly and reasoned work, and Hooker would almost certainly have studied Williams' position with equally great care in order to determine the best way of refuting it. All this took time, precious hours which the pastor of Newtown could have spent with his townsmen, strengthening the hearts of the faithful and persuading the reprobates to seek after Christ. Furthermore, as events were developing, Hooker saw that he could only expect greater involvements in controversy. As he had searched out the opinions of various Bay religious and lay leaders on contended issues, he had discovered divergences from his own theological and political conceptions. His treatise on the cross in the banner was by no means universally accepted, and he was also quite likely finding that he did not see eye to eye with either Cotton or Winthrop. To be at odds with the one minister who commanded equal respect with himself and also with the colony's most important political figure did not bode well for his own future. Just as Williams had been driven into exile, so he might have to take himself out of the limits of the colony to preserve the unity of the saints.

In dealing with Roger Williams, the Bay leaders learned a valuable lesson about the politics of coping with a dissenter who could marshal considerable popular support; they would soon have occasion to put their lesson to use. Although in a larger view the Williams affair is only an incident in Hooker's career—he never seems to have taken the threat of Williams as seriously as John Cotton did—he too learned from it. There were limitations to even his powers of persuasion, and ministers and magistrates had to work together to prevent both heresy and social disorder. Also, his aim had been, as always, to find some means to focus the undistracted power of his ministry upon the hearts of his people; he must have been concerned about shielding his congregation from the temptations of enthusiasts and demagogues. He might well have feared a reappearance in Massachusetts of the divisive and controversial spirit which had gripped the Amsterdam church a few years before; he may also have discovered some sympathy for John Paget.

SIX

Connecticut

IN his brief to the magistrates concerning the mutilation of the flag, Thomas Hooker had noted that, although "follow the truth we must, yet if it bee possible and as much as in us lyeth —bee at peace with all men."[1] His first years in America brought him little peace, and his involvement in the troubles of the first planters was not due to any love of contention but to his superior visibility among his colleagues as a man whose opinions mattered and as a man eminently qualified in the traditional art of disputing. All the disturbances with which he had to contend were not, however, outside the town and congregation of Newtown, and the most serious local troubles were not to be settled by pastoral counseling.

When Thomas Dudley chose the site of Newtown, he had in mind its possibilities as a defensive stronghold. In the first years of the Bay Colony the treacherous frontier was the sea coast rather than the edge of the wilderness, then only a few miles inland. The Indians were quiet and weakened by disease, but the warships of the French, Dutch, or, even worse, of King Charles on their way to retrieve the charter seemed an ever-present danger to the colonial magistrates. Newtown also recommended itself to Dudley as a possible commercial site; there were lengthy marshes along the river, and deep-draft ships could not navigate so far up the Charles, but with a certain amount of dredging lighter vessels could load and unload there.

Newtown never became a commercial center because the harbors of Boston and Salem were naturally better and more

[1] Hooker, "Crosse in the Banner."

convenient, and the earliest settlers were farmers rather than merchants. This latter fact brought about several problems. Newtown was settled after Watertown and Charlestown, and as a result its bounds consisted of the land left over after those two towns staked out their claims. The town in 1635 fell into a narrow, constricted shape, nearly eight times as long as it was broad. The village was at the extremity bordering the Charles, and as more and more families moved into Newtown, their fields lay farther and farther from their homes. The geographical peculiarity of the town was the annoyance which the planters most often complained of, but another hindrance to farmers wanting to make their way in a new world was the general marshiness around the village and the thick forest cover over the rest of the town. The Newtown planters could hardly complain of any inequity in the quality of their land, since Watertown and other nearby villages presumably had the same problem, but they could complain of the straitened bounds of their town and petition for relief.

About ten days before Hooker's arrival on the *Griffin*, Winthrop noted that "a bark was set forth to Connecticut and those parts, to trade."[2] This was only one of a number of trading and exploring enterprises sent out toward the Connecticut River in 1633. Plymouth had earlier requested the Bay Colony to join her in establishing a trading house on the Connecticut, which the Dutch had "often commended unto them for a fine place both for plantation and trade."[3] The Bay rejected the offer of an official partnership, and Plymouth went ahead on her own, but many individual entrepreneurs decided to get in on a good thing. By midsummer 1634 trading and exploring parties had gone out and returned from Connecticut by sea and by land, and at least one party made the overland trip in the middle of the winter, thus demonstrating the accessibility of the Connecticut Valley in all seasons. The Bay Colony settlers might have seen a grim sort of encouragement to emigrate

[2] Winthrop, I, 107.   [3] Bradford, 257.

in the reports of a smallpox epidemic among the western Indians; when the Plymouth planters discovered in 1620 that the Indian tribes along the coast had been decimated by disease, they attributed it to a special care of Providence. Providence might be at work once more, arranging a solution to the problems of Newtown.

> At the General Court in the spring of 1634, those of Newtown complained of straitness for want of land, especially meadow, and desired leave of the court to look out either for enlargement or removal, which was granted; whereupon they sent men to see Agawam and Merrimack, and gave out they would remove.[4]

This was the first public airing of the Newtowner's complaint, and it was presented at a convenient moment, since at this court their townsman, Dudley, replaced Winthrop as governor. Besides having a sympathetic governor, they were also able to work out their plans with little supervision from the magistrates, who seemingly didn't understand the fullest implications of the Newtown proposal. The Newtown group was perhaps practicing a certain amount of purposeful obfuscation; given permission to seek either an enlargement of town boundaries or a site for removal, they seem to have almost immediately opted for removal. They sent out parties to investigate two possible sites which were already within the neighborhood of existing Bay Colony towns, but in July they also sent six men on the ship *Blessing of the Bay* to investigate possible sites on the Connecticut River.

The men of Newtown wasted no time in completing their plans, and at the General Court held during the first week of September they asked for permission to emigrate to Connecticut. They advanced three reasons for their request:

1. Their want of accomodation for their cattle, so as they were not able to maintain their ministers, nor could re-

[4] Winthrop, I, 124.

ceive any more of their friends to help them; and here it was alleged by Mr. Hooker, as a fundamental error, that towns were set so near each to other.

2. The fruitfulness and commodiousness of Connecticut, and the danger of having it possessed by others, Dutch or English.

3. The strong bent of their spirits to remove thither.[5]

The first two reasons were obvious enough, although Hooker's feeling that the towns were set too close to each other needs some explanation, but the third reason conceals more than it reveals. The strong bent of the Newtowners' spirits was made evident during the course of the court, however, and a great deal of strong feeling was raised on both sides of the question. Before the court was adjourned, William Goodwin, "a very reverend and godly man, being the elder of the congregation of Newtown, having in heat of argument, used some unreverend speech to one of the assistants, and being reproved for the same in the open court, did gravely and humbly acknowledge his fault."[6]

Winthrop and several of the assistants argued against the removal of the people of Newtown, alleging five reasons in favor of their remaining. Curiously enough, the recognized importance of Hooker militated against his own cause; the Winthrop party pointed out that the colony was at that time "weak and in danger to be assailed," and "the departure of Mr. Hooker would not only draw many from us, but also divert other friends that would come to us." As a counterproposal, they offered the Newtowners either "some enlargement which other towns offered," or permission to "remove to Merimack, or any other place within our patent."[7] When the original motion for permission to emigrate to Connecticut came to a vote, the deputies were in favor of the proposal, but the assistants opposed it, with only Dudley and two other assistants casting

[5] Ibid., 132.   [6] Ibid., 134.   [7] Ibid., 133.

affirmative votes. At this point in the proceedings, the immediate problems of Newtown were superseded by more serious disputes over the fundamental authority of the colony's government.

The General Court of 1634 was the first meeting of the colony's lawmaking body which included the deputies, representatives elected by their own townsmen, in addition to the governor, deputy, and assistants, who were elected on an at-large basis. Simultaneously with this popular extension of the legislative privilege, Winthrop was for the first time not reelected governor, and apparently the original group of the colony's leaders began to feel threatened in their power and authority. When the vote on the Newtown motion was counted, "no record was entered, because there were not six assistants in the vote, as the patent requires."[8] Although the vote of the General Court as a whole was in favor of permitting the emigration, Winthrop and the other assistants used their negative voice as a veto to restrain what they felt was an anarchic tendency in the colony's political structure. True liberty, said Winthrop, in another controversy ten years later, "is maintained and exercised in a way of subjection to authority."[9]

The dispute over the negative voice was not settled for a decade, and the proposal of the Newtown people to emigrate to Connecticut was temporarily shelved. John Cotton preached a sermon attempting to satisfy everyone by explaining that the magistrates, the ministry, and the people all had their own peculiar sorts of negative voice. "The congregation of Newtown came and accepted of such enlargement as had formerly been offered them by Boston and Watertown." William Goodwin possibly grumbled all the way home, and John Winthrop optimistically noted in his journal, "and so the fear of their removal to Connecticut was removed."[10] The issue was by no

---

[8] Ibid.   [9] Ibid., II, 239.   [10] Ibid., I, 134.

means settled, however, since the enlargements were for the most part a futile gesture. The tract ceded from Watertown was meadowland already being used by Newtown grazers, and the Boston cession was on the south side of the Charles River, attainable only by small boat. In addition, the spirits of the Newtown planters were exacerbated by the controversies aired in this court and by certain events of the coming summer of 1635.

John Oldham and a small party from Watertown spent the winter on the Connecticut, and at the General Court in May of 1635 Watertown and Roxbury complained, as Newtown had before, that they needed more room and wished to emigrate. The General Court extended its permission "to remove whither they pleased, so as they continued under this government," and on June 3 the same permission was allowed to Dorchester.[11] At the court of the preceding September it had been held against Newtown that "in point of conscience they ought not to depart from us, being knit to us in one body, and bound by oath to seek the welfare of this commonwealth."[12] This covenant responsibility was suddenly no longer an issue in the spring of 1635, and the Newtown settlers saw others plucking the fruit they had chosen for themselves. In that summer John Pratt, one of Hooker's parishioners, wrote to friends in England, warning them against "excessive commendations" of New England's wealth and piety; the contents of his letter were discovered, and on November 3 he was called before the assistants to explain allegations such as the "Commonwealth [being] builded upon rocks, sands, and salt marshes." Hooker once more had to help settle a dispute, and he appealed "in humble desire unto the Court" that Pratt's explanation of the harsh terms of his letter might be accepted.[13]

[11] Ibid., 151.   [12] Ibid., 132.
[13] Paige, 25, 26. Also, *Records of the Governor and Company of the Massachusetts Bay in New England*, ed. Nathaniel B. Shurtleff (Boston, 1853), I, 358–60.

By November 1635 both John Pratt and Thomas Hooker could well afford to be conciliatory. It was clear that the Bay Colony had no effective restraint to emigration, and Watertown and Dorchester had both ignored the injunction to stay within the limits of the Massachusetts territories. In spite of the General Court's rebuff a year before of their request to emigrate, the Newtowners continued with their plans to move to Connecticut. At the end of the summer of 1635, several citizens in Newtown had arranged to dispose of their land and buildings, and in mid-October, "About sixty men, women, and little children, went by land toward Connecticut with their cows, horses, and swine, and after a tedious and difficult journey, arrived safe there."[14] This was the first contingent of the Newtown emigrants to Connecticut; they would prepare a beachhead at a place called Suckiaug while the rest stayed behind to finish their personal affairs and those of their friends.

The work of those wintering in Newtown was made easier by the arrival on October 2 of Thomas Shepard and a large party of his friends and followers. He had been intending to come to America for over a year and had probably exchanged letters with his old friend and adviser, Thomas Hooker. At any rate, he and his group settled in at Newtown and decided to stay after they "found many houses empty and many persons willing to sell."[15] The business of handing the town over to the new proprietors was completed during the following winter, and in May 1636 Hooker and the bulk of the remaining first settlers of Newtown marched through the eastern Massachusetts forests to their new plantation on the Connecticut.

II

The reason for emigrating which the Newtowners placed first in their petition to the General Court of May 1634 was the

[14] Winthrop, I, 163.   [15] Shepard, "Autobiography," 384.

desire for more and better land.[16] This was probably the motive most commonly held by the emigrants, including Hooker. He too had a large family to support, and for the last ten years he would have been unable to provide them with much security and comfort. He had served an arduous apprenticeship in the moral wilderness of the world, and he deserved a share in the New Canaan. Certainly his fellow settlers on the Connecticut later voted him a generous share of town lands. In addition to his personal responsibilities, he was responsible for the spiritual well-being of his congregation, and men who spent their whole lives grubbing a subsistence out of a stingy soil could not have the time or energy required to cultivate the seeds of grace.

Hooker had often advised his congregation, "We must never over-charge our spirits with multiplicity of worldly business, but keepe our souls in such a frame, that we may be able when ever we goe to converse with God in any holy ordinance, to set aside all worldly occasions, that neither our hearts, nor our thoughts, may run out upon them."[17] If by emigrating to Connecticut men could satisfy the material needs of life without overcharging their spirits, then it might be possible that providence beckoned thither. It is important to note that while both Hooker and his fellow emigrants might have been drawn by the promise of richer soil, the implications of that promise were not necessarily the same for all. Some men undoubtedly saw the Connecticut lands as an opportunity to become wealthy, but Hooker had previously warned Essex Christians not to follow the example of the man whom "God hath given . . . a pretty estate in this world, he is turned a very muck-

[16] See Sydney E. Ahlstrom, "Thomas Hooker—Puritanism and Democratic Citizenship: A Preliminary Inquiry into Some Relationships of Religion and American Civic Responsibility," *Church History* 32 (1962–63), 415–18 for a review of this running argument in terms of Hooker's political opinions and influence.

[17] Hooker, *Saints Guide*, 169–70.

worme, become covetous, or a loose one."[18] For Hooker the
benefit of more prosperous land might well have been the
promise of increased leisure time which his congregation might
turn to pious advantage.

When Hooker warned men not to overcharge their "spirits
with multiplicity of worldly business," he used the term "business" in the widest possible sense to include all the varied activities of life which were not immediately involved in man's
spiritual rapprochement with the divine. Besides avoiding any
entanglement in one's trade which might deaden the spirit,
men had to be wary of placing either an immediate or an ultimate commitment in a creature rather than in the creator. Yet
the difficulties of erecting a new society in the wilderness
posed just this threat to the human spirit; it was difficult to
set aside worldly occasions when to do so might mean civil
anarchy, starvation, death from Indian attacks, or a host of
other evils. John Pratt in his notorious letter to his English
friends had bemoaned "the danger of decaying here in our
first love." When called upon to explain this, he stated,

> I did it only in regard of the manifold occasions and busi-
> nesses which here at first we meet withal, by which I find
> in mine own experience (and so, I think, do others also),
> how hard it is to keep our hearts in that holy frame which
> sometimes they were in where we had less to do in outward
> things.[19]

Although Pratt might seem to be merely rephrasing the
warnings against worldly involvement given ten years before
in Essex by his pastor, he is perhaps the first layman in the
Bay Colony to express fears of a general decline in godliness.
His complaint is possibly not so much a reflection of a bur-
geoning wave of Puritan immorality as it is a response to the
strains of a new life on the edge of civilization.

[18] Hooker, *Faithful Covenanter*, 28.   [19] Paige, 26.

The worldly occasions which Pratt feared as a danger to the "holy frame" of his heart were the simple necessities of earning a living in a wilderness. Hooker confronted these same problems, both as a purely personal concern, like Pratt's, and as a pastoral concern for his people. His personal concern was if anything more pressing than that of John Pratt, for if Hooker were diverted from the divine source of power and truth, his public ministry would become impotent. "That a Minister may be Powerful," said Hooker, "an inward spiritual heat of heart, and holy affections is required, answerable and suitable to the matter, which is to be communicated."[20] The holy frame of the prophet's heart was essential to the holy frame of the hearts of the congregation; personal concern for his own heart inevitably became pastoral concern.

The holy affection required to render a ministry powerful was acquired by meditation, "a serious intention of the mind whereby we come to search out the truth, and settle it effectually upon the heart."[21] A social or political environment which distracted men from regular and frequent meditation would clearly, for Hooker at least, erode the inner sources of ministerial power. The lengthily detailed controversies of 1633–1636 might well have created just this sort of corrosive situation. From almost the moment of his arrival, Hooker had been involved in a seemingly endless series of major and minor quarrels, and his subsequent inability to concentrate on the growth of holy affections—he was a proud man with a hot temper which he usually managed to repress—would have become a hindrance to the unity of the saints. The preacher's holy affections were first raised so that those of his congrega-

[20] Hooker, *The Application of Redemption, By the effectual Work of the Word, and Spirit of Christ, for the bringing home of lost Sinners to God. The first eight books* (London, 1656), 213. *The Ninth and Tenth Books* under the same general title were published in a separate volume at London in 1659. For footnote identification purposes they will be designated as *Application* and *Application 2*.

[21] Hooker, *Application 2*, 210.

tion might be raised later: "He that mournes in speaking of sin, makes another mourn for sin committed."[22] "Bound by oath to seek the welfare of this commonwealth," Hooker could not in conscience evade the threats posed to the souls of men beyond this own church by dissension and heartburnings; he had several times in his sermons put the rhetorical question, "Am I my Brothers keeper?" and answered, "Yes, thou art, or else thou art his murtherer."[23] His primary allegiance was, nevertheless, to his own congregation; they had called him, they had ordained him to a position of spiritual power and responsibility.

Hooker's considerable talents as a peacemaker helped allay several potentially divisive and destructive controversies, but clearly it would have been preferable had no such broils ever arisen in the first place. Since it was obviously unlikely that even in the Bay Colony men would cease having violent disagreements, Hooker seems to have come to the conclusion that some way ought to be found to minimize the disturbing effects of such quarrels upon society as a whole. In the Newtown petition of September 1634, "it was alleged by Mr. Hooker, as a fundamental error, that towns were set so near to each other." This apparently supported the contended need for more land, but Hooker may well have considered the possibility that if towns were more isolated, they were less likely to contaminate each other with their home-grown squabbles or heresies. Hooker was not alone in believing that local issues should remain local, be settled promptly, and confined to their source; the magistrates wasted little time in arguing John Eliot out of his ill-advised opinions.

Hooker's credibility as a peacemaker was unfortunately depreciated with his involvement in each succeeding controversy. His advice on the business of the cross in the banner, dismissing Endicott's action as a pointless scruple, was not

[22] Hooker, *Application*, 213.   [23] Ibid., 445.

heeded, for example, and when Sir Henry Vane arrived in 1635, the newcomer appointed himself to reconcile differences between several leading men of the colony, including the clerics Hooker, Cotton, and John Wilson and the laymen Haynes, Winthrop, and Dudley. His role as reconciler of other men's differences had been transformed into that of a disputant. Cotton seems to have disagreed with Hooker over the flag affair, and although the first generation of New Englanders attempted to conceal all differences which had been reconciled, there is evidence that Cotton and Hooker were discovering radical disagreements which were never to be fully resolved.

In later years, while commenting upon the emigration to Connecticut, William Hubbard observed, "Two such eminent stars, such as were Mr. Cotton and Mr. Hooker, both of the first magnitude, though of differing influence, could not well continue in one and the same orb."[24] Following Hubbard, later historians have suggested that one significant reason for Hooker's removal to Connecticut was a rivalry with Cotton; in view of the involved set of controversies into which Hooker was drawn, this is clearly a simplistic explanation. There indeed were disagreements between Hooker and Cotton, although the serious and lasting differences would only appear after Hooker had already been in Connecticut for a year, but a theological quarrel between two men who had not yet publicly questioned each other's orthodoxy is hardly an explanation for the removal of a whole town. A more important reason for Hooker's encouragement of his parishioners' designs would be his desire to remove them from an atmosphere in which they were "apt to be disturbed with every little occasion, and not easily quieted again."[25]

The explanation for Hooker's removal which has been most vigorously argued by historians since 1860 has been the question of his democratic rejection of a theocratic polity. The

[24] Hubbard, 173.   [25] Hubbard, 142.

argument that Hooker left Massachusetts in order to found America's first democratic government has been convincingly demolished by Perry Miller, and historians have now gone on to argue whether the government of Connecticut had democratic effects despite its initial lack of democratic intentions. One problem with this argument is that the term "democratic" in a twentieth-century sense has no relevance in the seventeenth century, where it was considered to be but one remove from anarchy.[26] Another problem is the essentially political nature of the label.

John Winthrop in a document written for the political guidance of his fellow voyagers en route to America delineated "a double Lawe by which wee are regulated in our conversation one towards another." Christians were under, first, the law of nature or moral law, and, second, the law of grace or law of the Gospel. The first pertained to all men, being given to man "in the estate of innocency" before the fall; those "in the estate of regeneracy" were also governed by the second sort of law. The Massachusetts Bay Colony, as Winthrop saw it, was unique among the nations of his time in that, since the planters were "a Company professing our selves fellow members of Christ," the entire colony would be governed by both the moral law and the law of the gospel.[27] As a Christian magistrate, it would be Winthrop's duty to synthesize this double law into a unified legal corpus.

Winthrop had been a trained and practicing lawyer in England, and he approached the problem of integrating moral law and Gospel law from the standpoint of the English legal tradition. Hooker, on the other hand, was concerned directly and almost completely with Gospel law, the responsibilities and

[26] See Perry Miller, "Thomas Hooker and the Democracy of Connecticut," in *Errand into the Wilderness* (Cambridge, Mass., Harvard Univ. Press, 1964), 16–47.

[27] John Winthrop, "A Model of Christian Charity," *Winthrop Papers*, II, 283–84, 292.

duties of regenerate Christians. Gospel law or the law of grace bound men upon the grounds of their regeneration, and Hooker turned his attention primarily toward these grounds of Gospel law, secondarily toward the nature and demands of that law, and scarcely at all toward the affairs of moral law except insofar as it involved the regenerate men of his congregation. He urged men to discover their regenerate estate and then to live in accordance with the principles of grace; if they did this, they would in course observe the moral law. Winthrop perforce attempted to establish "a City upon a Hill" with political means, and his character and actions may be judged in political terms. Hooker's involvement with city-building was for him only incidental to his pastoral calling, and labels so fundamentally political as "democrat" cannot be appropriately used to describe his motivations for removal to Connecticut. He moved to the wilderness to build a more pure congregation of men living under Gospel law, and his significance was as a pastor rather than as a political leader.

Winthrop's "Modell of Christian Charity" presented a theory of law in society. The model which Hooker spent his life in elaborating was the pattern of redemption within the individual soul, and rather than speak to a commonwealth, he spoke to poor sinners in their particular conditions. Hooker took his congregation to the wilderness not that he might free them from oligarchic political control but that he might more effectively impress upon them his own peculiar kind of spiritual discipline. In Connecticut he could direct his attention more completely to that group of people who had submitted themselves to his spiritual leadership, and his influence was inescapable in their new isolation.[28]

---

[28] See Richard L. Bushman, *From Puritan to Yankee: Character and the Social Order in Connecticut, 1690–1765* (Cambridge, Harvard Univ. Press, 1967), 3–21 for a discussion of the oligarchic nature of seventeenth-century Connecticut government.

III

On the May morning of 1636 when they set out on the journey they had desired for over two years, the Connecticut emigrants were probably not altogether relieved to be departing from their first plantation. Newtown was by this time, after all, a settled town with protection from the perils of the wilderness, be they human or bestial, its fields at least produced a subsistence, and if the towns were planted too close, they did represent sources of aid and comfort in an emergency. Connecticut was isolated, exposed, uncultivated, and the advance party had just suffered through a particularly severe winter. Settlers from Dorchester had also gone out in the previous autumn, and in December a party of about seventy men and women returned, "which was a great mercy of God, for otherwise they had all perished with famine, as some did."[29]

The Newtown party already on the river was apparently better prepared, however, and there were the beginnings of an established community ready to welcome the Hooker contingent. Above all, in spite of the attendant dangers, the rich bottom lands of the Connecticut still held out the promise of being a sort of agricultural Eldorado to many of the Newtowners—the Indian name for their new settlement, Suckiaug, meant "black earth"[30]—and those who were not entirely convinced by the future bounties of the western settlements might take comfort in being with their friends and their pastor on their own for the first time in the new world. When Anne Bradstreet considered the American forests in her "Contemplations," she was aware of their ambiguous meaning, but before even her thoughts did "in the darksome womb of fruitful nature dive," Hooker's congregation had already made the plunge into a reality at once beckoning and fearsome.

[29] Winthrop, I, 166.
[30] William DeLoss Love, *The Colonial History of Hartford* (Hartford, 1914), 82.

The Hooker family and about a hundred men, women, and children followed the trail later known as the Old Bay Path across southern Massachusetts, striking the river near the present town of East Longmeadow. They moved down the east bank of the river from there to Windsor, where the Dorchester settlers were reestablishing themselves after the winter, and after crossing the river at Windsor, they continued on to rejoin their fellow planters at Suckiaug. They drove about one hundred and sixty cattle with them, and took almost two weeks to make the trip. Although Mrs. Hooker had to be carried in a litter, the journey seems to have been made without mishap, and the whole party probably arrived at their new home just after the first day of summer.[31]

When he arrived at Suckiaug, Hooker would have found a dozen or more small and fairly primitive houses set in front of the first of the hills leading away to the west from the river. Between this infant settlement and the river was a stretch of open bottom land called the Little Meadow, and to the south of it the Little River ran into the Connecticut. In the center of the plantation a large square area had been reserved for the meeting-house yard, and presumably the first meeting-house, a small and windowless structure, had been erected in the corner of it. Elder William Goodwin had come to Suckiaug in the previous autumn, as perhaps had Samuel Stone, and they would have led the Sabbath day services for this temporarily detached portion of the Newtown church. Across the Little River were more meadows, and, somewhat ominously, a fortified Dutch trading post known as the House of Hope. Most of Hooker's party settled south of the Little River, but the first comers had reserved large house lots on the north side for Hooker and Stone. Hooker's lot fronted on the Little River and had the meadow immediately to the east of it.

From the beginning the settlement at Suckiaug was divided

[31] See Love, 34–47 for details of the journey route.

by the Little River into north side and south side plantations. When the first townsmen were elected, the planters were careful to give representative parity to each side of the river, and when the first committeemen were chosen for the colony's General Court they followed this same principle of equal representation. Since conscious effort had to be exerted to keep the two parts of the town unified as a community, the importance of the church as a spiritual bond among the people was perhaps magnified. It is interesting to note that Hooker's house lot was almost immediately opposite the fordway across the Little River and that Stone's house was directly next to his on the west. Until a bridge was built farther up the river several years later, no one went from one side of the town to the other without being aware of the presence of the spiritual leaders.

After he arrived at Suckiaug, Hooker was no longer forced to act as a political front man for members of his congregation. There were no contentious Dudleys or Endicotts among the Newtown emigrants, and he was able to direct most of his efforts to fulfilling his pastoral duties. The settlers on the river avoided the mistake of the Massachusetts planters as Hooker saw it; by the end of the summer of 1636 there were five plantations on the river, all separated by generous amounts of untenanted space. For a variety of reasons—the difficulty of creating a town as a self-subsisting economic unit, trouble with the Indians, uncertainty about legal rights and privileges, the relative insularity of the towns—the river plantations tended to concentrate on creating effective local political structures before they established laws and institutions to govern a colony.[32] This process of development seems to have been well adapted to the inclinations and ideas of the settlers. Early seventeenth-century Englishmen were perhaps most aware of and involved in government on the local level, and these par-

[32] See Love, 49–58. Also Mary Jeanne Anderson Jones, *Congregational Commonwealth, Connecticut, 1636–1662* (Middletown, Wesleyan Univ. Press, 1968), 61–69.

ticular men had left England after parliamentary government had been unable to achieve their goals. The Connecticut settlers seem to have been committed to creating a political body from the bottom up. As for Thomas Hooker, his basic unit of social thought was always the particular church, and after 1636 his major concern was to make his congregation the effective spiritual heart of the community. There were many intelligent and able men at Suckiaug to regulate its political life; Pastor Hooker devoted himself to fostering the vitality of his church.

Beginning immediately upon his arrival, he and Stone would have reinstituted the regular order of Sabbath services. Now that ministers and people were once more together, they would have their usual two sermons every Sunday and one on lecture day. Hooker maintained his belief that the pastor's ultimate role was that of evangelist, and he adapted his other pastoral functions to the goals of awakening men to the presence of saving grace within themselves and of qualifying them for entry into the church covenant. Correspondent to his maintenance of an evangelical attitude, he never lost confidence in the efficacy of powerful preaching; the words that sought out the sinners in their pews at Chelmsford might also convey the Spirit into the hearts of sinners on the rude benches of the meeting-house by the Connecticut.

Hooker gave his congregation in the wilderness the same message he had preached to them in England, the soul's need for preparation, humiliation, and calling to Christ, and the fruit of its eventual ingrafting into the life-giving stock of Christ. Hooker wrote out the notes for these sermons he delivered in America, and they later became the basis for the two lengthy, posthumously published volumes entitled *The Application of Redemption*. Hooker's English reputation was based upon his handling of the matter of preparation, and many of his neighbors needed these doctrines still. Only a few of the Suckiaug planters had heard the whole persuasive course of sermons on the application of redemption, and in the community were many servants and young people who had not yet felt the stirrings of salvation. The emigration to Connecticut took with it many natural men who needed to be brought into a state of grace and the church.

The passage of time brought a continuing enlargement of the human community outside the church, and Hooker never lost sight of the consequent necessity to direct poor sinners to Christ and Christ's church. Although he might note that within the church covenant "every faithfull Minister is the father of the people and they are his children, they are the Stewards of the Lords house," the minister's responsibilities were ultimately to all of the elect whether in the church or not; he should give "to everyone their portion, terrour to whom terrour belongs, and comfort to whom comfort belongs."[33] He would occasionally preach sermons directed at nipping specific sins and follies in the bud:

> I have ever judged it most seasonable, if I would pursue a sinful course breaking out, not by the by to pull it into a discourse, but to take a Text on purpose, wherein it is plainly condemned. That the people may hear God in his Word speaking before we speak; this is to shew our Commission before we do Execution, and this wil stop mens mouths.[34]

The needs of sinners who were required by law to attend the sermons even though not members of the church were answered by sermons pointed with terrors of damnation and the bitterness of spiritual death. "Where are the teares that wee make for the slaine of our people?" Hooker asked; "If they will needs goe to hell, let us bury them with bitter lamentations."[35]

While the technique of aiming sermons at specific abuses was useful checking communal moral lapses, it was also an

[33] Hooker, *Preparation*, 73. [34] Hooker, *Application 2*, 204.
[35] Hooker, *Vocation*, 511.

effective method of safeguarding the public from heresy or other "corrupt and sinful practices" which were "like to grow and leven and that speedily and dangerously." Private sins were usually corrected privately, but where private error was in danger of becoming public delusion, "its lawful in way of caution and prevention to discover men's sins and errors in their own words, that others may avoid them the better, and they be ashamed of them more."[36] While the course of sermons on the application of redemption provided a somewhat abstract guide to the way of salvation, Hooker was always willing to come back again and again to the hard facts of personal and communal existence: "A Spade is a Spade, and a Drunkard is a Drunkard."[37]

Portions of terror were balanced by portions of comfort as Hooker followed the ebb and flow of his congregation's spiritual life. As a steward of the Lord's house, he preached sermons full of lessons of assurance designed to strengthen the saints in their piety. As Hooker unfolded the process of redemption, he gave comfort to the covenanted members of the church by confirming their redemptive experiences, reasserting the new structure of their lives. His sermons tended to unite the just-awakening but still reprobate members of the community with the covenanted elect as they shared in the homiletic experiences. Many of his sermons upon special occasions were specifically designed to enhance the Suckiaug planters' image of themselves as a community unified by God's love for them. In a sermon of thanksgiving after the Pequod War, he offered "as a cordial to releve the hearts of the servants of God in thir depest tryales" a reminder that "all such as seeke God in his ordinances and in the humiliation of thire sowles they are under the strength of Gods providence, and all the creatures are appointed for the relefe of such so that if heaven or earth can aford it they shall have it."[38]

[36] Hooker, *Application 2*, 205.   [37] Hooker, *Application*, 210.
[38] Hooker, "Thanksgiving Sermon," in Andrew Thomas Denholm,

No matter what the message on any given day, the sermons Hooker and Stone delivered from their Connecticut pulpit were always the most preeminently visible and audible guides for the lives of the planters. Men came together in lesser and greater numbers for varieties of civil functions, but on the Sabbath virtually all men, women, and young people assembled in the meeting-house to receive their individual and collective portions.

A significant number of the natural men who required special portions from the minister were children and young people who had not yet experienced the revivifying motions of saving grace. Although some of these children were the sons and daughters of reprobates, many were the offspring of members of the congregation, and they were in a unique spiritual position requiring particular attention. Under the general rubric of the covenant of grace, Hooker discovered two different sorts of covenant. The inward covenant was held between the indivdual souls of the elect and God; it was this covenant which created the invisible church of the saints in verity, the type of the visible church which admitted members upon a reasonable assumption of their tenure of the inward covenant. The outward covenant was established between God and a people in a larger, more nearly national sense; in the inward covenant God undertook to create unfailing, saving faith in man, but in the outward covenant He only "takes speciall notice of them, and he waters them every moment, and keeps them night and day; hence they are said to come under the wing of God, that is under the speciall expression of his favour."[39] In the outward covenant there was no saving grace; God merely protected his chosen people from many of the shocks and disasters of the world and provided them with the

---

"Thomas Hooker, Puritan Preacher, 1586–1647," Diss. Hartford Seminary Foundation 1961, 424–25. Denholm has printed a transcription of several useful Hooker texts.

[39] Hooker, *The Covenant of Grace Opened* (London, 1649), 2–3.

ordinances useful in seeking saving grace. When "Beleeving Parents" were received into the inward covenant, they secured "federall holiness," the advantages of the outward covenant, for their children, because "they enter not for themselves alone, but for all that come of them."[40]

A child who had the foresight to be born to one of the saints thus gained spiritual advantages over his less fortunate mates, but at the same time he found his spiritual and intellectual life to be an object of unusually intense interest as he grew up. "God engages himself to use the Covenant as a means to doe good to them, as he sees fit," said Hooker, and the covenant seed were often reminded that they had been chosen by the deity to be his particular people.[41] Since God's way of using the covenant to do good to the children of the saints was to bring home to them continually the power of the Word, the pastor often presented to them in his sermons a portion especially adapted to their needs. The covenant seed were uniquely eligible, or so Hooker thought, for the ministrations of their pastor because their federal holiness made them more susceptible than natural men to either the eventual realization of saving grace or the workings of a restraining grace which would keep them from the "wildness" that was destructive of self and community. Hooker observed that, though the Jews were wicked, "they were not wild, but they were under Gods hand ordering them: and hence they were preserved under his hand."[42] One of the most important ways in which the minister could secure the safety of his community was to subject the covenant seed to the power of the Word and remind them of their responsibilities under the outward covenant. Hooker's concern for the outward covenant extended to urging "Beleeving Parents" scrupulously to attend the spiritual

[40] Ibid., 35. The basic work on New England covenant theory is Perry Miller, *The New England Mind, The Seventeenth Century* (1939; rpt., Boston, Beacon, 1961), 365–491.

[41] Hooker, *Covenant*, 40.   [42] Ibid., 51.

welfare of their children within the home. He often reminded parents that their ultimate responsibility toward their children was spiritual:

> Lets bring our Children as neer to Heaven as we can, it is in our power to restrain them and reform, and that we ought to do.
>
> . . . . . .
>
> Oh you tender Mothers, would have those little ones saved? Oh bring them up hither, traine them up to be souldiers of Christ, it is admirable being here. Oh husbands and wives, you have a care to leave Legacies to your children.[43]

While the intense scrutiny and direction of children's lives was especially apt for the covenant seed, the children of Hartford's reprobates were not overlooked.[44] They might not have federal holiness, and their parents, being natural men and women, might shirk their spiritual responsibilities, but Hooker was concerned for their souls almost equally with those of the covenant seed. Hooker's favorite tropes show the inclinations and interests of the private man, and some of his most moving metaphors are images of the soul as child. Hooker had long been sensitive to the importance of youthful experiences for the adult mind—witness the fact of his turning to school-teaching when unable to preach in the 1620s—and in Hartford he attempted to provide a comprehensive spiritual and intellectual program for the community's children.

Hooker was instrumental in the establishment of Hartford's early schools. John Higginson was apparently the first teacher on the grammar school level (in 1636–1637), and he was drawn to Hartford more out of an interest to study with Hooker than by any desire to become a schoolmaster. Samuel Stone as

---

[43] Hooker, *Chief Lessons*, 34–35; *Application* 2, 357.

[44] The name Hartford was adopted in February, 1637, in honor of Stone—it was his birthplace in England. Hereafter the settlement will be referred to under its modern name.

teacher probably took the primary role of catechist to the young, but Hooker undoubtedly shared in this labor. He also took under his care several young men who were preparing for the ministry, such as Higginson and James Fitch. He concerned himself with the moral behavior of the young in order to insure the proper admonition of any juvenile peccadilloes; young sinners were as dangerous to the community as old ones. In the seventeenth century the period of childish irresponsibility did not last long (although the age of reason for capital crimes in New England was sixteen), and Hooker treated children as small men and women, admonishing them to face up to the moral consequences of even childish sins. This attitude might seem harsh to a more sentimental era, and at times it was, but it could be tremendously effective in creating a sensitive yet tough-minded adult, for to treat a child in this way was to challenge him to fulfill all his potentialities.

Cotton Mather recorded an interesting anecdote illuminating Hooker's sensitivity toward children:

> . . . there happened a damage to be done unto a neighbor, immediately whereupon, Mr. Hooker meeting with an unlucky boy, that often had his name up for the doing of such mischiefs, he fell to chiding of that boy as the doer of this. The boy denied it, and Mr. Hooker still went on in an angry manner, chargin of him; whereupon said the boy, "Sir, I see you are in a passion, I'll say no more to you:" and so ran away. Mr. Hooker, upon further enquiry, not finding that the boy could be proved guilty, sent for him; and having first by a calm question, given the boy opportunity to renew his denial of the fact, he said unto him: "Since I cannot prove the contrary, I am bound to believe; and I do believe what you say:" and then added: "Indeed, I was in a passion when I spake to you before; it was my sin, and it is my shame, and I am truly sorry for it: and I hope in God I shall be more watchful hereafter." So, giving the boy some good counsel,

the poor lad went away extremely affected with such a carriage in so good a man; and it proved an occasion of good unto the soul of the lad all his days.[45]

This incident shows both Hooker's choleric temper and his overriding commitment to rational charity. A lesser man, having discovered his error, might have forgotten the encounter since the target of his anger had been only a boy, and apparently a Tom Sawyerish sort at that. Hooker's apology established for the boy a much-needed model of contrition and humility, and, more importantly, it revealed his fundamental willingness to see every human as soul as a potential citizen of the city of God even if not yet enfranchised in the city of man.

While Hooker's sermons exhorted children to obey their parents, he more frequently urged parents to exercise educative and disciplinary forces upon their children. The disciplined community was to be a shelter for posterity against a wicked and threatening world: "When we leave the world, if we leave our children here in trouble, this will be a comfort to them, they shall be safe from Devils; he that is hidden shall be safe; leave them therefore under the faithfulnesse of that God, what he hath promised, he will bestow."[46] Ultimately the community was a refuge for all men who came into it, children and adults, and participated in its life. Hooker's program for posterity was simply a part of his attempt to create a total, spiritually self-sustaining community.

Just as Hooker's concern for the spiritual condition of the community's children operated on the public level of the sermon and the private level of personal discourse, so his care for the adults of Hartford functioned by public and private acts. Because Hooker's sermons are the only part of the man to survive into our century, it is all too easy to imagine him only in his pulpit and not among his people as well, above his con-

[45] Mather, I, 345–46.   [46] Hooker, *Covenant*, 84.

gregation rather than in it. As pastor, he undoubtedly made periodic visits among all the residents of Hartford, for "a faithfull Minister must deal with poor sinners, as with the Sheep commended to his care and custody."[47] He also made himself readily available for those seeking to understand their troubled consciences. Cotton Mather noted that Hooker

> has a singular ability at giving answers to cases of conscience; whereof happy was the experience of some thousands: and for this work he usually set apart the second day of the week; wherein he admitted all sorts of persons, in their discourses with him, to reap the benefit of the extraordinary experience which himself had found of Satan's devices.[48]

The Devil's rhetoric was spoken even in Connecticut, and these weekday conferences in Hooker's study were an essential part of his care for both the saints and the natural men of Hartford as he encouraged, assured, counseled, and admonished.

Hooker's care for his fellow townsmen was both a traditional pastoral responsibility and his appropriate response to the duty of the brotherly watch by which he was bound through his participation in the covenant. The double responsibility of pastoral care and brotherly watch was of particular importance to Hooker, for he conceived of the covenanted church as a spiritual society approximating the ideal human community. The strength of this society was in great measure upheld by the strength of heart of its most pious members; in turn, the strength of the individual was supported by the entire group, including even the weakest Christians.

> The strongest bones need sinewes, an Arme cannot lacke the least bone; the greatest Pillars have need of the lesse things: So in the Church, the strongest members in the same need

[47] Hooker, *Application* 2, 196.   [48] Mather, 1, 346.

advice and support; the richest man must use the Market; so none can live without the Market of the society of Saints; and there is need of help to the best.[49]

In Hooker's hands the brotherly watch became an evangelical instrument, for as a Christian community the church had responsibilities to the world at large. He stressed the importance of the watch in his sermons, but he gave even greater emphasis to the duties of Christians toward the unregenerate. He kept the definition of "brother" open to embrace all of humanity, and he reminded the saints that St. Paul "makes a Christian to be as busie as a Bee, that he should go no whither, but should see, and find occasion of doing good to one or other."[50]

Just as the Christian pastor's concern for his brethren began in his congregation and extended outward, so the Christian layman's concern should begin in the family where his natural love bound him and his opportunities were most ready. "You that have wicked husbands or wives, feare every night when you goe to bed, lest the judgement of the Lord should come upon them, yet ere morning, and cut them off and send them to destruction."[51] The saint must remember that he was himself once a sinner and must act accordingly to his natural brethren: "Wee ourselves were once haters and hated of God, and ran the broad way to Hell and everlasting destruction, therefore shew pitty and compassion to such poore soules."[52] By expressing concern for the souls of sinners, the spiritually renewed saint could imitate Christ. "This is the course that God takes, and .this ought to be a coppy and pattern to you in the meane time, as you are of the Elect people of God, to put on the bowels of mercy and compassion towards your brethren, if ever mercy, here it ought to be expressed and discovered."[53] When Hooker stressed this extension of Christian love to sin-

[49] Hooker, *Chief Lessons*, 3. [50] Hooker, *Application*, 445.
[51] Hooker, *Faithful Covenanter*, 6.
[52] Hooker, *Foure . . . Treatises*, 71.
[53] Hooker, *Unbeleevers*, 104₂. Faulty pagination.

ners, he affirmed his belief in the church as an evangelical institution; he as minister imitated Christ by bringing the divine message to man in public sermons and private conferences, and the church members brought the divine message to the world by living Christian love toward their fellow man. Pastor and people were engaged in a common quest: "We should use all the cords of mercy, and love, and anger, and indignation; so that if it were possible we might hale the soules of poore sinners to God."[54]

The New England Puritans believed that the stability of the commonwealth was providentially and directly dependent upon the stability and vitality of the church. Hooker's attempts to encourage a dynamic spiritual life among the citizens of Hartford did have political connotations, even if for him they were distinctly secondary to his vision of the church as an aid to salvation. On the most practical and trivial level the church promoted civil righteousness among the unregenerate whereby "a mans corruption may bee restrained and kept in from any actual breaking out, not for any good that in himselfe shall reape thereby, but for others benefit, for the good of society in generall, the good of some in speciall."[55] The minister and church might aid the magistrates in keeping sinners in line, thus providing civil peace in which the saints could work out their salvation, but at the same time the prevention of actual breakings out of corruption tended to preserve the community in a larger sense. "The multitude of sins bring the dangerest times," Hooker said.[56] Sodom was destroyed when Lot could not find ten good men, and Hooker could point to the recent troubles in Bohemia and the Palatinate. "Our Liberties and Priviledges are precious we enjoy in New England," he reminded his people, "I pray God we may profit by them."[57] The liberty God gave to New England saints was to do his

[54] Ibid., 111$_2$. [55] Hooker, *Chief Lessons*, 218.
[56] Hooker, *Foure . . . Treatises*, 3.
[57] Hooker, *Application 2*, 248.

will, and by doing his will, they preserved their liberties and privileges, both spiritual and political.

Hooker's conception of the relevance of the church to the commonwealth was not, however, simply conservative. In the church's proper realm of the spirit the covenant extended a preserving sense of assurance to its members while at the same time it functioned as an agent for the conversion of the natural men without. Similarly in the commonwealth, the well-ordered church protected external peace and harmony, but it also tended ultimately to transform the commonwealth into a more nearly perfect state. Hooker's charitable presumption was that the church member had saving faith in Christ, and faith "is a working grace, where there is faith, there is work, and what work is it? It is a work of love."[58] As faith worked in elect individuals, it produced love for God and also love for one's fellow man, the second part of Christ's redaction of the commandments. As the evangelical church discovered more and more of the faithful within the community, it produced a body of men and women who were governed by a new and more perfect conscience, people whose wills were motivated by a love of God. The hostilities natural men exercised toward each other in civil society would disappear, or so Hooker expected.

> . . . the disobedient child, the stubborn and careless servant, were their hearts brought to this detestation of these their distempers you would see a new world, they would mind themselves of their miscarriages, though you never remembered them, they would check themselves from carelessness though you never reproved them, they would be heart sick of the stirrings of such rebellions, though you never reckoned with them in that behalf.[59]

As the membership of the covenanted church more closely approximated the town's total population, the community would come to be defined by the Christian love for man which the

[58] Hooker, *Saints Dignitie*, 5.   [59] Hooker, *Application 2*, 683.

saints were to exercise. The commonwealth would be transmuted into

> the union of love and concord with the faithful, as the members of the same Body ought to maintain in their hearts and consciences, and in their converse societies one with another; keeping that unity of spiritual agreement in the bond of peace: to think of the same thing, and speak the same thing: to be of the same mind and Heart, as it was said of them in Primitive times.[60]

Hooker believed with Winthrop that a New England town should be a city upon a hill in a political sense, that it should be a model for the spiritually and morally imperiled society of Old England, but he emphasized even more strongly the traditional image of that city as the New Jerusalem. When the final thousand years of peace began, Hooker hoped and believed that they would be initiated by the reformed churches of Christ.

Despite the relevance of the covenanted church to the commonwealth at large, the central fact for Hooker, as for all the Puritan ministers, was the church itself. John Cotton noted approvingly, "Mr. Hooker doth often quote a saying out of Mr. Cartwright . . . that no man fashioneth his house to his hangings, but his hangings to his house. It is better that the commonwealth be fashioned to the setting forth of Gods house, which is his church: than to accommodate the church frame to the civil state."[61] If we are to assess Hooker's success as a minister, it is only proper to examine first his successes within

[60] Hooker, *Comment*, 38–39. This is an idealization of Hooker's position. He went on here to emphasize that this union was to be a spiritual one among saints in verity. He had no realistic expectations that the political state would be subsumed by the church *in toto*, yet there was always the promised apocalypse.

[61] John Cotton, "A Copy of a Letter from Mr. Cotton to Lord Say and Seal in the Year 1636," in Perry Miller and Thomas H. Johnson, *The Puritans* (1938; rpt., New York Harper, 1963), I, 209.

his own church. As is too often the case in discovering his career, the records of the Hartford church for his period have not survived, but it does seem that under Hooker's pastorate the church became the evangelistic instrument he wished it to be. His concern for keeping the doors of the church open influenced the process of admission of new members to the Hartford church. In the second half of the 1630s the Massachusetts churches, responding primarily to the ideas of John Cotton and Thomas Shepard, began to require of candidates for membership a public profession showing "the work of grace upon their soules, or how God hath been dealing with them about their conversion."[62] Hooker realized that not all men were equally articulate about their experiences, and wishing to judge men by rational charity, he seems to have eased this most difficult hurdle to membership. "Some, that could unto edification do it, he put upon thus relating the manner of their conversion to God; but usually they only answered unto certain probatory questions which were tendered them."[63] While Hooker was clearly not willing to dispense with the requirement that candidates show some evidence of a gracious change within their hearts, the sort of evidence he was willing to accept was more varied. The man who could hold out hope of salvation to Mrs. Drake was not prepared to reject any person who lived "not in the commission of any known sin, nor in the neglect of any known duty, and can give a reason of his hope towards God."[64] The comparative openness of Hooker's church tended to keep it from becoming an elitist and isolated society and at the same time made it a viable institution for the enrichment and purification of its members' spiritual experiences.

Hooker also seems to have been exceptionally successful in maintaining within his parishioners a continuing sense of the necessity of gracious spiritual experiences. His success in this

[62] Thomas Lechford, *Plain Dealing, or News from New England*, ed. Darrett B. Rutman (1867; rpt., New York, Johnson, 1969), 19.
[63] Mather, I, 349.   [64] Hooker, *Survey*, III, 6.

strengthened the fellowship of the church by making men more sensitive about how they behaved toward each other; it encouraged "the union of love and concord" which was the church's social end. As a result the Hartford church was free of much of the internal dissension which racked other churches, including that of neighboring Wethersfield. This internal peace was in large part of the pastor's arranging. Cotton Mather recorded that Hooker was quick to reconcile errant church members "with sensible and convenient acknowledgements of their miscarriages" and thus prevent embarrassing and aggravating formal church censures. "There was but one person admonished in, and but one person excommunicated from, the church of Hartford, in all the fourteen years that Mr. Hooker lived there."[65] Peace in the Hartford church was supported by the force and effectiveness of Hooker's personality and ministry; within a dozen years of his death the church was hopelessly fragmented. In the meantime the loving fellowship of the saints was a foretaste of heaven, and Hooker advised all hearers, natural and elect, "Go into their Societies as men that resolve to go to the Court; for where God is, Heaven is."[66]

Thomas Hooker's success in his church was temporary; it was achieved by repressing hostilities and aggressions which reappeared elsewhere, but it was nonetheless no mean achievement.[67] For the fourteen years he was among his people in America, he was able to bring genuine peace and harmony to many men. During his eleven years in Hartford he was able to create an integral harmony in church and town which gave men who had to face a very real and forbidding external wilderness time to come to grips with the no less real world within themselves. "There is no greater hindrance to be found on Earth to holy Meditation than froathy Company and Com-

[65] Mather, I, 349.   [66] Hooker, *Application 2*, 13.
[67] See John Demos, *A Little Commonwealth, Family Life in Plymouth Colony* (New York, Oxford, 1970), 135–38 for a discussion of Puritan displacement of repressed hostility.

panions, while a man is in the crowd amongst such wretches there is no possibility in reason that one should search his heart and examine his own way."[68] Moving to the banks of the Connecticut was as far as a seventeenth-century Englishman could go in literally coming out of the world; in the communal love and concord of the Hartford church Hooker could persuade him to take the ultimate step of coming out of the world spiritually.

Hooker had no illusions about his church members—there were certainly hypocrites among them—nor did he deceive himself about the natural men who listened or were required to listen to his Sunday sermons. Restraining grace did not and would not restrain all men; there would always be sinners like Walter Gray, who was punished for "labouring to inveagle the affections of Mr. Hookers mayde."[69] Although "the union of love and concord" in church and town was more an ideal than a social reality, Hooker's rational charity in judging candidates for the church did have wider implications which were realized in the political life of the colony. His generosity in accepting men with their faults and weaknesses argues a somewhat greater confidence both in the possibilities of human nature, at least for natural acts, and in God's directing and preserving grace than that shown by the ministers and magistrates in the Bay. Thus on May 31, 1638, when the General Court of Connecticut was meeting to discuss the drawing up of formal articles for the government of the river plantations, Hooker could preach them a sermon with the following doctrines:

    I. That the choice of public magistrates belongs unto the people, by Gods own allowance.

    II. The privilege of election, which belongs to the people, therefore must not be exercised according to their

[68] Hooker, *Application 2*, 240.
[69] *Public Records . . . Connecticut*, I, 124.

humours, but according to the blessed will and law of God.

III. They who have power to appoint officers and magistrates, it is in their power, also, to set the bounds and limitations of the power and place unto which they call them.[70]

As Perry Miller has noted, he was telling the magistrates nothing new but simply reminding them of conventional truths of political theory with which they were already familiar.[71] He was, however, holding them to the practice of these concepts of government to which they had previously subscribed in theory and, in their experience as dissidents in the Bay, in fact. The political leaders of Connecticut now had the opportunity to refashion their hangings to fit their new house.

Winthrop had warned Hooker that in regard "to the body of the people, . . . the best part is always the least, and of that best part the wiser part is always the lesser." Although this seemed to be a practical, even if somewhat pessimistic, analysis of fallen man's society, Hooker countered it with a different sort of practicality: "In matters of greater course, which concern the common good, a generall counsell chosen by all to transact businesses which concerne all, I conceave under favour most sutable to rule and most safe for releif of the wholl."[72] Both Winthrop and Hooker would have concurred with the planters' statement in the Fundamental Orders that their first purpose in "Combination and Confederation" was "to mayntayne and preserve the liberty and purity of the gospell of our Lord Jesus which we now professe, as also the disciplyne of the Churches, which according to the truth of the said

[70] Hooker, "Abstracts of Two Sermons by Rev. Thomas Hooker, From the Shorthand Notes of Mr. Henry Wolcott," transcribed by J. Hammond Trumbull, in *Collections of the Connecticut Historical Society* (Hartford, 1860), I, 20.
[71] Miller, "Thomas Hooker," 38.
[72] *Winthrop Papers*, IV (Boston, M.H.S., 1944), 54, 82.

gospell is now practiced among us." The Connecticut planters went on, however, and stated a second purpose for combining and confederating: "in our Civell Affaires to be guided and governed according to such Lawes, Rules, Orders, and decrees as shall be made, ordered and decreed."[73] Winthrop had tried to make the civil covenant, the agreement made among men to govern themselves, coincide with the national covenant, the agreement a people made with God to be His people. Hooker had always presented the national covenant as a function of both the covenant of grace and the church covenant and thus separate from any sort of civil covenant;[74] the Connecticut writers of the Fundamental Orders had upheld Hooker's distinction, and in making an agreement to conduct "Civell Affaires" they might legitimately consult the body of the people which included civil, natural men. One immediate result of this was that in 1639 when the Orders were promulgated church membership was not a prerequisite for the franchise as it was in Massachusetts.

When Winthrop, Hooker, and other men of the early seventeenth century referred to the body of the people, they were not using an empty figure of speech. The medieval allegory of the state as an institutional man still shaped men's thinking. Winthrop and Hooker thought of the commonwealth as an organic entity, and the problem they faced was how effectively and securely to align the head, Winthrop's "wiser part," and the body. As Hooker saw it, the concept of soul he had known so intimately from study and pastoral experience, the model

[73] *Public Records . . . Connecticut*, I, 21.

[74] Hooker observed in the *Survey*, concerning "the difference betwixt civill and Ecclesiastical power, *Dominuum* and royal Soveraignty may be seated in the one, . . . because they can communicate power from themselves to others, and inable others to attain civill ends, and to accomplish Civill work, and in that respect they are called . . . a humane Creation. But in the Church there is only ministerium received from Christ alone, and therefore they cannot delegate from themselves, and by their own institution an Officer, but only attend the institution of Christ." I, 7.

of the human mind restored to truth by grace, provided the most suitable organic model for the commonwealth. The General Court was the head, the organ of understanding, judging, and remembering, and the people were the heart, the willing, motivating force of the organism. Thus, the organic reason why the people should choose their magistrates and should set limits to their power was "because, by a free choice, the hearts of the people will be more inclined to the love of the persons chosen and more ready to yield obedience."[75] This conception reflected Hooker's confidence in the abilities of himself and his ministerial colleagues to "preserve the liberty and purity of the gospell" in their churches, for the churches, the house in which the civil government was the hangings, were the only adequate regulatory agency of the hearts of the people.

The mark of perfection in man, shown absolutely only in unfallen Adam and Christ, was the unerring relationship between reason and will; the perfect commonwealth—only an ideal in a society of fallen men, but all bodies of laws were ideal—would also be marked by this interaction between heart and head. According to Hooker's second doctrine in the sermon of May 31, 1638, the people were to align their choices, their wills, with God's will, and then they were to yield complete obedience to their chosen magistrates. This particular sermon was only one of several that Hooker preached in the years 1638 and 1639 to direct the hearts of the people as they drew up their orders for a civil government. The people of Hartford and Connecticut were well instructed in the necessity of obedience to their leaders; earlier in May of 1638 Hooker had preached a series of lectures on Ephesians 5:17, "Therefore be you not unwise but understanding what the will of the Lord is," in which he warned his listeners: "Take heed that you do not distract yourselves with more occasions than your

---

[75] Hooker, "Abstracts of Two Sermons," 20.

calling, or God's command, or your abilities is able to bear."[76]
He buttressed this with a more explicit statement on December 26, 1638, in a lecture on Romans 13:5: "Wherefore ye must needs be subject, not only for wrath, but for conscience's sake."[77] In their role as the heart of the commonwealth the people's only active deed was to choose the good—and all magistrates were required by law to be church members, just as in Massachusetts—and then submit to the government of the enlightened understanding. In Connecticut political government was separate from the covenant of grace, but it was modeled upon that spiritual experience. In politics as in conversion the will should submit to right reason.

Consideration of the political sermons Hooker preached in 1638 in addition to the famous one of May 31 supports Perry Miller's conclusion that Hooker cannot be interpreted as a democrat among theocratic oligarchs. He has simply discovered a method of controlling the body of the people which was at once more subtle, better adapted to his own peculiar strengths of personality and technique, and perhaps even more theocratic than the scheme of Winthrop and the Bay ministers and magistrates. Consideration of the political sermons of 1638 clarifies Hooker's role in the creation of the Fundamental Orders; there is no need to presume that he had in any way a direct hand in drawing up these first laws of the new colony. Hooker never descended from his pulpit. He reminded the magistrates of the necessity to engage the affections of the people in the commonwealth, but left them to arrange the mechanics of it, and he repeatedly instructed the people in their duty to acquiesce to the laws their elected leaders made.

The political and social legacy of Hooker's religious insight was thus not "democracy," an irrelevant term concerning

[76] Hooker, "Notes on Sermons by Henry Wolcott, Jr.," transcribed by Douglas Shepard, in Denholm, 413.
[77] Hooker, "Notes on Sermons," 414. This was preached just before the official enactment of the Fundamental Orders.

seventeenth-century Connecticut, but the ideal of a "union of love and concord" between people and magistrates. Hooker came to the wilderness to establish the unity of the saints among his people. His basic definition of this union was theological and ecclesiological, but love was not to be extended to church members alone. Hooker knew from long experience that the God of justice was also the God of mercy, and New England liberties were the gift of a loving God.

SEVEN

The New England Way

THOMAS HOOKER began coming out of the world to Christ when he experienced conversion as a young man at the university, but he knew full well the journey to the city of God would not be completed this side of death. By the summer of 1636 he had come out of the world, almost as far as it was possible to come. The distance between England and Connecticut was more than just an ocean and a hundred miles or so of uncharted wilderness; it was also the distance between a mixed society in which the sinners and saints were jostled willy-nilly together and one in which individual spiritual priorities were to be reflected by social priorities, the distance between the social and intellectual diversity of London and the comparatively stark homogeneity of Hartford. This village on the Connecticut was as near as Hooker would come to re-creating Canaan, the promised land, although he realized that Canaan was only intelligible as a spiritual antitype of the land that Moses sought. Thus, even here in the forest Hooker was not free of the world beyond his congregation, and the workings of history, or providence as he would have seen it, called him back again and again from his refuge to face external threats to his community.

Just a year after Hooker arrived, the first great danger presented itself when "the old Serpent according to his first malice stirred [the Pequot Indians] up against the Church of Christ" in Connecticut.[1] The Pequot War arose through a long series of provocations, retaliations, and counterretaliations—the same

[1] John Underhill, *Newes From America* (London, 1638; facsimile rpt., The Underhill Society of America, 1902), 22.

process of "escalation" so terribly familiar to Americans who came of age in the nineteen-sixties—but the immediate causes were a raid upon Pequot towns by Massachusetts men and subsequent attacks by the Indians upon the river settlements. In 1636 John Oldham, a trader from the Bay, was murdered on his boat near Block Island, the home of the Niantics, allies of the Pequots. A punitive expedition was sent out by the Massachusetts General Court in August under the command of John Endicott, a courageous man but not noted for his tact or policy. Endicott was unable to engage the Indians but ravaged towns on Block Island and the mainland. He merely infuriated the Pequots and failed to impress them with the military power of the English; that winter it was unsafe for men at Saybrook to go farther than a musket-shot from the fort's walls, and on April 23, 1637, the Pequots made a surprise attack on a work party near Wethersfield, killing nine people and capturing two girls.

The skirmishes at Saybrook had been serious enough, but the river plantations could hardly ignore an attack upon one of their central towns. They were a small and isolated group of settlements, and the lack of decisive action might only offer further encouragement to repeated Indian harassment. On May 1 the General Court at Hartford declared war upon the Pequots and levied a ninety-man army under the command of Captain John Mason, a man "tall and Portly, but nevertheless full of Martial Bravery and Vigour."[2] The men convened at Hartford about the fifteenth of May, and Hooker delivered a sermon for their edification and encouragement. His text was Numbers 14:9, "Only rebel ye not against the Lord, neither fear ye the people of the land; for they are bread for us: their defence is departed from them, and the Lord is with us: fear them not." This sermon and his prayers for the absent men

[2] Thomas Prince, Introduction to John Mason, *A Brief History of the Pequot War* (Boston, 1736; facsimile rpt., Ann Arbor, University Microfilms, 1966), iii.

constituted Hooker's personal role in the war; the aggressive tone of this sermon might be inferred from the text, but in view of later events, Hooker was perhaps too successful in encouraging the militia's martial ardor. Samuel Stone went with the army as chaplain and as an adviser about God's will concerning their movements.

Mason was far more successful than Endicott; he staged his own surprise attack upon the Indians by sailing past Pequot country, landing on the shores of Narragansett Bay, and marching westward from there in order to come upon the Pequots from behind. The English together with their Mohegan and Narragansett Indian allies—the Pequots terrorized their red neighbors as well as their white—managed to surround one of the principal Pequot forts just before dawn on a Friday morning in late May. The fort was a circular palisade with entrances at opposite ends blocked by brush; within were wigwams laid out in an orderly fashion on either side of a main street. "There were about foure hundred soules in this Fort, and not above five of them escaped. . . . Great and dolefull was the bloudy fight to the view of young souldiers that never had beene in Warre, to see so many soules lie gasping on the ground so thicke in some places that you could hardly passe along."[3] This was the first massacre of the Indians by the English, and it destroyed the Pequot nation as a threat. The attack on the fort at Pequot was made by Connecticut men, although Mason replaced twenty of his original ninety with a like number of Bay Colony men who were at Saybrook under Captain John Underhill. When the military contingent sent by Massachusetts to prosecute the war arrived, the remaining Pequots were a frightened and disorganized lot of refugees. The war continued for several more months, but it was mostly a matter of collecting brutal trophies. An assortment of severed hands and heads were sent back to Boston to show the Bay Court that they had received their money's worth from their belated mili-

[3] Underhill, 39–40.

tary expedition. If Hooker did not intend this cruel show when he preached that the Indians would be "bread for us," he publicly never said otherwise. Indian brutality was answered with English brutality; Puritan scripturalism balanced the New Testament message of a loving, spiritual community with an Old Testament lesson of severity toward the enemies of Israel.

Before the summer of 1637 was even two-thirds over, Hooker had to return to Massachusetts in order to confront a more subtle and, for him, more serious threat to the peace and concord of his people. While the Old Serpent was encouraging the savages to attack the saints in the flesh, he had apparently also been raising contentions in Boston to subvert the spiritual life of New England. Writing in October 1636, scarcely five months after Hooker's departure, John Winthrop traced various "doubtful disputations" then disturbing the Bay churches to one "Mrs. Hutchinson, a member of the church of Boston, a woman of ready wit and bold spirit, who brought over with her two dangerous errors: 1. That the person of the Holy Ghost dwells in a justified person. 2. That no sanctification can help to evidence to us our justification. — From these two grew many branches."[4] The crisis provoked by Anne Hutchinson and her followers fundamentally reshaped the religious life of New England, and it affected the content of nearly all of Hooker's preaching after 1637. To understand the significance of the controversy, we must digress momentarily from the immediate context of Hooker's life in order to consider the background of the antinomian crisis.

The first erroneous opinion noted by Winthrop implied that a justified man, one of the saints, was more than a mere man because he shared directly and immediately in the godhead. If this were so, then human laws would no longer apply to such a person, but his behavior would be regulated entirely

---

[4] Winthrop, I, 195. Winthrop may be reading later events back into his characterization of Mrs. Hutchinson. Note Cotton's characterization of her in *Way . . . Cleared*, 238.

by the promptings of the spirit within. This was the anti-nomian heresy, which rejected, as a so-called covenant of works, both human law and the divine law as expressed in the decalogue and elsewhere in Scripture. The second of these dangerous errors turned out to be the thornier of the two; all of the ministers rejected the first, but at least one very important theological spokesman in the Bay, John Cotton, affirmed the second. Man "must not trust in any spiritual gift he hath received," said Cotton, "though his mind be inlightened, sometimes to feare, sometimes to joy, to humiliation, to inlargements, to zealous reformation."[5] This, of course, ran counter to Hooker's contention that apparently sanctified behavior was one ground upon which rational charity might judge a man to be a probable saint.

By thus warning men against trusting in their apparent sanctification, Cotton's intent was, first, to emphasize fallen man's inability to save himself and to exalt Christ's free grace as the ultimate manifestation in this world of divine love. Secondly, since "reformation is no assurance that God hath made an everlasting covenant with us," he wished to exhort men to distinguish between spiritual changes caused by the presence of a divine regenerating spirit and those moral changes of human origin. This distinction would enable men to determine if they were truly saved or self-deluding hypocrites. "Common graces may and will deceive you, a man may have all these, and yet not prize Christ, as his chiefest good."[6] This was all well and good, but Mrs. Hutchinson and her followers subverted the doctrine by saying, in effect, that sanctification, living a moral life, was irrelevant to salvation. In their hands the second of Winthrop's "dangerous errors" reinforced the first; it doesn't matter what a man does, only what motions of the spirit he might feel within himself. The Massachusetts

[5] Cotton, from *Christ the Fountaine*, in Miller and Johnson, I, 383.
[6] Cotton, "A Sermon at Salem," in Ziff, ed., *Cotton . . . the Churches* 62; Miller and Johnson, I, 333.

antinomians did not in fact reject morality or even relax their moral sense in any way, but their solipsistic doctrine looked in this direction, whether they admitted it or not.

Winthrop was probably mistaken in claiming Anne Hutchinson brought her errors over with her, although on board ship in 1634 she did display to the Reverend Zechariah Symmes a taste for dubious theological speculation. Most of her errors seem to have been nurtured in the free air of the New World by some of the subtler doctrines preached by John Cotton. Mrs. Hutchinson emigrated in order to follow Cotton and his preaching, and in New England as in Old she preferred his sermons to all others. She was a midwife, "wherein she was not only skillful and helpful, but readily fell into good discourse with the women about their spiritual estates."[7] These good discourses rapidly became regular meetings of women in her home in order to discuss the sermons of the previous sabbath or lecture-day. Mrs. Hutchinson led these discussions, working from notes taken in church, and they offered an opportunity to explicate her own understanding of the nature of conversion and salvation. She soon realized that there were important differences between the doctrines of John Wilson, the church's pastor, and Mr. Cotton, its teacher. She tended more and more to criticize Wilson as a legal preacher who preached a covenant of works—he taught the necessity of sanctification for the assurance of justification—and at the same time she distorted and exaggerated Cotton's insistence upon man's fundamental passivity in salvation.

These meetings came to be comparatively large, seventy or eighty people at times, and they began to include people from nearby towns as well as from Boston. With the presence of members of other congregations (although not all who attended were formal church members), the critical discussion of ministers expanded to a consideration of most of the notable

[7] Cotton, *Way . . . Cleared*, 239.

preachers of New England, and they all failed to measure up to the standards of John Cotton and the covenant of grace. Many of the men who were attracted to Mrs. Hutchinson's teaching, either through attendance at her meetings or through hearing their wives' reports, were respected merchants and artisans, and their support provided political muscle for antinomian views. Eminent supporters of her activities included Henry Vane, governor of the Bay in 1636–1637, William Coddington, an assistant, and John Wheelwright, her brother-in-law and a minister who had been silenced in England for his nonconformity. The group's most eminent supporter, however, was one who realized only too late what the meetings in Mrs. Hutchinson's house were all about; Cotton insisted for as long as possible that these gatherings were exemplary of the high level of piety in Boston, and in the meantime the Hutchinsonians justified their doctrines by ascribing them to Cotton.

Sometime in the late winter or early spring of 1636 Thomas Shepard, then living in Newtown with Hooker, wrote to Cotton asking him to clear several problematic doctrines which had been supposedly of his teaching. Shepard warned his colleague, "You may meet in time with some such members (though I know none nor judge any) as may doe your people and ministry hurt, before you know it." Shepard saw at that time, or thought he did, exactly where the danger was, and he attempted to enlist Cotton's support for ministerial consensus in order to forestall quarrels "which are secretly begun and I feare will flame out unless they be quenched in time."[8] Cotton answered politely, if not in sufficient detail, and dismissed the idea of secret quarrels as well as the possibility of doctrinal controversy: "But I suppose wee differ not here in, nor any of my Brethren if wee understood one another. Nor

[8] David Hall, ed., *The Antinomian Controversy, 1636–1638: A Documentary History* (Middletown, Wesleyan Univ. Press, 1968), 29. Hall's collection of primary sources supersedes that of Charles Francis Adams, Jr.

doe I discerne (though after diligent search) that any of our members, (brethren or sisters) doe hold forth Christ in any other way."[9] Cotton agreed less with his brother ministers than he believed, for Shepard's was only the first query he received about his views. Peter Bulkeley of Concord wrote later on in the year, and there were probably other, unrecorded conferences and letters; finally in December 1636, "the rest of the ministers, taking offence at some doctrines delivered by Mr. Cotton, . . . drew out sixteen points, and gave them to him, entreating him to deliver his judgment directly in them . . . Some doubts he well cleared, but in some things he gave not satisfaction."[10] Cotton was becoming testy over the continuing examination; his prefatory statement to his answers of the sixteen points ended with the usual avowal of learned humility, but the first sentence referred to the questions as "interrogatories" and likened them to the high priest's questioning of Christ.

While the ministers were sounding out Cotton, the situation in the Boston church was becoming more explosive. An attempt to call John Wheelwright as a second teacher in the church was defeated through the opposition of Winthrop and Wilson, and the Hutchinsonian party subjected Wilson to a variety of humiliations in revenge—dozing during his sermons, walking out of church when he rose to preach, etc. Cotton and some members of the church had even attempted to admonish Wilson formally for making "a very sad speech of the conditions of our churches" before the General Court. The magistrates called a fast to be held in all the Bay churches on January 19, 1637, for, among other reasons, "the dissensions in our churches."[11] The fast was a conventional act of piety in which a faithful people sought divine assistance, but it was also an attempt by the court to remind the people of the possible consequences of their dissension by linking with it troubles

[9] Hall, 33. [10] Winthrop, I, 206–7.
[11] Ibid., 208.

in Germany, England, and with the Indians. This attempt at persuading the various disputants to lower their voices failed absolutely because of a sermon preached by John Wheelwright during the afternoon of January 19 in Boston.

Wheelwright's sermon was the turning point in the antinomian controversy: after it, the troubles in the Boston church could no longer be settled informally, and legal proceedings by the court together with united action by all of the ministers were required to reestablish peace. Whether intentionally or not, Wheelwright's sermon was an insult to the orthodox ministry and the members of the court. The very fact that a fast had been called for proved they were all under a covenant of works: "Must we especially looke after the removing those evill things, and procuring those good things? This an hipocrite will do, . . . those that do not know the Lord Jesus, they are usually given most unto fasting."[12] Papists and Pharisees, all under a covenant of works to a man, were well-known for their fasting, Wheelwright pointed out; so much for those who believed in any spiritual efficacy in a fast. More alarming than the aspersions cast upon the colony's ministers and magistrates were Wheelwright's exhortations to those who "belong to the election of grace." "If we would have the Lord Jesus to be aboundantly present with us, we must all of us prepare for battell and come out against the enimyes of the Lord, and if we do not strive, those under a covenant of works will prevaile."[13] Although Wheelwright warned that "the weapons of our warfare are not carnall but spirituall," the rhetorical weight in his lengthy development of the spiritual combat metaphor fell upon "warfare" rather than "spirituall."

The Hutchinsonians were quick to grasp the nuances of Wheelwright's sermon. It was the custom in the Bay Colony churches before the antinomian affair to allow questions from the congregation after the delivery of the sermon; the self-

[12] Hall, 156–57. [13] Hall, 158.

styled free-grace party seized these opportunities to harass and undermine the ministers with whom they disagreed. Thomas Weld reported,

> Now after our Sermons were ended at our publike Lectures, you might have seen halfe a dozen Pistols discharged at the face of the preacher. (I meane) so many objections made by the opinionists in the open Assembly against our doctrine delivered, if it suited not their new fancies, to the marvellous weakning of holy truths delivered (what in them lay) in the hearts of all the weaker sort.[14]

The emergence of an active, publicly disputatious minority turned secret quarrels into a crisis; by interfering with the effective transmission of the Word from the ministers to those people seeking grace, the antinomian truth squads seriously disrupted the history of redemption as perceived by the orthodox. The Reformation had reopened the channels of grace by restoring powerful preaching to its central role in the church services, and the Hutchinsonians threatened to reverse this achievement by rejecting the orthodox view of salvation as a covenant of works. These attacks were at the same time a danger to the prestige of the ministry as they ridiculed the concept of the preacher as an ambassador of God. If salvation was accomplished by an immediate union with Christ, what need of a ministry educated in order to reveal Christ in Scripture?

There was a powerful anti-intellectual tendency in antinomism; the opinionists responded eagerly to Wheelwright's quotation of Proverbs 26:12 in his sermon, "Seest thou a man wise in his owne conceit, more hope there is of a foole then of him." Edward Johnson, no friend to heterodoxy, portrayed one of their spokesmen as saying, "Come along with me, . . . i'le bring you to a Woman that Preaches better Gospell then any of your black-coates that have been at the Ninne-versity."[15] The antinomians' tactics in defense of their beliefs

[14] Hall, 209.   [15] Johnson, 127.

ultimately verged onto political anarchy as well as religious
disorder. There was nearly a riot at the election of May 1637,
and Boston militiamen who were to join that year's expedition
against the Pequots almost refused to go when John Wilson
was named as the military chaplain. The General Court began
to assert its control in the spring of 1637 by rejecting Vane
from the magistracy and by politically isolating the deputies
from Boston. The court then moved to enlist the support of the
ministry in order to reduce the dissenters' sustaining theological core; the court consented to the ministers' wish that the
first synod in New England be called to meet on August 30,
1637. This, then, was the situation when Thomas Hooker
arrived in Boston on August 5. He had traveled by way of
Providence, where he had conferred with Roger Williams about
the Indian troubles—it is tantalizing to wonder what these two
old friends and antagonists said to each other about the Bay's
present religious troubles. With Hooker were Samuel Stone
and John Wilson, who brought back "a part of the skin and
lock of hair of Sassacus and his brother, and five other Pequod
Sachems."[16]

The main business in the month of August before the synod
convened was to persuade John Cotton to see the dangers of his
stand and to return him to consensus with the rest of the New
England ministry. Once again Hooker had been brought out
of his congregation to arbitrate Bay Colony dissensions, but
the explosive antinomian affair was very unlike the previous
comparatively polite disagreements among the colony's leaders.
Instead of a closet controversy like that between Dudley and
Winthrop, the Hutchinsonians initiated a crisis which involved
the lower classes as well as the social and economic elite and

[16] Winthrop, I, 229. The Indian problems Hooker and Williams discussed concerned the disposition of the few surviving Pequots among
Narragansetts and Mohegans. These two tribes were united only in their
rivalry with the Pequots, and after the war they often quarreled. Williams was the white spokesman for Narragansett interests, and the
Mohegans dealt through the River Plantations.

which generated overt dissent in at least half a dozen Bay communities. Mrs. Hutchinson's eventual fate was clear by the summer of 1637; the colony had exiled Williams when he began to recruit activist followers of his opinions, and barring a last-minute repentance, the lady was almost sure to follow. John Cotton was a different case, however, for he never explicitly subscribed to Mrs. Hutchinson's excesses, and he was, after all, the one Bay Colony divine who enjoyed a large reputation in the home country—only Hooker was his rival. Fearing for their patent, the Massachusetts leaders could not afford to scandalize their English supporters by banishing Cotton. He had to be—or at least seem to be—brought into line with the rest of the ministers, and in this effort Hooker's reputation and his talents for disputation, persuasion, and diplomacy were indispensable.

By the middle of the summer of 1637 the points of difference between the orthodox ministers and Cotton were whittled down to three questions. The problem was that as the ministers backed Cotton into a theological corner, he simply reworked his previous answers into more elusive and obscurantist terms; of all the surviving documents of the antinomian crisis, *A Conference Mr. John Cotton Held at Boston with the Elders of New England*, containing his answers to the three questions of mid-1637, most nearly justifies Charles Francis Adams, Jr.'s characterization of the controversy as one "carried on in a jargon which has become unintelligible."[17] After Hooker arrived, the elders renewed the task of reducing Cotton to some semblance of agreement with themselves, and in the month of preparation for the synod they were finally successful, at least up to a point. They gave Cotton a new set of questions, five this time, which were more narrowly phrased and which enabled Cotton to answer in a satisfactory manner. The answers were acceptable because, apparently realizing the gravity of the

[17] Charles Francis Adams, Jr., *Three Episodes of Massachusetts History* (Boston, Houghton, 1893), I, 367.

situation at last, Cotton was also willing to compromise his expressions, if not the beliefs themselves.

During the whole course of examining Cotton's doctrines, the issues changed and clarified themselves from their initial statement. The first questions were based upon versions of Mrs. Hutchinson's errors and attempted to discover Cotton's agreement or nonagreement with them; by August of 1637 the questions were over differences of opinion between Cotton and the other ministers regarding the nature of the meaning and process of salvation. Cotton emphasized man's passivity in salvation and made a complete separation between common and saving grace; for Cotton there was no such thing as preparation. The first act in the drama of redemption was Christ's union with the elect soul, and even faith came subsequent to that. As Cotton viewed it, Adam's fall was such a complete disaster for man that regeneration was possible only by re-creating man in the image of Christ; therefore, since no acts of fallen man could be holy—only Christ did holy acts in man —proof of salvation had to be obtained by a direct awareness of the divine presence.

Although Hooker, the chief architect of the preparationist theology in New England, agreed with Cotton on man's passivity in salvation, he conceived of regeneration as the reawakening of man in the image of prelapsarian Adam and the perfecting of him in the image of Christ considered as the second Adam. In the process of regeneration God restored man's ability to perform holy action; grace made man act, for "by the worke of his Spirit hee doth bring all the riches of His grace into the soule truly humbled, so that the heart cannot but receive the same, and give answer thereto, and give an echo of the subjection of itselfe to be governed thereby."[18]

[18] Hooker, *Vocation*, 34. The difference between Hooker and Cotton here is very similar to that between Shepard and Cotton as delineated by Jesper Rosenmeier, "New England's Perfection: The Image of Adam and the Image of Christ in the Antinomian Crisis, 1634 to 1638," *William and Mary Quarterly* 27 (1970), 435-59.

God prepared man for regeneration through forms of common grace, and man cooperated in the preparation, but for Hooker the crucial point in the process was God's offer of saving grace as the ability to believe and man's instantaneous response of faith. Union with Christ, "ingrafting" in Hooker's earlier terminology, began with that and was completed only after death. In Cotton's version the union with Christ was perfect and complete; man received his whole portion of Christ in that one moment of regeneration. Ingrafting into Christ, as Hooker saw it, was perfect only in the sense that it perfected the image of Adam in man; the regenerate man gained a strength of grace which Adam never had.

> If mercy should put a man into the same estate that Adam was, a man should bring himself into the same misery that Adam was brought into. But there is that fullnesse of that mercy that is in Christ, that it will bestow all good needful for me; so also, it will dispose of that good in me so that Satan shall never prevail, . . . but the Lord shall rule me forever.[19]

In spite of his thinking that, once accomplished, man's salvation was irreversible, Hooker maintained that ingrafting into Christ was progressive in time and experience after the reception of faith, just as preparation was before. Man's holy acts, his sanctification, therefore revealed more of Christ, and, more important, they supplied evidence of justification. The initial presence of Christ might well be shadowy to human understandings, but holy actions both argued this presence and in time tended to clarify it.

These differences of opinion between Cotton and Hooker were not theological nit-picking, for they had important intellectual and practical consequences. Cotton's version of the nature of salvation encouraged antinomians like Mrs. Hutchin-

---

[19] Hooker, *Vocation*, 42.

son, but more alarming to Hooker were its consequences for
the admission of members to the churches. If one had to explain one's assurance of saving faith, Cotton's emphasis upon
direct knowledge of Christ might lead to all sorts of direct
revelations, inner voices, etc.—and did so lead Anne Hutchinson. It would also restrict participation in the church, and thus
eventually in the civil government, to the most imaginative,
hypersensitive, and introverted members of the community.
Besides being a doctrinal crisis, the antinomian affair provoked
a crisis over church government. Prior to 1637 the New England Way had been defined upon the whole pragmatically and
inexactly, but the difficulties in dealing with Cotton and the
antinomians called for a more careful definition of the relationship between churches. This took a decade to produce, but
a new period in the intellectual life of New England began
in the first nine months of 1637 with the conferences between
the ministers and John Cotton.

Hooker, Shepard, and the other preparationists never arrived
at an absolute consensus with Cotton; eleven years later when
Cotton reported his answers to the five questions of August,
he covered over residual disagreements, saying, "How far there
arose any consent or dissent about these questions, between my
fellow brethren (the elders of these churches) and myself, it is
not material now to particularize."[20] He was able to maintain
modified expressions of his beliefs, but Hooker and the rest of
the ministers held the field. When the synod convened on August 30, Hooker and Peter Bulkeley, who after Hooker and
Shepard was the next leading preparationist theologian in New
England, were elected moderators, and the first self-definition
of New England Puritanism was created by ministers in agreement with their position. The elders' self-definition was of
necessity a negative statement; with Cotton returned to the
ranks in August and Wheelwright lying under sentence of

[20] Cotton, *Way . . . Cleared*, 233.

banishment, the synod moved against the popular wing of the antinomian heresy by drawing up and condemning a list of eighty-two errors and nine "unsavoury speeches." The New England ministers had to define their position at this time in terms of what they did not believe because they had so narrowly escaped a disastrous confrontation over the doctrines they did hold. Cotton made one or two scrupulous protests over some of the particular errors, but he quickly fell back into line and admitted he was mistaken. The resulting list of errors and unsavory speeches formed an explicit balance to the implicit negation the ministers had made earlier by fleeing from Old England; their rejection of the Laudian, formalist church laid out one parameter of their faith, and their confutation of the antinomian enthusiasm defined its limit in the opposite direction. There was neither salvation in human works without faith nor security in a supposed faith without sanctifying works.

No one of the Hutchinsonians, not even Anne herself, subscribed to all eighty-two errors, but the antinomian heresy tended to fragment into a plurality of diverse heretics entertaining a variety of opinions. The basic problem facing the ministers in the synod was not to dispose of particular religious dissenters, which they had no civil or religious power to do, but to restore a credible image of themselves as a spiritual brotherhood of godly preachers united in the one truth. This they did under the leadership of Hooker and Bulkeley, defining themselves and their truth by imagining and refuting the whole spectrum of errors which could be inferred from the antinomians' known tenets. After they had established their position *vis-à-vis* the popular wing of the antinomians in this way, they turned their attention to the ministerial supporters of Mrs. Hutchinson. They gave public expression to the private conferences with Cotton and also gave the stubborn Wheelwright one last chance—although there was little likelihood that he would concede anything at this late date—by raising five points in question "put into such expressions as Mr. Cotton and they agreed, but Mr. Wheelwright did not."[21] These questions were similar to but not the same as the ones Cotton had answered privately; the important fact about them is that they indicate the extent of Cotton's concession to his opponents. Earlier Cotton had maintained that the soul's union with Christ was "not without, nor before the habit (or gift) of faith, but before the act of faith"; in the synod "the consent was, that there was no marriage union with Christ before actual faith, which is more than habitual."[22]

On the last day of the meeting points of practice were resolved; the first resolution condemning set meetings of large groups of women to discuss sermons, clearly aimed at Mrs. Hutchinson, and the other three strengthened the authority of ministers over their churches and of churches over recalcitrant individual members. The synod broke up on September 22. Its success in restoring the public image of a harmonious ministry was evidenced by the fact that four days later in Boston

> Mr. Davenport (as he had been before requested by the assembly) preached out of Phil. 3:16, wherein he laid down the occasions of differences among Christians, etc., and declared the effect and fruit of the assembly, and, with much wisdom and sound argument, persuaded to unity.[23]

In November and later in March of 1638 Wheelwright and Mrs. Hutchinson were banished, and Mrs. Hutchinson was excommunicated from the Boston church with no great clamor on the part of their erstwhile supporters. Some of their followers were also banished, and most were disenfranchised and

---

[21] Winthrop, I, 233.

[22] Cotton, *Way . . . Cleared*, 227; Winthrop, I, 233.

[23] Winthrop, I, 235. Davenport was a friend of Cotton's, opposed to preparationist theology, but also strongly opposed to antinomian enthusiasm. His attempt at peacemaking in this sermon was less than successful.

disarmed. By bringing the Boston church, a hotbed of heresy and sedition as late as June and July of 1637, back into line with the other churches of New England in less than six months, the synod proved that the congregational system of particular independent churches was feasible. The right hand of fellowship when given synodical form was powerful enough to preserve unity of doctrine and practice in the churches.

When the synod was over, Hooker went home before the trial of Mrs. Hutchinson began. That, after all, was Bay Colony business and not his, but the experience of the antinomian controversy was not forgotten. The events of 1637 shaped Thomas Hooker's pulpit career for the remaining decade of his life. He was not alone in his sensitivity to the implications of the crisis, for the major ministerial disputants went on justifying themselves for years—nearly half of Shepard's collected works, for example, are detailed refutations of the grounds and practices of antinomianism, and Cotton went on defending moderate versions of his early opinions. It was Cotton's ultimate refusal to accept the preparationist theory of conversion which in many ways led to a subsequent passion for elaborately systematized descriptions of religious experience upon the part of the orthodox ministers. In addition the drawn-out debates had raised such heartburnings among the ministers that the synod's show of unity was in 1637 and 1638 little more than a formality. In an undated marginal entry to the manuscript of his autobiography Shepard noted angrily, "Mr. Cotton repents not, but is hid only," and Hooker had "melancholick suspicions" about Cotton's continued defense of Mrs. Hutchinson.[24]

When Hooker was safely home at Hartford, he turned his attention to the problems faced by his people in erecting their new civil order; his backstage role, so to speak, in the creation

[24] Shepard, "Autobiography," 386; Hooker letter quoted by Thomas Hutchinson, *The History of the Colony and Province of Massachusetts Bay*, ed. Lawrence Shaw Mayo (Cambridge, Mass., Harvard Univ. Press, 1936), I, 63.

of the Fundamental Orders has been discussed in the previous chapter, but it is important to recognize the possible effects of his recent involvement in the Bay Colony's disorders upon his attitudes toward Connecticut order. When he first arrived in Massachusetts in 1633, Hooker was disturbed by the unregulated exercise of authority by the magistrates: "After Mr. Hooker's coming over," said William Hubbard, "it was observed that many of the freemen grew to be very jealous of their liberties."[25] When, however, he exhorted the men of Hartford the following spring to "take heed that you do not distract yourselves with more occasion than your calling, or God's command, or your abilities is able to bear,"[26] he reminded the commonalty of their civil and spiritual limitations, thus redressing the balance between the rights of the freemen and the authority of the magistrates. In spite of his continuing distrust of unlimited authority, Hooker after 1638 preached submission to the spiritual and civil powers; during these years he consolidated his control over his congregation at the same time as the civil government became more and more conservative about extending the franchise.

His concern for Connecticut's emerging government did not distract him from the primary issue of the moment; before June 1638 he had begun to preach the sermons which were issued posthumously in two volumes as *The Application of Redemption*. This book was Hooker's final statement, both in point of time and in manner of expression, of his doctrine of preparation, and he evidently wished it to supersede his other earlier books covering the same material.[27] He did not modify

[25] Hubbard, 165.

[26] Hooker, "Notes on Sermons," 413.

[27] Thomas Goodwin and Philip Nye in their epistle "To the Reader" of The Application of Redemption state that Hooker's previous works, "having been taken by an unskilful hand, which upon his recess into those remoter parts of the World, was bold without his privity or consent to print and publish them," were "utterly deformed and mis-represented in multitudes of passages; And in the rest but imperfectly and crudely set forth" (sig. C3ᵛ).

the ideas preached over a decade before and published under the titles of *The Soules Preparation, Humiliation,* and *Vocation for Christ*—he even used some of the same scriptural texts and illustrated his doctrines with the same favorite tropes— but he did tailor their expression for a postantinomian New England.

The first important change was simply one of emphasis. In the earlier preachings on conversion he struck a balance between natural man's passivity in the work of salvation and his concurrent need for voluntaristic action, but he was more forceful when urging men to react under the influence of preparing grace than when reminding them of their essential helplessness before union with Christ. This rhetorical, if not doctrinal, imbalance was what laid him open to the Hutchinsonians' charge of preaching a covenant of works. Now in the 1640s he was much more careful to articulate the precise relationship between supernatural and natural action in the process of salvation. The very titles of the books discussing conversion indicate what he has done; *The Soules Preparation* is a much more ambiguous title than the later version. It can be read as the soul's preparing itself for salvation as well as the soul's being prepared by Christ, whereas when Hooker came to define Application, there was no such uncertainty about the origin of the spiritual energy involved in salvation: "Application is that special part of our Recovery from our lost Condition, whereby all that Spiritual Good which Christ hath Purchased for us, is made Ours."[28]

During his controversy with his fellow ministers, Cotton had continually represented the works of preparation, and even faith itself, as sanctifying works coming after the saving union with Christ. At the same time he insisted that repentance for one's sins and humiliation, the two main stages of preparation according to Hooker, were works of common grace and thus no evidence of a justified faith; for that matter, even that moral

[28] Hooker, *Application*, 4.

behavior which was a sanctifying work might be produced in hypocrites by restraining common grace, and it could never be a sure sign of the presence of saving grace. By thus disregarding the order of the workings of redemption in man (as understood by Hooker and like-minded divines) and by denying the epistemological value of *any* human experience, Cotton substituted for Hooker's description of conversion as a psychological process an abstract, theological description. The nature of the differences between Cotton and Hooker is revealed by comparing their emphasis on the idea of the covenant of grace as the divinely established basis of redemption. Cotton was far more of a covenant theologian than Hooker, and he articulated the conversion process in terms of the covenant as revealed in Scripture. Hooker discovered in Scripture, as Cotton and the rest of the Puritans had, divine revelation that entrance into the covenant was the method of salvation, but for him Scripture was the means of regeneration as well, at least when the Spirit accompanied the Word. In order to understand the process of conversion and thus receive assurance of personal salvation, Hooker insisted that man need not concern himself too much with the nature and terms of the covenant as God has framed it—it was enough to know that Christ would save man—but that he ought to observe the effects of supernatural work in natural man. Hooker, unlike Cotton, rarely spoke of the covenant, even though it was the divine basis for human salvation, for man knows God not directly but reflexively by analysis of God's work in himself.

Hooker countered Cotton's attack on his theory of conversion and regeneration by revising in *The Application* his usual order of explication of the conversion process. *The Application* was divided into ten books, and not until the third book did Hooker explain preparation in detail. He began by affirming with Cotton the Calvinist theological axioms concerning man's passivity in conversion, but he explicated them in terms of the psychology of both fallen and regenerated man. The first two books preached doctrines emphasizing the primacy of Christ's role in the redemption of fallen humanity, and in the uses he drew from them, Hooker discussed the stage of vocation, God's calling of man which initiated his rebirth as a spiritual creature. Hooker granted as doctrine that "Christ hath purchased all spirituall good for His" and that "Christ puts all his into possession of all that Good that he hath purchased for them,"[29] but he explained Christ's purchasing and his giving in terms of the human mind. Of a certainty supernatural truth could not be experienced by natural man; no man "can challenge any interest in any Spirituall Good in Christ, or can bring in any proof to himself of any Spirituall Good received . . . before he beleeve." The perceived experience of spiritual good was reserved for those who had been regenerated, "But (I assume) no man can be under the Covenant of Grace that is not under the Condition of Faith, for it is that only which brings him into it, and estates him in it."[30] If faith thus preceded union with Christ and was a prerequisite to it, then it was faith, and not union with Christ as Cotton would have it, which was the essential fact in redemption, and in addition there was a divine working in the human soul prior to union. Since faith was created in the soul before union with Christ in the covenant, there were clearly two different sorts of gracious acts being performed in the soul, those culminating in faith and those beginning with it. Hooker was thus able to refute Cotton's confusion of evangelical preparation and sanctification and to establish both the possibility and the necessity of describing grace in terms of the motions of the soul. Divine causes could only be understood in terms of human effects.

At this point in Hooker's explication of the first doctrine of *The Application of Redemption*, his Hartford congregation must have been aware of his strategy. He was not simply restating his doctrine of conversion in terms acceptable to John

[29] Ibid., 5, 71. [30] Ibid., 23, 25.

Cotton; he was launching into a full-scale attack on his Boston colleague. When his listeners heard Hooker warn, "To affirm that the Spirit should say to any man that he is in a state of Grace, when he is in a state of Sin, that he is justified when he is Condemned, is little less than Blasphemy," they knew whose ox had been gored. Lest there be any doubt about whom he referred to and why this opinion was so dangerous, he moved into a vigorous and scathing rejection of the consequences of Cotton's theory of conversion.

> Hence its cleer: That manner and order that men have devised to make known the mind of God to a man, and to give comfort to the soul in distress, being cross to these truths now delivered, is an Erroneous and False way: As for example, you being in distress about your Sins, and lying under the Spirit of Bondage, you must first lay Christ in the bottom, lay him in the foundation, Christ must first be yours, and so united to you, and your Sins forgiven by him, before you have any Faith or gracious qualification wrought in you; This Opinion that sayes, That Christ may be united to the Soul, and so he be Justified and Adopted before he have any Faith; it is a dangerous Opinion, a desperate Delusion; that I may say no worse of it. Mark what follows, here's the plot of all prophaneness, the ground of all looseness and familism: A man may have Christ and be Justified and Adopted while he is without Faith, and therefore while he is under the power of his Sins and the Spirit of God may witness this, And hence though a man fall into any Sin, or live in any sin whatever it be, he may have recourse to this Revelation, this witness of the Spirit, and that's enough.[31]

In all of Hooker's writings this is the closest thing to a personal attack. He would often apply his sermons to particular sinners in the audiences but never in published works with such

---

[31] Ibid., 28, 29.

acridness, and even in polemic works he kept the argument out of the realm of personalities.

This unusual and even startling attack upon a historically identifiable person reveals an antagonistic undertone below Hooker's publicly correct and brotherly relationship with Cotton. It has often been surmised that Hooker left the Bay because of rivalry with Cotton; the outcome of the antinomian affair shows that each man was stubborn enough and talented enough to hold up his own end of an argument, and at the same time each proved his Christianity by forgiving, if not by forgetting. Hooker's indignation at Cotton in 1638 and 1639 eventually was turned against the Hutchinsonian remnants as "false Teachers" who "make a trade to wind into mens affections and win them to the entertainment of their erroneous conceits,"[32] but it was probably just as well that the two men were no longer preaching in adjacent towns.

Hooker spent several years in preaching over *The Application of Redemption*, and when he had finished, he had made preparationist theology a permanent element of New England religion. He also worked to stamp out lingering traces of antinomianism by preaching two very different series of sermons. The first and shorter of these was later published in 1651 under the title of *The Saints Dignitie and Dutie*. This was made up of six sermons on different texts but clearly conceived as a unified series, and its intent was to clarify the paradoxical nature of grace whereby only Christ's supernatural working could save men although He insisted at the same time that men must save themselves. The ultimate purpose of this treatise was to refute the antinomian contention that works of sanctification were irrelevant in the redemptive scheme. More immediately for Hooker's congregation, it held out to the unregenerate the image of human fulfillment through Christ and instructed the

---

[32] Hooker, *Application 2*, 591. As seen from my quotations from Cotton's *Way . . . Cleared*, he still maintained his old position in a quieter, less aggressive manner.

saints in the necessity of an unceasing and internally consistent moral behavior. "The heart will be inlarged, the soul quickened, and there will be a change in the whole life and conversation, if ever faith take place in a man," said Hooker, once again pointing out that conversion was an emergence of the divine pattern into the human. Hooker was quite capable of instructing his people that they should be ready to lovingly embrace damnation in order to glorify God, but *The Saints Dignitie*, like several of Hooker's other late works, was a book of hope and joy. By believing in the Scriptural promises of salvation, Hooker said, "the promise is made ours," and "all strength to obey commeth by promise." Divine union with the faithful soul brought man "the joy of the Lord" by enabling him to perform holy works in this life, to "imitate the actions of faithfull Abraham."[33]

The other long work upon which he labored, in many ways the most speculative and radical of his life, was *A Comment Upon Christs Last Prayer in the Seventeenth of John.* "The more eminent Matter of these Sermons, [is] *our mysticall Union with God and Christ*; a Subject but *rarely* handled by Divines."[34] Hooker had formerly discussed the stages of redemption coming after justification, i.e., adoption and glorification, in *The Soules Exaltation*, but his treatment of the matter is far more complex and lengthy. The antinomians had maintained that a "man is united to Christ onely, by the worke of the Spirit upon him, without any act of his."[35] The implication of this was that man could be saved but not regenerated in the usual sense, since even after justification he remained entirely passive. *The Saints Dignitie* argued that this was untrue for the re-created saint in a moral sense, and *A Comment* went to the root of the matter to prove it untrue in a spiritual sense also.

[33] Hooker, *Saints Dignitie*, 166, 88, 166.
[34] Thomas Goodwin and Philip Nye, "To the Reader," in *Comment*, sig. Br.
[35] Hall, 202.

Although Hooker did not usually discuss covenant theory directly in his sermons, he inevitably fell back on it when his beliefs were threatened in their foundations, for he, like the rest of his New England colleagues, built his faith upon it. So here again he rehearsed the familiar story of the fall, the loss of the first covenant, the advent of Christ, and the gift of the new covenant. He sharpened the distinctions between the two covenants—distinctions which the antinomians had blurred with their accusations of preaching a covenant of works. "As the first *Adam* conveyed his sin and wrath by a covenant of works: the second must convey holiness and life by a covenant of Grace, and the free gift thereof." In this new covenant God offered a different and more perfect form of grace than he had offered Adam: "*This grace is Inward and spiritual,* not that which orders a mans carriage in regard of himself," as Adam's did.[36] Man was not simply re-created by Christ in the process of regeneration but made after a new and grander model than that of unfallen Adam.

The vital difference in regenerate man, as Hooker had explained when he first began preaching his final and definitive statements on experimental religion, was that in giving man faith, God also gave him "*sanctified reason,* or reason exercised about divine truths." This was supposedly different from natural human reason, for "being exercised about the Word and Work of the Spirit, it brings in the light of the truth as a mighty stream with more strength and plainness to the heart."[37] This gracious gift of sanctified reason made possible man's first act of faith, the answer to the divine offer; it also enabled man to perform subsequent holy acts and gave him the power to perceive divine truth in himself and in the world. In effect, although Hooker did not explicitly make the point, sanctified reason was a new sense which enabled regenerate man to perceive a whole new order of reality hidden from fallen man: "Before a man can discern spirituall objects, he must have

[36] Hooker, *Comment,* 93, 88.   [37] Hooker, *Application,* 35.

spirituall light; therefore wicked men being (as all hypocrites are) but bare nature, and wanting spirituall light, are not able to perceive and discern the things of God."[38] As the saint beheld God's glory in this spiritual light, his ideas of the divine were made fact within himself, for "not only a mans apprehension comes to be exercised, . . . but the quality and nature of the thing, comes so to be taken into our observation and consideration that the heart comes to be experimentally affected therewith."[39]

What made *A Comment Upon Christs Last Prayer* Hooker's most speculative and visionary work was his explication of the intimate relationship between the soul's sanctification in this life and his glorification in the next. In the covenant of grace, "Here is the suburbs of happinesse, and of the New Jerusalem. Grace is the *Porch*, as it were, Glory the *Palace*."[40] The saints of Hartford were indeed creating the heavenly city, but it was a city in the heart where bit by bit men assembled that perfect community of affection which would only be realized after death. Hooker showed them the glimmerings of "the unconceivable beauty and brightness of the place" in themselves, and thus gave them the strength to bear up under the trials of this world. The terrors of preparation, the agony and despair of humiliation were thus revealed as culminating in this communication of "al His glorious excellencies to the Soul."[41] This image of the heaven in the soul of justified man, however, could have been a terrible hindrance to the poor doubting Christians of Hartford. If experiences like these were required for assurance of salvation, who could ever hope to find peace, who could ever presume so much as to offer themselves for church membership?

Hooker turned these sermons to an evangelical advantage by pointing out to these troubled spirits how weak a faith

---

[38] Hooker, *Saints Dignitie*, 208; cf. *Vocation*, 74.
[39] Hooker, *Comment*, 371.   [40] Ibid., 79.
[41] Ibid., 527, 524.

would qualify to set the soul upon the road to the New Jerusalem. "Our Savior hath a speciall care for those that shal beleeve on him, even in the worst condition of their Unbeleef," he told them in the very first of the sermons in this series,[42] Even a rational, historical faith was a sign of encouragement that they were enroute to an experimental, saving faith. The suburbs of happiness were large in Hooker's map of the heavenly city, and this was the radical element in *A Comment* and in most of the pulpit statements of Hooker's last years. His sermonic response to the antinomian crisis was buoyant and encouraging; victory in the synod almost seemed a sign of God's benevolence toward the people of New England, and the gates of the church were expectantly opened for those still outside. Had a man historical faith? Fine, let him and those like him once realize that "they are not yet in a right state, and that all their vain hopes and imaginarie conceits are false, . . . there were a great deal of likelihood that they would obtaine true grace, and so consequently come to be everlastingly saved."[43] *A Comment Upon Christs Last Prayer* revealed to man a world of grace which was attainable not through mystic "witnesses of the Spirit" as the antinomians had claimed but through faith in action. In the 1640s in Connecticut the visibility of saintliness—although it required constant nurture, and recalcitrants continued to draw their share or reproofs—was a source of measured satisfaction to the pastor of Hartford.

Hooker also published during these years a curious book that is somewhat out of the stream of his central concern for experimental piety. *The Paterne of Perfection* appeared in London in 1640, but it is not clear just when he preached this series of sermons from Genesis 1:26. The subject, however, the image of God in Adam and in us as heirs of Adam, connects it to the controversies between Cotton and the other ministers

---

[42] Ibid., 22.   [43] Hooker, *Saints Dignitie*, 67.

at the time of the Hutchinson crisis; this book was one more quiet, implicit criticism of Cotton in an attempt to protect men from the antinomian errors. God created man in his image, "that spirituall ability put into Adam, whereby hee was able to worke as God wrought, after the manner and measure of a creature."[44] Since "it was not Adams soule, but the image of God, that inabled him to obedience, therefore he must have this image, before either his body, or soule could obey." Thus it was clear that human redemption began with a recovery of the "spirituall light" first given to Adam and culminated in union with Christ, not beginning with a perfect union as Cotton believed.[45] Also interesting here is Hooker's use of the traditional idea of the book of Nature as an ancillary to the revealed truth; characteristically he concentrated on its meaning for the wounded heart and ignored its more conventional use as a proof of God's existence:

> When thou findest they heart sluggish, quicken thy selfe thus; Aske the fowles of the ayre, and they will tell thee, thou receivedst all from God; returne all unto him againe. When thou seest the heavens turne in their compasse, consider thy soule, that thou art so dead hearted in duty. The Sunne rejoyces like a Gyant to runne his course, because God commands it; the sea ebbes, and flowes, because God will have it so.[46]

None of Hooker's friends and parishioners doubted the existence of God; they only doubted their knowledge of him. One advantage of living in the western wilderness was the clarity of outline in the book of nature, and here a man might consider his soul and God's power over it with corresponding clarity.

<hr>

[44] Hooker, *The Paterne of Perfection* (London, 1640), 8.
[45] Ibid., 37, 44. [46] Ibid., 25–26.

II

Hooker was happiest in his pulpit and in his study, and the Connecticut years afforded him time for both; his late sermons reveal a notable increase in philosophical and theological insight over the earlier ones, partly because of his more sophisticated audience, partly because of his own maturity and greater depth of scholarship. He had made his mark upon New England with his role in the antinomian controversy, however, and the last years of his life were nearly as busily occupied with public concerns as the first half of the 1630s had been. Isolation might be conducive to the trade of meditation, but the wilderness had always been a place of temptation as well as of purification for Christians. The churches of New England had hardly disposed of a threat from within when they were suddenly brought under fire from without, not by Laud this time but by many of their erstwhile sympathizers at home. In 1637 the ministers had received two sets of questions about the organization and administration of their churches. These were variously answered by John Davenport, John Cotton, and Richard Mather, but by 1643 or so their replies began to meet rebuttals. The disputants on the other side of the water were Scotsmen and Englishmen favoring a presbyterian, or classical, church polity. While these men were preparing their criticisms of the New England Way, the Civil War began, bringing with it a religious ferment that would eventually make the enthusiasms of the Hutchinsonians look tame. One of the first manifestations of the many radical sects to come was the reappearance of anabaptism. The New England ministers suddenly found themselves under simultaneous attack by presbyterians for excluding people from the church and by anabaptists for admitting too many.

If the charges of either of these groups were vindicated, they would seriously disrupt the effectiveness of Hooker's church as an eschatological, regenerative institution. In a series of sermons probably preached in 1644 he faced up to "a generation of Anabaptists" by going back once more to the foundation of the covenant; these lectures were later published as *The Covenant of Grace Opened* in 1649. He proved herein the validity of infant baptism by presenting the Old Testament Israelites as a type of the church of Christ and circumcision as a type of baptism. He utilized the distinction between the inward, spiritual covenant and the external, federal covenant to explicate the relationship between type and antitype. For Abraham the two covenants were concurrent, but the first included only his elect descendants, while the second, national covenant contained all his seed. Christ had turned the national covenant of the Jewish nation into the spiritual version of the church covenant. By marshaling these well-established bits of covenant theory, Hooker was able to argue that baptism, the "seals of our first entrance into the covenant," was to be extended only to the children of church members, the New Testament version of the seed of Abraham. *The Covenant of Grace Opened* thus defended the practice of the New England churches against both the anabaptists, who wished to limit baptism to the visible saints alone, and the presbyterians, who wished to extend it to any child whose parents requested it. In Hooker's view the anabaptist position misread the meaning of the sacrament by making it a seal of the inward covenant alone, thus ignoring its typical use in the Old Testament, and the presbyterians tended to reduce it to a mere formality.[47]

The presbyterian critique of the New England Way was far more extensive than this, however, and Hooker's sermons on Genesis 17:23 refuted only a small part of their position. Furthermore, the anabaptists were a relatively insignificant minority, while the English Puritan movement was predominantly of presbyterian sentiment before 1645. When Cotton,

[47] Hooker, *Covenant*, 1. Hooker's specific target was to answer John Spilsbury, *A Treatise Concerning the Lawfull Subject of Baptisme* (London, 1643).

Davenport, and Hooker were invited to join the Westminster Assembly in 1642, "Mr. Hooker liked not the business, nor thought it any sufficient call for them to go 3,000 miles to agree with three men, (meaning those three ministers who were for independency, and did solicit in the parliament, etc.)."[48] Even in the Bay Colony, that city upon a hill, there were ministers who held presbyterian opinions, most notably James Noyes and Thomas Parker of Newbury, and there were definite stirrings of support for presbyterian church order among some of the laymen who were not as yet able to give evidence of their election in order to enter into a covenanted church. Two months after the Westminster Assembly convened, the ministers of New England responded to the presbyterian threat by holding an assembly at Cambridge where the principal occasion was the opinions of the Newbury ministers. Cotton and Hooker were chosen moderators of the assembly which, all in all, turned out to be fairly inconclusive. The assembly was the beginning of greater things, however; just as the antinomian affair forced the ministers to take a definite stand on doctrine, so the presbyterian critique impelled them to articulate their ideas about church polity.

The first result was the appearance within a year or two of a number of books which were written by the most eminent and able of the New England ministers and which defended independent congregational church polity. Most notable among these were Thomas Shepard and John Allin's *Defence of the Answer*, Cotton's *Way of the Churches of Christ in New England*, and Hooker's *Survey of the Summe of Church Discipline*. Hooker returned to the issues first raised nearly fifteen years before by John Paget in Amsterdam, but now he addressed himself to a considerably more talented opponent, Samuel Rutherford, professor of divinity at the University of St. Andrews. In 1643 Rutherford had published his *Due Right of Presbyteries*, wherein he "proved himself familiar with a

[48] Winthrop, II, 71.

wide range of Congregational literature, and showed himself able to put his own case clearly and effectively."[49] Hooker composed his reply in 1644 and presented it for approval to an assembly of the ministers held at Cambridge in July 1645. He had previously gained the approbation of all the elders of Connecticut, and the Cambridge meeting expressed the desire that he publish the treatise.

His finished copy was lost, however, when the ship to which he had consigned it perished at sea; being "overborn and condescended to what now is again endeavored," he began to prepare a second draft, and although he died before he could give it its final polishing, it was published in 1648. This book was, nevertheless, the master statement on the theory of the church polity in New England in the first years. As of 1640 there were no firm statements about the theory and nature of church government in New England because the development of forms of church discipline had been pragmatic and experimental within the particular churches themselves rather than on a wider, theoretical basis. The New England ministers did have a large stock of theoretical knowledge before they ever left the homeland, but in the actual practice of setting up the churches, praxis inevitably modulated theory.[50]

When Hooker sat down in 1644 to defend the constitution of his church, he produced a document which provided at once a theological and philosophical validation of the form of church government which he and his colleagues had developed in the 1630s, a complete model of this government, and a closely reasoned, scholarly, and scriptural refutation of the presbyterian concept of a national church.

He divided the *Survey* into four parts, "which as so many pillars principall, bear up the whole frame." He first looked

[49] Williston Walker, *The Creeds and Platforms of Congregationalism* (New York, Scribners, 1893), 140.
[50] On English backgrounds and New English adaptations see Miller, *Orthodoxy*, and Morgan, *Visible Saints*.

"at the Church *in its first rise and essence*, The causes of it, in the efficient, Matter, and Form; The Qualifications of it, in its precedency, power, priviledges." He then described "the *Church*, as compleated with all her Officers, the number and nature of them, in her elections, and Ordinations." Thirdly, he considered "the Church thus constituted, *The power that she exerciseth in admissions, dispensations of Sacraments, and censures.*" In the final section he briefly discussed "the consociation of Churches in Classes, Synods, and councels,"[51] The first of these sections was strategically the most important and correspondingly amounted to a bit more than half of the total content of the treatise; could he bring his opponents to agree upon the true nature of the church, then the defense of congregational practices detailed in the last three parts would be the logical consequence. It was also perhaps the most important part theologically for Hooker, for it justified the policies of church admission which followed from his evangelical practices. The *Survey* was written "out of the wildernesse" as much, if not more, for the edification of a New England audience as for the reduction of stubborn Scotsmen; in an "Epistle To The Reader, Especially The Congregation and Church of Jesus Christ in *Hartford* upon *Connecticut*" Hooker's parishioners, William Goodwin and Edward Hopkins, claimed, "There were some workings in his thoughts before the sending away of the first Copy, to have recommended these his labours in an Epistle to this Church, and thereby left them (to use his own expressions) as his last legacy to us."[52]

Hooker began the *Survey* with unexceptionable Christian doctrine, making a crucial distinction between the visible and invisible church. Christ was the head of the church both mystically "by Spirituall influence" and politically "by his especiall guidance in the means, and dispensations of his Ordinances." Hence, the church was a "*mysticall Body . . . the*

---

[51] Hooker, Preface, *Survey*, sig. b2r.
[52] Hooker, *Survey*, sigs. a4v, c2v.

Church of true Beleevers, . . . *the Invisible Church*" as well as a "Politicall body or Church visible" which "results out of that relation, which is betwixt the professours of the faith, when by voluntary consent they yeeld outward subjection to that government of Christ, which in his word he hath prescribed."[53] It was with this latter, visible church that Hooker had to deal in refuting presbyterians and instructing his fellow New Englanders. It is interesting to note that just as he had separated the civil covenant embodied in the Fundamental Orders from the covenant of grace, so here he has sharpened the emphasis on the visible church as a political and administrative body formed by the merely human wills of "professours of the faith" (who are not necessarily the same as the faithful).

The efficient or *"Principall cause* and Institution of a visible Church," said Hooker, "Issues from the speciall appointment of *God the Father, thorow the Lord Jesus Christ,* as the head thereof, *by* the *holy Ghost,* sent and set on work for that end."[54] Hooker affirmed the direct correspondence of the church as both mystical and political body and the covenant of grace seen as spiritual process. In *The Application of Redemption* he told the men of Hartford, "There are but three great works in the World, Creation, Redemption, and Application, which are given to the three Persons of the Trinity according to the special manner of their working."[55] The church was a macrocosm of spiritual man just as the state was a macrocosm of civil man. When he argued in the *Survey* that the material cause of the church was the visible saints, who "only are fit Matter appointed by God to make up a visible Church of Christ," he thus justified the contention by appealing to the essential distinction of the covenant of grace into an inward and an outer covenant; they were the saints

---

[53] Hooker, *Survey*, I, 3.   [54] Ibid., 12.

[55] Hooker, *Application*, 123. See Perry Miller, "The Cambridge Platform in 1648," in *The Cambridge Platform of 1648, Tercentenary Commemoration,* ed. Henry Wilder Foote (Boston, Beacon, 1949), 66.

"in appearance: for when the Scriptures so terms and stiles men, we must know that *Saints* come under a double apprehension. *Some* are *such* according to Charity: Some according to *truth*."[56]

One of the charges that Rutherford leveled against the independents was that they confused the distinction between the invisible and visible churches and thus fell into the errors of separatism. Hooker was able to refute this by reasoning, "*Those* who by God are *excluded* from *his covenant* and meddling with *that* as *unfit, they* are *not fit* to have *communion* with the *Church*: For to *that* all the holy *things of God* do in an especiall manner *appertain*." He thus put the ball back in Rutherford's court, saying, "The Church consists of some who are faithfull and sincere hearted: Some counterfet and false hearted. Some really good, some really bad, onely those who appear so bad and vile should not be accepted. And doth not *Mr. R.* say the same?"[57] While Hooker was thus defending himself and his colleagues from the charge of enthusiastically attempting to realize the millennium by human means, he was also able to remind his fellow ministers in New England of the need for liberal admission policies to their churches. Because men's "*judgement*, then, of *others sincerity, est tantum opinio, non scientia,* and therefore the most discerning may be deceived therein," they must judge of others by "*Love* directed by the rules of reason and religion" which always "inclines to *the better* part, unlesse *evidence* come to the *contrary*." Entrance into the church, the visible manifestation of the gracious covenant's larger form, must be adjudicated on larger grounds:

> He that professing the faith, lives not in the neglect of any known duty, or in the commission of any known evill, and hath such a measure of knowledge as may in reason let in Christ into the soul, and carry the soul to him: These be

[56] Hooker, *Survey*, I, 14.   [57] Ibid., 17, 22.

grounds of probabilitics, by which charity poised according to rule, may and ought to conceive, there be some beginnings of spirituall good.[58]

"Some beginnings," that is the critical expression, for the church, like the covenant supporting it, was dynamic and evangelical; the "three great Works in the World" were God working, the Word in the active voice, present tense.

The formal cause of the church according to Hooker was the "Mutuall covenanting and confoederating of the Saints in the fellowship of the faith according to the order of the Gospel."[59] The church covenant was a "spirituall combination," uniting visible saints into "spirituall cities and corporations."[60] Because the covenant of grace brought together the truly godly and worldly hypocrites, the church was in a peculiar sense a divine beachhead in the world. It was not strictly supernatural or mystical, for that was the invisible church of the elect, but at the same time a natural relation between men "is not the foundation of a *free covenant*." The church covenant was an ordinance of the Gospel, said Hooker, designed to bring souls to grace and regeneration.

Many duties flow from the generall and necessary duties of morality, which reach a man as a *creature*, with reference to *God* as a *Creatour*, or else to his *fellow creatures*. And hence *this* relation from a rule *of nature*, it hath nothing to do with a *free covenant* betwixt parties and parties by mutuall and free consent, before either can take up *another sort of duties*.[61]

The covenanted, particular church was God's way of redeeming man from nature: "Those who are *converts in the judgement of charity*, may yet in Gods intention be brought into the Church, that they may be truely converted."[62]

[58] Ibid., 24.   [59] Ibid., 46.
[60] Ibid., 50, 51.   [61] Ibid., 68, 70.
[62] Ibid., 31.

Having thus established the model of the true church intended by the divine first cause, Hooker went on in the rest of the *Survey* to prove that the particular church had both ministerial authority and power to perform all the acts required of a church by Scripture. It could elect officers with the power to dispense all the allowed and required ordinances; it could admit members and exercise discipline over them by means of the brotherly watch, formal admonitions, and excommunications, and it could extend the right hand of fellowship to other true churches. Power to do all this was delegated by means of the covenant of grace directly to the particular churches from God; to erect hierarchical structures, be they popish or presbyterian, above the only body authorized to exert spiritual power would be to exalt fallen human reason in the face of divine wisdom. Hooker refrained from all *ad hominem* accusations, but behind his arguments lurked the independent's fear that new presbyter might well be old priest writ large. The possibilities of both spiritual and political tyranny increased as the exercise of power was progressively alienated from its foundations.[63]

In 1645 Hooker published in London three other titles which were apparently attempts to influence the resolves of the Westminster Assembly. *A Briefe Exposition of the Lords Prayer* and *Heavens Treasury Opened in a Fruitfull Exposition of the Lords Prayer* were slightly divergent forms of the same text issued by two different booksellers. The books are exactly

[63] Winthrop S. Hudson, in *The Great Tradition of the American Churches* (New York, Harper, 1953) has noted that "the congregational type of church organization, with its insistence upon the autonomy of the local church was due in part to this principle of limitation. A concern for the restriction of church power quite as much as a belief in the rights of the local church led to the advocacy of only an 'associational connectionalism.' Usurpation of the divine sovereignty by national, provincial, or episcopal institutions was what their experience had led them to fear; they had yet to learn that a local church could be quite as wayward and that perhaps some more positive check than 'brotherly counsel' might be necessary" (54n).

what the titles would lead one to expect, detailed analyses and openings of the Lord's Prayer, and, interestingly enough, not in a sermon form but in one more nearly catechetical. The third title, *An Exposition of the Principles of Religion*, was a catechism, and a recent scholar has surmised that all of these works were intended to influence the Assembly's final choice of a standard catechism.[64] Hooker's catechism was only one of more than a dozen new catechisms appearing in the early and mid 1640s, and insofar as his work was traditionally Calvinistic, the Westminster Larger and Shorter Catechisms followed his example. But his example was in this respect much like that of several other writers, and the theological direction of the Assembly was determined by the political successes of the English Independents and not by advice from New England. More important, Hooker's expositions of the Lord's Prayer and his *Exposition of the Principles of Religion* display his concern for the psychology of conversion and his pastoral interest in the wounded soul, qualities notably lacking in the Catechisms' dry definitions of first principles.

The manuscripts for these volumes seem to have been delivered by John Hooker, his eldest son, who went to England apparently at this time to continue his education at Oxford.[65] Hooker's family was beginning to leave the Hartford home; with John gone to England and Joanna married to Thomas Shepard in 1638, it is no surprise that some of the most moving passages in *A Briefe Exposition* are on the prayer's first words and the meaning of fatherhood. These considerations on the divine Father and His heavenly kingdom are all the richer, however, for Hooker's involvement during these years with the problems of worldly patriarchs, magistrates, and ministers in the New England settlements. To pray to Our Father, said Hooker, "notes a bond of society between

[64] Sargent Bush, "Thomas Hooker and the Westminster Assembly," *William and Mary Quarterly* 29 (1972), 291.
[65] Ibid., 295.

the faithfull children of the same Father." Later, discussing the kingdom of Heaven, he verged upon the apocalyptic: "We beseech Christ that his Gospel may be spread and be strong, and these dayes of sinne may be wasted, and that he may come in the clouds, *Revel.* 22. and then, *come Lord Jesus*, come quickly."[66] As he approached his own end, he was mindful of the coming end of all things and wanted to strengthen the bonds between the saints and their Father. The strength of the covenant bonds was the strength of the saints' Christian liberty.

III

Hooker had previously demonstrated his dislike for improperly limited power by the decision to remove to Connecticut, out of reach of the negative voice and Winthrop's discretional exercise of authority. This distrust of the Bay Colony's use of civil power was shared by many of his fellow emigrants, and it disturbed the peaceful relationship between the two colonies for several years after the Pequot War. The troubles with the Indians revealed the necessity of a more efficient, coordinated method of exerting military and diplomatic controls, and in 1637 the New England colonies still had cause to fear the imposition of a governor general and the subsequent loss of their privileges. After the Antinomian Synod adjourned, Hooker remained in the Bay for a week or two, and he discussed with the magistrates terms of confederation between the colonies. Hooker took the Bay Colony's suggestions home to Connecticut, and the magistrates there lost little time in rejecting them, possibly with his recommendation to do so.

The original draft provided that "upon any matter of difference, two, three, or more commissioners of every of the confederate colonies should assemble, and have absolute power (the greater number of them) to determine the matter." Ab-

---

[66] Hooker, *A Briefe Exposition of the Lords Prayer* (London, 1645), 7, 22.

solute power was not the going thing in Connecticut, and in the early summer of 1638 they sent by way of John Haynes a counterproposal stating that in case of lack of unanimity among the commissioners they were to return home for advice, meet again, "and so to go untill the matter might be agreed." The Massachusetts General Court was irritated by "their alteration, and the inconvenience thereof," and an exchange of progressively more acrimonious letters began between parties in the two colonies.[67] Winthrop made the mistake of informing Haynes that through a basic error of Connecticut policy "the main burden for managing of state business fell upon some one or other of their ministers, . . . who, though they were men of singular wisdom and godliness, yet stepping out of their course, their actions wanted that blessing, which otherwise might have been expected."[68] Winthrop was clearly warning Haynes against Hooker's influence—there were only three ministers in the colony at the time, and only Hooker figured in "state business" in any way. Winthrop's concern might almost seem to be somewhat hypocritical on the part of a colony which requested John Cotton and Nathaniel Ward, minister of Ipswich, to draw up model legal codes for the court's consideration. Winthrop did not help matters any with his letter to Hooker written at the end of August 1638; we have already noted his remarks contained therein about the unsafeness of referring matter of counsel to the people, and the letter also complained about Connecticut's behavior concerning the Indians and about jurisdictional disputes over the plantation at Agawam (now Springfield).

Hooker's reply to Winthrop was an angry response, implicitly accusing the governor of Massachusetts of being an unwitting tool of Satan because he failed to prevent defamatory accounts of Connecticut "with which the heads and hearts of passengers come loaded hither." He recounted the

[67] Winthrop, I, 288.   [68] Ibid., 288–90.

various stories Bay men supposedly were telling newly arriv-
ing immigrants in order to persuade them not to settle on the
river; this rumor-mongering was an economic threat to the
infant colony, since its economic welfare depended upon immigrants, and even worse it evidenced a "sesmatical spirit."
The disparagement of Connecticut was one more high-handed
attempt upon the part of the Bay to maintain exclusive control of the New England enterprise: "If these be the wayes
of God, or that the blessing of God to follow them, I never
preached God's wayes, nor knew what belonged to them."[69]
The rest of the letter justified the practices of Connecticut
and included Hooker's famous comments upon the proper relationship between the people and their magistrates.

Many of Hooker's charges were exaggerated, but it apparently helped the negotiations to bring them into the open.
He returned along with John Haynes to the Bay Colony in
the following spring to renew the talks about confederation.
There was a new urgency to smooth over relations with the
larger colony, for the Dutch in New Netherlands were becoming more aggressive about their rights on the Connecticut.
The House of Hope was still squatting in the middle of Hartford, a Dutch thorn in the English garden. Discussion in 1639
was apparently correct but cool, although Winthrop was careful to give no further cause of offense. When Hooker was invited to preach in Cambridge on the Sabbath, Winthrop went
to listen, "though the governor did very seldom go from his
own congregation upon the Lord's day."[70] The breach was not
healed so easily: in 1640 Hooker tried to persuade Thomas
Shepard, his son-in-law, to remove to Connecticut, thus re-
taliating for Massachusetts' discouragement of immigrants. It
was not until 1643 that the colonies of Massachusetts, Plymouth, Connecticut, and New Haven, calling themselves the

[69] Hooker to John Winthrop, *Winthrop Papers*, iv, 77–78.
[70] Winthrop, i, 306.

United Colonies of New England, accepted a compromise set of articles of confederation.

Hooker ended the old quarrel between himself and the Massachusetts governor when he wrote commending Winthrop for his "christian readines" and "enlarged faythfullness in an especiall manner to promote so good a work." As for his own share in the political business of the colonies, he told Winthrop, he only wished "to be in the number, and to have my voice with those, that whyle your self and your faythfull Assistants, . . . be laying the first stone of the foundation of this combynation of peace, I may crye grace grace to your indeavors." In the earlier letter he had defended his political ideas in a bitter context; here he generously extolled Winthrop as a man who had fulfilled ideals of a a higher priority than mere politics: "To be the repayrer of the breach, was of ould counted matter of highest prayse and acceptance with God and man: much more to be a meanes not only to mayntayne peace and truth in your dayes, but to leave both, as a Legacy to those that come after, untill the coming of the Sonne of God in the clouds."[71]

Hooker had grown old contending in the cause of peace, repairing breaches between men and men and men and God. "I confess my head grows gray and my eyes dim, and yet I am sometime in the watchtower," he wrote to Winthrop in 1638, and two years later he told Shepard, "I know, to begin plantations is a hard work; and I think I have seen as much difficulty, and came to such a business with as much disadvantage as almost men could do."[72] While giving the Cambridge sermon of May 26, 1639, which Winthrop heard, he suddenly "was at a stand, and told the people, that God had deprived him both of his strength and matter, etc. and so went forth, and about half an hour after returned again, and went on to very good

[71] Hooker to John Winthrop, *Winthrop Papers*, IV, 401–2.
[72] Ibid., 76; Letter to Shepard quoted by Paige, 49.

purpose about two hours."[73] This mental lapse could have occurred to anyone, and his recovery hardly suggests much loss
of his powers, yet the duties of a family, a church, and a colony
were taking their toll. The ague he had contracted in the
Netherlands would not have been appreciably helped by living
on the bottomlands of the Connecticut. Still, he went on in his
work, making at least three and possibly four difficult trips
to the Bay, going to Saybrook on colony and church business,
preparing treatises, counseling the afflicted, and through it all
holding forth in the pulpit week in and week out.

These years in Connecticut were, however, probably the
happiest since the days of his courtship in Esher; no more
dodging bishops and hiding from pursuivants, no more Indian
troubles after 1637, he was where he wanted to be, working
in the heart of a religious community and doing "a great deal
of good." The Palace of Glory seemed close to Hooker in
those days; the enemies of Christ's church were being defeated
on all sides, and "the coming of the Sonne of God in the
clouds" was growing nearer. Connecticut in the early 1640s
was the suburb of happiness; in addition to the spiritual rewards, God had seen fit to give him material comforts. A grate-
ful town voted him large shares in Connecticut lands; under
the watchful hand of Susannah his herds increased. His children were becoming godly young men and women; Joanna
was married to Thomas Shepard, John was preparing for
Cambridge University, Mary had wed Roger Newton, the
pastor of Milford. Sarah and Samuel were still at home, having
their educations perfected by their father. Hooker's children
had grown up for the most part while the family was on the
move, and it must have been difficult for him to give them the
time and attention they deserved. In Hartford he was given
a second opportunity to enjoy the growth of a child; Thomas
and Joanna Shepard had sent their small son Samuel to live
with his grandfather, and Hooker's reports of him in his letters

[73] Winthrop, I, 306.

to Shepard show us the Puritan as doting grandparent. "My little Sam is very well, and exceedingly cheerful, and hath been so all this time—grows a good scholar. The little creature hath such a pleasing, winning disposition, that it makes me think of his mother almost every time I play with him." And again, "My little bedfellow is well. I bless the Lord, and I find what you related to be true; the colder the weather grows, the more quiet he lies. I shall hardly trust any body with him but mine own eye."[74]

But as the old man played with his grandson and heard his lessons, mortality drew on. Joanna Shepard died in 1646, and he himself was wearing down year by year. When a synod was called to meet at Cambridge in 1646 to begin consideration of an explicit, unanimous statement of church polity, he wrote Shepard, "My years and infirmities grow so fast upon me, that they wholly disenable to so long a journey." In another letter he apologizes, "My eyes grow dim, and my hand much worse, though never good, and therefore my pen is very unpleasant"; the years of close study had begun to exact their price.[75] When the synod reconvened in 1647, he was again unable to consider the trip, although he was still taking his regular turn in the pulpit. Samuel Stone did go to the meeting, and Hooker would have taken his duties in the pulpit as well. The synod adjourned early because of an "epidemicall sickness" throughout the country, and when Stone returned to Hartford, he found Hooker on his deathbed.

God refused to heare our prayers for him, but tooke him from us July 7, a little before sunne-set. Our sunne is set, our light is eclipsed, our joy is darkened, we remember now in the day of our calamitie the pleasant things, which we enjoyed in former times. His spirits and head were so op-

[74] Hooker to Shepard, quoted by John A. Albro, *The Life of Thomas Shepard*, in *The Works of Thomas Shepard* (1853; rpt., New York, AMS, 1967), cliii.

[75] Hooker, in Albro, clxvi, cliv.

pressed with the disease that he was not able to expresse much to us in his sicknesse, but had exprest to Mr. Goodwin before my returne, that his peace was made in heaven, and had continued 30 years without alteration, he was above Satan. . . . I gave thankes to my God dayly for his helpe, and no man in the world but my selfe knowes what a friend he hath been unto me.[76]

His end was peaceful, surrounded by friends and family and assured of his salvation. A short time later, "a worthy spectator, then writing to Mr. Cotton a relation thereof, made this reflection, 'Truly, sir, the sight of his death will make me have more pleasant thoughts of death, than ever I yet had in my life!' "[77]

Hooker was unshaken to the very end in his principles and in his confidence that he was about to enter the perfect state he had for so long only discerned in brief flashes of spiritual joy. According to Mather, "When one that stood weeping by the bed-side said unto him 'Sir, you are going to receive the reward of all your labours,' he replied, 'Brother, I am going to receive mercy.' "[78] He was not to be trapped into Arminianism at the last moment, and heaven was much more than the completion of a business transaction. It was mercy he lived for and lived by; this divine expression of rational charity, love ordered by perfect reason and perfect religion, was more sure than mere human labor. Thomas Hooker was finally home.

In addition to a heart-stricken church, Hooker left behind a widow, four surviving children, and an estate valued at £1136, a considerable sum in 1647. Of the total value of his estate £300 alone were assessed for "Bookes in his studdy, etc.," which would have made a considerable library, perhaps

[76] Samuel Stone to Shepard, *Collections of the Massachusetts Historical Society*, Fourth Series, 8 (Boston, 1868), 544–45.
[77] Mather, I, 350.   [78] Ibid.

as many as a thousand volumes.[79] In many ways Hooker died just in time—although he was only sixty-one, many men who had the strength to survive that long lived on into their seventies or eighties—the old serpent was about to break into the happy suburbs once more. Hartford discovered its first witch only months after he died; within a decade his church was irrevocably and bitterly divided; what would have been most disappointing of all was his eldest son's refusal to return to New England after he graduated from Cambridge and his eventual conformity to the Church of England at the Restoration. He was spared these shocks to his expectations of the coming glory of Christ, and he left behind in his published works and in his example a powerful heritage for the covenant seed.

[79] Hooker, Will, in *Public Records . . . Connecticut*, I, 502. The number of books in Hooker's library has been estimated from the valuation in the will in accordance with suggestions in Thomas Goddard Wright's *Literary Culture in Early New England* (New Haven, Yale Univ. Press, 1920), 25–61.

EIGHT

Heritage

EIGHTEEN days before his death Hooker supplied the pulpit in Windsor, "whilst Mr. Warham was absent in the Bay." He sought to keep the people up to the mark in the absence of their pastor, reminding them of the dangers of carnal security and of the necessity of continually exercising whatever graces they might have. He chose as his text Romans 1:18, "For the wrath of God is revealed from Heaven against all unrighteousness," and found as a doctrine "that there be stirrings of truth in the hearts of all men naturally, and carnal men labor to beat them down." He went on to urge the congregation:

> Wonder therefore at the goodness of God to man fallen, that he hath not left him wholly in darkness, without any means to help him, but hath left him some recoilings of heart to recover him. So long as a prince leaves his ambassador in another country, it is a sign he maintains peace with them, but if he call him home, they must expect war.[1]

There was an ironically prophetic sense in this; God's ambassador, as Hooker intended it here, was the conscience, "those relics that are left in the mind of man fallen from Adam," but previously he had often used the figure of the preacher in his pulpit as God's ambassador to the unconverted. The Prince recalled His ambassador in Hartford eighteen days after this sermon, and it was only the first of a disturbing sequence of

[1] Hooker, "Notes of Mr. Hooker's Sermon. From Deacon Matthew Grant's MSS Notes," transcribed by J. Hammond Trumbull, in George Leon Walker, *History of the First Church in Hartford*, 1633–1883 (Hartford, 1884), 429–30.

deaths. Within a bit more than ten years all of the major disputants at the Antinomian Synod of 1637 would be dead—Shepard, Cotton, Bulkeley, Anne Hutchinson, only Wheelwright lived on until 1679. In the same period many of the most influential men among the laity were being removed from the scene, notably John Winthrop, and the civil and religious life of New England came to be dominated by a few old diehards and by a younger generation. The old men, such as John Davenport and John Endicott, had never been noted for their generous application of rational charity, and the younger generation failed to measure up to the spiritual standards of the founders, or at least to the standards defined by the old men who represented the founders.

Almost exactly thirty years after Thomas Hooker's death his son Samuel delivered the Connecticut election sermon in Hartford. In the interim the younger Hooker had graduated from Harvard and become the pastor of the church at Farmington; at the election of 1677 he returned to exercise his prophetic gifts in Hartford where his father had triumphed before. The burden of his ancestry sat heavily upon him, and it was heightened by the recognition that all was not well with New England. "In what awful and tremendous manner the Lords anger hath been of late in special, made to appear against us wilderness people, is not soon or easily forgotten." This most recent manifestation of divine anger at the failings of his covenanted people was King Philip's War, but there had been previous displays of God's wrath, and there would surely be more: "for certain our sufferings will be greatned if our sins be not lessened."[2] What particularly bothered Samuel Hooker was his realization that God's anger at the covenant seed was intensified exactly because they were the children of an elect paternity. Reminding the General Court of their pious fathers, he asked,

[2] John Whiting, "To the Christian Reader," in Samuel Hooker, *Righteousness Rained from Heaven* (Cambridge, Mass., 1677), sig. A2r.

. . . were not their faces set for Heaven, their language the language of *Canaan?* Was not holiness to the Lord written on their wayes? and will you bee worldly and prophane, drink and swear, riot and be wanton, deride Religion; scoffe at the wayes or servants of God: O take heed, take heed, lest the names you bear, the houses you dwell in, the estates you inherit, the places you sustain, rise up in judgement against you, and increase your condemnation at the last.[3]

Hooker's sermon was not unusual in the New England of the 1670s, and variations upon his jeremiad were heard from every pulpit. The message was clear, according to the ministers; the great plan for erecting the city of God in the wilderness had been frustrated by the sins and heedlessness of a wayward people.

The message has turned out to be, however, less than clear for twentieth-century students of these sermons. Perry Miller and others of his generation tended to read the jeremiads as journalism or social criticism; these sermons indicated the declension of New England religious life as external affirmations displaced inner experience. In the terms of Joseph Haroutounian moralism triumphed over piety.[4] The religion of Thomas Hooker and the first-generation Puritans in New England was indeed a mixture of voluntaristic moralism and inspirational piety—one way of understanding the antinomian crisis is to see it as a dispute over the proportions of this mixture—and in the long run moralism did displace piety as the more popular version of religion. But this displacement did not occur in the seventeenth century, or even in the first half of the eighteenth.

[3] Samuel Hooker, *Righteousness*, 18.
[4] Joseph Haroutounian, *Piety Versus Moralism: The Passing of the New England Theology* (New York, Holt, 1932). For other versions of the decline of religion in New England see Miller, *The New England Mind: from Colony to Province* (1953: rpt., Boston, Beacon, 1961), 19–146; Pettit, 158–216; Joy Bourne Gilsdorf, "The Puritan Apocalypse: New England Eschatology in the Seventeenth Century," Diss. Yale 1964, 162–94.

While it is misleading to speak of religious declension in seventeenth-century New England, we must realize that modes of expressing piety did change in response to changing conditions in the churches. Thomas Hooker's "language of *Canaan*" had to be reinterpreted for later generations.

When Hooker had laid down the rules for administering baptism in congregational churches, he had expected that infants of believers would grow into true holiness themselves and thus become qualified to receive the sacrament of the Lord's Supper, the second seal of entrance into the covenant. Hooker restricted infant baptism to the children of covenanted church members, but he did not expect that all of the covenant seed would eventually become regenerate. Entrance into the covenant of federal holiness was merely the first step in preparing children for entrance into the internal covenant of saving grace and did not replace the church's traditional evangelical efforts. Baptism was thus analogous to preparation, and like preparation, it did not of itself qualify a person for participation in the privileges of church membership. Hooker's church remained pure because all genuine members, whether recruited from the federally holy covenant seed or from the civil community beyond the church, had satisfactorily evidenced the experience of saving faith. The membership status of the baptized covenant seed, however, was largely undefined.

The practical flaws in this theory, which Hooker shared with his New England colleagues, began to appear in the 1640s, and became critical in the following decade. Many of the covenant seed, more than Hooker had anticipated, failed to experience saving grace; they themselves were in an anomalous position in the church—members, but not entitled to all the privileges of members until they had obtained experimental assurance of their salvation—but that of their children was yet more tenuous. Were they even entitled to baptism? The problem was theoretically settled in 1662 by the Half-Way Covenant Synod which declared that baptized but unregenerate people were entitled to church membership, but not to the privilege of the Lord's Supper, and that their children were in turn eligible for baptism.

The Half-Way Covenant seemed to its opponents to be an untenable compromise of the standards of church purity defined by Hooker and the other theoreticians of the first generation, and yet it was in many ways in profound accordance with important characteristics of his theology. He had tailored his practice to the spiritual conditions of his flock, and he was not above innovation in the accidentals of his faith—indeed, the *Survey of the Summe of Church Discipline* was a distillation of a lifetime of innovation and experiment.[5] The Half-Way Covenant Synod maintained this experimental spirit; Hooker and his associates had been so successful in establishing the paramount value of experiential piety that the synod's seeming compromise with church purity encouraged rather than hindered the practice of personal piety. A recent scholar has argued convincingly that the slowness with which the laity embraced the terms of the Half-Way Covenant and the caution with which they approached the Lord's Supper shows the immense importance New Englanders placed on the experience of saving faith and not the decline of religion.[6]

The Half-Way Covenant did change the conditions of spiritual life in New England by displacing the point of conversion in relation to a person's membership in the church. Conversion in Hooker's terms qualified the natural man who was nominally Christian for participation in the church covenant. Although this earlier sense of conversion in respect to natural men was not lost, conversion after the Half-Way Covenant

---

[5] It is interesting to note that Robert G. Pope, *The Half-Way Covenant: Church Membership in Puritan New England* (Princeton, Princeton Univ. Press, 1969), found that the widest variety of innovative responses to the half-way covenant was in Connecticut. Pope has presented convincing data that argue against a decline in New England religious life.

[6] Pope, 272–73.

was also understood as qualifying the half-way member for full membership and the Lord's Supper. As a result the ministers tended to focus their attention upon the growth in piety of those who were half-way members. The Half-Way Covenant, especially in its most liberal interpretations, had brought large numbers of well-behaved people into the church, and the point of individual spiritual crisis was transposed with it.

Cotton Mather, in many ways the most innovative and inventive of all the New England Puritans, was one of the first ministers to realize what had happened. Preparation for salvation now corresponded to preparation for communion, and ministerial demands for experiential piety had to be adjusted accordingly. "The *Churches* which will always esteem it their *Glory;* To make the Terms of *Communion* and the *Terms of Salvation* run as parallel as 'tis possible: and found their *Communion* on the *Everlasting* MAXIMS OF PIETY: wondrously consult their own safety in it."[7] In 1690 Mather published *A Companion for Communicants*, a treatise which initiated a flood of manuals of evangelical sacramental piety in New England. Mather encouraged all members of the church who had not yet come to the Lord's Table, regardless of their scruples or hesitations about the saving nature of their faith, to undertake "a very Industrious and Conscientious *Preparation . . .* for that *Fellowship* with the Lord Jesus." Communicants should labor after a *"sense* of Truth" in order that they might *"Tast* and *See,* that the *Lord is Good."*[8]

By 1690 eased standards of admission to the church had changed the nature of preparation for conversion, but Cotton Mather had not sacrificed Hooker's emphasis upon the importance of the experience of piety. Mather's diaries, particularly the accounts of his monthly fasts, show the role piety

[7] Cotton Mather, *Malachi, or The Everlasting Gospel* (Boston, 1717), 58.

[8] Quoted by E. Brooks Holifield, "The Renaissance of Sacramental Piety in Colonial New England," *William and Mary Quarterly* 29 (1972), 38.

held in his own life. The *Magnalia* displays the first-generation magistrates and ministers as models of practical, intensive piety for their descendants, and the popularity of manuals for communicants that developed after his *Companion* reveals the success which he and his colleagues had in maintaining the practice of piety in the "Assemblies of *Zion*."

Although Mather had for the most part discarded Hooker's elaborate system of preparation in redefining it as preparation for the sacrament, he maintained the centrality of experiential piety, and he also maintained Hooker's evangelical stance toward the world at large. Like Hooker he balanced piety with moralism, but the way in which he supported these two concerns, although logically consistent and practically effective, was rather curious. Modern readers have often found it difficult to balance Mather's intense, private piety and his optimistic, do-gooding moral projects such as the *Essays to Do Good*, and they have too readily dismissed him as a crank.[9] If we see first, however, the centrality of piety, particularly sacramental piety, to all of his concerns, then we understand the nature of his moralism. Moral living qualified men for church membership, and made them ready for the exercise of piety which brought them to the Lord's Table. Although Hooker's moral and pious concerns were more tightly related, Mather's were equally consistent but organized on a more extensive plane. Puritan moralism did threaten to subvert Puritan piety, but Mather's use of evangelical moralism in the service of piety avoided the danger, and it was another example of his innovative mind turning a possible aberration in New England religious life to good account.

If Hooker occupies a prominent place at the head of a tradi-

[9] For historians' prejudices against Mather, see David Levin, "The Hazing of Cotton Mather: The Creation of a Biographical Personality," reprinted in his collection of essays, *In Defense of Historical Literature* (New York, Wang, 1967), 34–57. Also see Levin's Introduction to Mather's *Bonifacius: An Essay upon the Good* (Cambridge, Harvard Univ. Press, 1966).

tion of New England piety, he also figures largely in the tradition of moralism, particularly in the formalism of the *Survey of the Summe of Church Discipline*. He had not been very enthusiastic about composing the *Survey*, looking on it "as some what unsutable to a Pastor, whose head and heart and hands, were full of the imploiments of his proper place." The church was formed by experience rather than written platforms or scholarly treatises, and truth revealed itself to the world through experience interacting with meditation upon previous experience: "Either we do, or may erre, though we do not know it; what we have learned we do professe, and yet professe still to live, that we may learn."[10]

The New England ministers were, however, progressively forced by events in England and by the inclination of Cotton and a few other leading men into a legalistic approach to the conceptions of the church. In 1648, only a year after Hooker's death, they produced the Cambridge Platform, their first attempt at a formal solution to spiritual problems. It was undoubtedly a necessary and effective document, but it initiated a faulty method of response to later spiritual crises; thereafter when it appeared that there were serious problems with the spiritual life of New England, the ministerial technique was to lay down the law from their particular pulpits, especially in the notorious jeremiad sermons, and then to gather in synod to make a unanimous statement of principle.[11] Hooker's vital ability to function as a pastor among his people seems to have been more and more replaced by pastors attempting to hold themselves above their people. The speaking aristocracy of the pulpits tended to turn the silent democracy of the congregation into presbyterian subjects of clerical authority. Hooker's

---

[10] Hooker, *Survey*, "Epistle to the Reader," sig. C2ʳ; Preface, sig. a4ʳ. In the second quotation I have replaced a comma after "know it" with a semicolon for clarity.

[11] This was especially true in the case of the Reforming Synod of 1679. Hooker had initially expressed doubts about the wisdom of calling together the Antinomian Synod. See letter quoted by Hutchinson, I, 60.

real authority over his people resulted not from his office but from his personality; later ministers insisted much more emphatically upon the formal basis of their powers.

The Cambridge Platform arranged a skillful compromise between Cotton's and Hooker's positions on admission of new members to the churches. Although the Platform insisted that "such *charity* and tenderness is to be used, as the weakest christian if sincere, may not be excluded, nor discouraged," it also held that "a personall and publick *confession*, and declaring of Gods manner of working upon the soul, is both lawfull, expedient, and useful," for "we are to be ready to render a reason of the hope that is in us, to every one that asketh us."[12] The statement about confession is explicit, but who is to say how far rational charity must extend? The language concerning the required confession allowed both for Hooker's theory of conversion after preparation and for Cotton's demand that the saints know faith in themselves directly and immediately. Problems could be created for the church's evangelical missions, however, when a minister brought his measure of rational charity to his conception of the kind of assurance of conversion required for admission to the full rights of the church.

Since Cotton demanded as evidence of salvation a brief, intensive awareness of an inner difference in the soul, he could legitimately set high standards for the quality, as well as for the saint's detailed awareness, of that experience. Hooker's conception of regeneration, as a process extended over what might quite possibly be a considerable time, had to make allowances for the saint's natural weaknesses; if conversion took a year or more, then it was unlikely that most people would be able to recount all the significant details. What mattered was continuance in a new way of life, and the church and the elders were justified in using a great deal of rational charity as they judged candidates for admission.

[12] *A Platform of Church Discipline*, in Williston Walker, *Creeds*, 222–23.

Both Hooker's and Cotton's concepts had their weaknesses. Cotton's requirements could conceivably be more easily faked, either intentionally or unintentionally; John Underhill, for instance, was apparently taken into the Boston church as a matter of course, but after becoming involved in the antinomian heresy, he described his conversion thus: "He had laid under a spirit of bondage and a legal way five years, and could get no assurance; till at length, as he was taking a pipe of tobacco, the Spirit set home an absolute promise of free grace with such assurance and joy, as he never since doubted of his good estate, neither should he though he should fall into sin."[13] A church might need very high standards indeed to sift out a beguiling fraud like Underhill, but his case points up one sort of problem in the way of discovering the materials for a pure church. Hooker's requirements were much more formidable in that they prescribed a pattern of experiences to be undergone, and ironically the man who so often addressed himself to poor doubting Christians was later criticized for seriously hindering the approach to salvation of convicted and humbled sinners. Giles Firmin, who had lived in Massachusetts from 1632 until the mid-1640s and had been a deacon in the Boston church, remembered that

> when Mr. Hooker preached those Sermons about the Souls preparation for Christ and Humiliation, my Father-in-law, Mr. Nathaniel Ward, told him; *Mr. Hooker, you make as good Christians before men are in Christ as ever they are after,* and wished *would I were but as good a Christian now, as you make men while they are preparing for Christ.*[14]

Hooker's rigorous program of preparing for and discovering justification could indeed be an almost insurmountable hurdle

[13] Quoted by C. F. Adams, Jr. in *Three Episodes*, II, 552.
[14] Giles Firmin, *The Real Christian, or a Treatise of Effectual Calling* (London, 1670), 19.

for one seeking admission to the church, but in practice the liberal exercise of rational charity obviated this problem.

Firmin's primary target in his attack upon the preparationist theology was Thomas Shepard rather than Hooker, for Shepard had introduced a new emphasis (or rather reintroduced an old emphasis) in evangelistic preaching which would later bear strange fruit in New England. Hooker had taken his flock out of the world, as it were, and in Hartford he was apparently able to keep them hot after salvation by means of his preaching and pastoral attention. In a wilderness town visible sainthood was just about the only sort of security available, and it was accordingly treasured along the river, although not necessarily more common there than anywhere else. Back in the Bay, however, worldly affairs began to occupy the minds of the planters, and Shepard quickly realized that carnal security, a defining of religion in terms of a merely moral life and a simplistic trust in the external aspects of saintliness, was the greatest hindrance to genuine conversion, an authentic change of personality within the heart. His solution was to sharpen drastically the emphasis in his sermons upon the bondage of the Law for those entering the preparatory phases of conversion. In a word, he discovered that men must be terrified before they could be saved, and by far the most powerful rhetorical passages in sermons such as those contained in *The Sincere Convert* were his descriptions of the pangs of hell and their certainty for all sinners who rested in carnal security.

Not until Jonathan Edwards, himself an admirer of Shepard, could anyone surpass his rhetoric of terror—indeed, when Shepard reminds the unregenerate that "thou hangest but by one rotten twined thread of thy life, over the flames of hell every hour,"[15] he immediately puts one in mind of Edwards' most famous sermon. After Shepard's example terror became a favorite tactic of the New England ministers, but because

[15] Thomas Shepard, *The Sincere Convert*, in *Works*, I, 35.

they were preaching for the most part to half-way members and not the clearly unregenerate, terror became a less effective technique in their hands for persuading men to seek conversion. Shepard threatened sinners with an eternal hell; the sons and grandsons threatened Indian wars, earthquakes, droughts, and hail storms. More important, the descendants in their jeremiads inveighed against external peccadilloes and lapses, while Shepard held up to men their essential depravity, not just the sins they had committed but all those they would commit given the opportunity:

> O, thou art full of rottenness, of sin, within. Guilty, not before men, as the sins of thy life make thee, but before God, of all the sins that swarm and roar in the whole world at this day, for God looks to the heart; guilty thou art therefore of heart whoredom, heart sodomy, heart blasphemy, heart drunkenness, heart buggery, heart oppression, heart idolatry; and these are the sins that terribly provoke the wrath of almighty God against thee.[16]

Shepard, like his father-in-law and friend, knew the fundamental importance of experimental religion—God looks to the heart—but their descendants used the rhetoric of terror to guard the entrance to the church rather than as a stimulant for conversion. Terror undercut the half-way members' trust in carnal reason, but it did not necessarily produce, as it had in Shepard's sermons, the degree of heightened anxiety which was a precondition for conversion.

In 1654 the preparationist theology of Hooker and Shepard received an unlikely convert in John Norton, pastor of the church at Ipswich and a later successor to Cotton and Davenport in Boston. In that year he published *The Orthodox Evangelist*, intended as a sort of small-scale *summa* of Puritan doctrine as held in New England, and it held three chapters on

[16] Ibid., 29.

preparation. This break with his generally Cottonian view of things had a curious background. In the 1650s the Bay underwent a veritable invasion of proselytizing Quakers, or at least it seemed like an invasion to the Bay ministers, and one of the Quakers' most revolutionary tenets was the abolition of any established, authoritative ministry. Norton wrote his book in part to defend the necessity of a learned ministry and also to justify ministerial power over the laity. Orthodox evangelists, said Norton, are at one with St. Paul in being "Instrumental Saviors of Mount Sion; This Ministerial Spirit rested not only upon that great Doctor of the Gentiles; but also rests, and acts in its measure, in all the Ministers of the Gospel, for the calling and compleating of the Elect, until we all come to be a perfect man."[17] If ministers were legitimate in their authority because their role was typified by Paul in "calling and compleating of the Elect," then Norton had to admit a human, voluntaristic element in conversion, and this is exactly what the preparatory theory did in contrast with that of Cotton.

Norton did not make any significant change in Hooker's general pattern of preparatory phases, but he did change the whole nature of preparation theology for later New England ministers by the attitude he held toward it. Although he endorsed and systematized Hooker's scheme, he defined preparation in a Cottonian sense. Hooker had recognized two varieties of preparation, what he called "legal" and "evangelical": "legal preparation . . . may befall Reprobates, . . . nor is it appointed by God for this end, to make way for the form of Faith, but for other ends."[18] Evangelical preparation was worked in the souls of the elect by the Spirit, and it was always followed by salvation; it was this latter version of preparation which Hooker preached, and this was the element of his theology which so dis-

[17] John Norton, *The Orthodox Evangelist* (London, 1657), sig. (?)3ʳ. The first signature is not marked; the second is signed A, the third B, and the rest of the book is regularly signed.

[18] Hooker, *Application*, 152.

turbed the Cottons and the Wards of the Bay. Norton, however, defined preparation as "the common work of the Spirit" in distinction to "saving work . . . the effect of free special grace."[19] Preparation for Norton was what Hooker had meant by legal preparation, and thus he could enjoin it upon all men regardless of their election or reprobation. In attempting to compromise the doctrines of Cotton and Hooker, Norton had unwittingly subverted their shared belief in the essential nature of religion as inner experience.

In Norton's hands preparation ceased to be a program of experimental religion and tended to become a scheme for moral living. This development is particularly evident in the pronouncements of the Mathers and Samuel Willard upon the subject later in the century.[20] By the beginning of the eighteenth century, Cotton Mather could lead an aspirant to godliness through the vexing business of conversion in a page or two: "Hearken to the *First Steps* of a CONVERSION unto GOD. Behold yourselves perishing Sinners. . . . Behold then your SAVIOR."[21] Religion was, in this particular presentation of it at least, no longer a divine recreation of the self but a human choice to be reasonable: "a Religion which lies in *Fearing* of GOD, and *Prizing* of His CHRIST, and *Doing of Good* unto *Men;* Here is a *Reasonable Religion*; And it is most certain, the more that Men improve in Reason, the more they will see *Reason* for a Compliance with it."[22] Preparation for Mather was only half of what it had been for Hooker; it qualified men for the external covenant of the church but not for the internal covenant of grace. Norton had reduced preparation to a moral duty, a reform of reason which did not touch the will, but as we have seen, Mather preserved the psychological consistency

[19] Norton, *Orthodox*, 130, 139.

[20] See Perry Miller, " 'Preparing for Salvation' in Seventeenth-Century New England," in *Nature's Nation* (Cambridge, Harvard Univ. Press, 1967), 71–76.

[21] Mather, *Malachi*, 9–10.   [22] Ibid., 43.

of Hooker's preparatory scheme by urging communicants to labor after piety in addition to morality, to complete their rational reforms by acquiring a *"sense* of Truth" in their hearts.

If we see Hooker simply as a preparationist theologian and a defender of an impossible standard of ecclesiastical purity, then his influence was negated within fifteen years of his death, first by Norton's restatement of preparation, then by the Half-Way Covenant. Cotton Mather's innovations had preserved the spirit but had thoroughly rewritten the letter of Hooker's message. But for Hooker preparation and church purity were means to an end, and the end was powerful religious experience in the individual hearts of his people. Despite his son's seeming confession of defeat in 1677, Thomas Hooker's tradition of experimental religion and evangelical ministry lived on in the Connecticut River Valley. Worldliness and carnal security had inevitably come to the valley, but the model of Hooker's evangelical community survived, and there were a few ministers who displayed some of his ingenuity in discovering techniques suitable to induce radical religious experience. Most inventive and successful of them all was Solomon Stoddard, the pastor of the church in Northampton from 1669 to 1729. Stoddard saw the progress of Christ's kingdom in the world as uncompleted, even by the great first generation of New England reformers, "those holy men who first planted his land," and he demanded of his colleagues in the pulpit, "Surely it is commendable for us to Examine the practices of our Fathers; we have no sufficient reason to take practices upon trust from them."[23] New England's spiritual problems were not framed in terms of a decline but of progress; by keeping open the idea of history as continual activity, Stoddard could keep open the idea of the continual activity of grace in men.

Stoddard realigned the positions of New England orthodoxy in his attempt to answer the problem of half-way members who

[23] Solomon Stoddard, *The Inexcusableness of Neglecting the Worship of God* (Boston, 1708), Preface (no pagination, signature illegible).

never discovered saving faith. His first major change was to open the church doors to anyone able to make a mere "Profession of the faith joyned with a good Conversation," utterly doing away with the old experiential tests insisted upon by Cotton—and devalued by Hooker.[24] At the same time he removed the distinction of the Half-Way Covenant; all members of the church were full members, entitled to all of its ordinances, including the Lord's Supper. By insisting that church members need only be defined by a historical faith, he negated Hooker's concept of a pure church, but he did it in order to purify men. "The Lords Supper is Instituted to be a means of Regeneration," Stoddard said. "All other Ordinances are appointed for Regeneration, . . . it would seem strange if the Lord's Supper alone should not be appointed for that end, whereas it hath a proper tendency thereunto."[25] Stoddard, like Hooker, saw the church as an eschatological institution, intended by Christ to call men to salvation, and not as a conservative force designed simply to treasure up the tribes of the elect. The difference between the two men was that Stoddard, like Mather, placed regeneration as happening ordinarily within the church rather than upon its doorstep as Hooker had it.

Stoddard's success as an evangelist was attested to by the five harvests of souls reaped in Northampton during his long career. In the course of these extraordinary outpourings of grace, he discovered in his pastoral experience the importance of the doctrine of preparation for salvation, and he later set his insights down in a small book "composed upon the desire of some *Younger Ministers.*" *The Guide to Christ* provided these pastoral novices with thirty-nine directions for treating "wounded consciences." What distinguished Stoddard's little manual from

[24] Stoddard, *The Doctrine of Instituted Churches* (London, 1700), 19. Opening the church was not new, for Gershom Bulkeley and John Woodbridge, Jr., had done it in Connecticut before him, but it was still a radical step. See Pope, 102–6.
[25] Stoddard, *Doctrine,* 22.

the work of John Norton was its insistence on the "great variety in workings of the Spirit, and in workings of mens' hearts under the convictions of the Spirit."[26] Stoddard did follow Norton in giving a Cottonian emphasis upon the commonness of common grace; like Norton he denied the distinction between legal and evangelical preparation, for "they that are to be Converted, are not capable of any strivings of the Spirit, but what are common, till they come to be humbled, and to believe."[27]

Although he specifically rejected Hooker's suggestion that the truly humbled soul could contentedly accept his own damnation as his just end, Stoddard did follow Hooker in defining the minister's responsibilities functionally rather than formally. Like Hooker he kept open the possibilities of reaching into the ungodly community surrounding the core of the regenerate. Both men agreed that the minister's legitimacy in dealing with his people stemmed from his election and calling by Christ, and this calling was the authentic source of his power as a preacher and a guide to the spiritually distressed. "There is great need of *experimental* knowledge in a Minister," Stoddard said, thus echoing Hooker's insistence upon a regenerate ministry.[28] Although the Northampton church of 1700 might accommodate virtually all who sought membership, it was vivified just as the Hartford church of 1640 was by the experimental religion lived within it.

These points of comparison between Stoddard and Hooker are, however, almost equally true concerning Cotton Mather and Hooker. Although Mather and his father, Increase, took public exception to Stoddard's open communion, they tolerated his position and Increase Mather wrote the preface to *The Guide to Christ*. The serious point of difference between Stoddard and the Mathers concerned the nature of conversion; whereas the Mathers saw communicants as slowly growing

[26] Stoddard, *A Guide to Christ* (Boston, 1714), 9–10.
[27] Ibid., 57.   [28] Ibid., 9.

into genuine piety, Stoddard argued that conversion was a memorable, shattering experience:

> *If any be taught that frequently men are ignorant of the Time of their Conversion, that is not good Preaching.* . . . surely men that are Converted must take some notice of the Time when God made a Change in them. . . . Conversion is the greatest change that men undergo in this world, surely it falls under Observation.[29]

As a recent scholar pointed out, "The Mathers insisted that Stoddard was too demanding, that there was too great an *'Exactness*, in his Thoughts about a Work of *Regeneration.'* . . . Stoddard, however, thought that the Mathers' charity would produce complacent communicants, blind to the danger of their unregenerate state and satisfied with a mere hope of conversion."[30] Cotton Mather conceived of the church as engaging in a continuous process of "pietizing" the civil community, and he thus reflected Hooker's concern for the communal significance of the church. Stoddard's demands for intense personal experience carried on Hooker's concern for the importance of the church to its individual members.

But while Stoddard brilliantly continued Hooker's tradition of heart religion, he discarded as dead letters great parts of his intellectual forebears' teachings. The church convenant which Hooker had so carefully defended as the social manifestation of the covenant of grace Stoddard rejected as unscriptural. Simultaneously with his attempts to revive the pastor's function as evangelist, he was formalizing his authority over the

---

[29] Quoted by Thomas A. Schafer, "Solomon Stoddard and the Theology of the Revival," in *A Miscellany of American Christianity: Essays in Honor of H. Shelton Smith*, ed. Stuart C. Henry (Durham, Duke Univ. Press, 1963), 355.

[30] Holifield, "Renaissance," 47. Also see James P. Walsh, "Solomon Stoddard's Open Communion: A Reexamination," *New England Quarterly* 43 (1970), 113.

congregation after the presbyterian manner, and the Saybrook Platform of 1705 signaled the end in the Connecticut River Valley of the completely independent churches Hooker described in the *Survey*. It remained for Stoddard's grandson and successor to create the last and greatest statement of experimental religion as Hooker knew it and at the same time to inter the last bits of Hooker's theology.

In his last years Hooker was working out the boundaries of his theology in *The Saints Dignitie and Duty* and *A Comment upon Christs Last Prayer in John*. The former of these treatises developed the voluntaristic side of Hooker's ideas, demanding human action of all those who hoped to gain a more certain assurance of their conversion. The present point of conversion, after all, was to provide a new basis for action in life. In the *Comment* Hooker at once described in great detail the change in human nature which legitimated his voluntarism and portrayed the coming vision of divine glory the soul achieved as it discovered through experience its union with Christ. It is in his discussion of life after conversion that Hooker defined the central realities of Puritanism. The Palace of Glory had always been the definitive Puritan concern in America, and it supplied the primary metaphor for all their hopes and acts.

"The things and relations of this life are like prints left in Sand, there is not the least appearance or remembrance of them," said Hooker. "There must be ever some print of some operation and impression of his Excellencies, or Relation left upon us, before anything can be discerned."[31] The print God left on the soul was a "direct act of knowledge which turns the eye of the Soul to look to the fulnesse of power and freeness of mercy, by which the heart is drawn to beleeve."[32] This was the saint's first vision of glory with which "the heart comes to be experimentally affected," and it was the first step into

[31] Hooker, *Comment*, 367, 403.   [32] Hooker, *Application*, 38.

that palace where men beheld "the lustre and beauty of such excellencies" of the Absolute, "Here by re-tale, as persons who are poor buy and bring in their Provisions, Then by whol-sale."[33] The experience of receiving the divine imprint initiated the saint into the experience of a universe of truth beyond nature:

> Take but an Apple, there is never a man under heaven can tell what tast it is of, whether sweet or soure, untill he have tasted of it; he seeth the colour and the quantity of it, but knoweth not the tast; . . . A carnall man may talk of repentance, and faith, and obedience, yet notwithstanding, there is a sappinesse, which I call the spiritualnesse in these blessed works, that no man can tell and understand, but onely those that indeed have found by experience the work in themselves.[34]

The apple of grace had been catalogued and quantified no end by men like Norton, but, although his thirty-nine articles on preparation were the final step in turning the doctrine of preparation into a dead form, Stoddard had kept experimental religion alive on the river.

When Jonathan Edwards took over his grandfather's pulpit, he also accepted the burden of his success as an evangelical minister; he measured up to it in a degree far beyond what Stoddard might reasonably have expected. Although circumstances had forced Stoddard into accepting speculative, historical belief in Christ as the hallmark of a Christian, he insisted upon experimental faith as the only assurance of salvation, and his insistence upon an assured, experimental faith encouraged the development of revivalism. Edwards restored experimental religion to the central position it had occupied in Hooker's preaching, and he stated it in terms resonating the

33 Hooker, *Comment*, 371, 368, 372.
34 Hooker, *Saints Dignitie*, 209.

doctrines of the first great preacher in the Valley. In 1734 everyone in Northampton "seemed to be seized with a deep concern about their Eternal salvation; all the Talk in all companies, and upon occasions was upon the things of Religion, and no other talk was anywhere Relished."[35] In that same year Edwards published by request of his parishioners a sermon in which he argued that "there is such a thing as a Spiritual and Divine Light, immediately imparted to the soul by God, of a different nature from any that is obtained by natural means."[36] This supernatural light was the "seal of the Spirit . . . a kind of effect of the Spirit of God on the heart, which natural men, while such, are so far from a capacity of being the subjects of, that they can have no manner of notion or idea of it."[37]

When Edwards came to explain natural man's failure to penetrate supernatural truth, he illuminated his point with an image much like that which Hooker had used over ninety years before.

> . . . there is a difference between having an opinion that God is holy and gracious, and having a sense of the loveliness and beauty of that holiness and grace. There is a difference between having a rational judgment that honey is sweet, and having a sense of its sweetness. A man may have the former, that knows not how honey tastes; but a man cannot have the latter unless he has an idea of the taste of honey in his mind.[38]

Edwards' appeal to his congregation to base their faith upon their sense of God's holiness and graciousness, their experi-

[35] Jonathan Edwards, "A Narrative of Surprising Conversions," in Clarence H. Faust and Thomas Johnson, eds., *Jonathan Edwards* (1935; rpt., Wang, 1962), 75.

[36] Jonathan Edwards, "A Divine and Supernatural Light," in Faust and Johnson, 102.

[37] Jonathan Edwards, *A Treatise Concerning Religious Affections*, ed. John E. Smith (New Haven, Yale Univ. Press, 1959), 231.

[38] Edwards, "A Divine . . . Light," 107.

mental knowledge, rather than upon opinion was for a time remarkably successful; by the middle of 1735 men and women from Deerfield in the north to New Haven at the south were experiencing their faith for the first time.

The revival of 1734 and 1735, interestingly enough, stayed geographically within the limits of that sphere of influence wielded first by Hooker and then by Stoddard. When the Great Awakening of the 1740s hit New England, it was most deeply experienced in this same area. Hooker had come to the river partly as a refuge from the doctrines of John Cotton; Stoddard had maintained for years a dispute with the Mathers, and Edwards in his turn was questioned by Charles Chauncy and other leading divines of Boston who feared the excesses of enthusiasm more than those of moralism. When he at last came to his most carefully reasoned and elaborate defense of experimental religion, the *Treatise Concerning the Religious Affections*, Edwards introduced as a chief witness for his views Thomas Shepard, and his principal Boston supporter, Thomas Prince, furthered the cause of heart religion by reprinting Hooker's *Poor Doubting Christian*.[39] The tradition which Hooker left behind of evangelical preaching and experimental religion flourished on the river. Edwards was simultaneously its last great exponent and the initiator of a new spiritual era.

During his career Edwards tended more and more to take his theology back to its roots in the seventeenth century. In the late forties he rejected Stoddardism and attempted to limit full communion in the church to those who could show evidence of a new heart. In his *Religious Affections* he made a detailed distinction between true and false signs of saving faith, thus in a sense reviving Hooker's distinction between legal and evangelical preparation. (However, when he distinguished

[39] See Shuffelton, "Thomas Prince," 73. Mather was Prince's sponsor and guide, and Prince's career as friend of Mather and supporter of Edwards exemplifies a unified Puritan heritage which embraced both Mather and Edwards.

between legal and evangelical humiliation, the latter was anything but preparatory; preparation in Hooker's sense had been
left behind in the seventeenth century.) Edwards acted for
reasons other than a merely conservative attempt to reinstate
the past. The writers of the first generation he had read with
respect, but if their theology was impressive, it was equally
in need of a radical restatement. Although he presented the
narrative of his own conversion in a way conformable to
Hooker's stages of preparation, he could no longer accept the
preparatory theology of Hooker and Shepard, for he had seen
the Arminian excesses to which their voluntarism might lead.
Hooker and Shepard did reveal to him an attempted resolution
of "the dichotomies which constantly beset the Puritan who
preached preparation by man and conversion by God," and
Edwards' doctrines "of grace as divine love, of excellency as
harmony of being, of spiritual light as changing the sense of the
heart, of true virtue as consent to being in general" were in
many ways attempts to restate their ideas in terms valid for
his century.[40]

Hooker's and Shepard's psychology was in many ways still
useful—there are striking similarities between Edwards' and
Hooker's discussions of the faculties of the mind; undoubtedly
they were familiar with many of the same sources—but it was
somewhat unsystematic, and their epistemology was fuzzy.
Compare the explosive connotations of Edwards' post-Lockean
use of the term "sense," in the image about the taste of honey,
to Hooker's much more generalized and loose appeal to "experience" in his trope about the apple (although Hooker's apple has a typological dimension absent in Edwards' comparable
image). When Edwards wrote out his own theology, he preserved Hooker's psychological orientation and his concern
for preaching the need of a new heart, but the argument was
erected upon a new frame. Perry Miller has shown us how this

[40] Schafer, "Solomon Stoddard," 360.

radical Edwards rewrote New England theology with the aid
of Locke and Newton, but before we concur with Miller's
rhetorical puzzlement over how such a genius could have
sprung up on the banks of the Connecticut, we ought to remember that there was a conservative Edwards well versed
in the traditions of experimental piety. Hooker was making
his explorations of human consciousness contemporaneously
with Descartes' formulation of *cogito ergo sum*, and as Leon
Howard has revealed, the young Edwards was as attracted to
Cartesian ideas as he was to the philosophy of Locke. A century in advance of Edwards' "A Divine and Supernatural
Light," Hooker had told the people of the valley, "Before a
man can discern spirituall objects, he must have spirituall
light."[41]

With the Great Awakening, however, Hooker's light became Edwards' light; his tradition of experimental piety was
displaced by the sermons and treatises of a more rigorous theologian, indeed, a greater theologian if not necessarily a better
pastor or a more winning man. Hooker left behind friends
and admirers but, unlike Edwards, no disciples, and the descent
of his ideas, as we have just followed them, is not a personal
tradition but the tradition of certain strains of Puritan piety of
which Hooker was a chief exponent. Hooker's more enduring
bequest was an image of heroic piety, the figure of the man
rather than a configuration of ideas. One measure of this phenomenon has been the continuing debate about his significance
in the tradition of American democracy. One of the first
Americans to move west from an "old" settlement, he stood
out among his fellows for all those historians from Hubbard
to Parrington who wanted to find champions for liberty. Ignoring most of his published statements about poor doubting
Christians and faithful covenanters, they created a mythicized

[41] Leon Howard, *"The Mind" of Jonathan Edwards: A Reconstructed
Text* (Berkeley, Univ. of California Press, 1963), 7; Hooker, *Saints Dignitie*, 208.

proto-patriot at the expense of the pastor concerned for his Father's children. The historians' biographical figure displaced the historical character.

Yet the image of the pastor was not entirely overshadowed; Timothy Dwight in the 1790s linked the character of Connecticut, that Land of Steady Habits, with the character of its first great religious leader: "A distinguished share of the same moderation, wisdom, and firmness which adorned Mr. Hooker has been conspicuous in the public measures of Connecticut down to the present day."[42] Dwight goes on to relate an "anecdote, transmitted among his descendents":

> In the latter part of autumn, Mr. Hooker, being suddenly awakened by an unusual noise, thought he heard a person in his cellar. He immediately arose, dressed himself, and went silently to the foot of the cellar stairs. There he saw a man with a candle in his hand taking pork out of the barrel. When he had taken out the last piece, Mr. Hooker, accosting him pleasantly, said, "Neighbor, you act unfairly; you ought to leave a part for me." Thunderstruck at being detected, especially at being detected by so awful a witness, the culprit fell at his feet, condemned himself for his wickedness, and implored his pardon. Mr. Hooker cheerfully forgave him, and concealed his crime, but forced him to carry half the pork to his own house.[43]

Hooker has in this case been perhaps more faithfully remembered in folklore than he has in history, and we could do far worse than to look to our forefathers and founders for like examples of rational charity. At its most tranquil moments so-

---

[42] Timothy Dwight, *Travels in New England and New York*, ed. Barbara Miller Solomon (Cambridge, Harvard Univ. Press, 1969), I, 172. See Sydney E. Ahlstrom, "Thomas Hooker—Puritanism and Democratic Citizenship: A Preliminary Inquiry into Some Relationships of Religion and American Civic Responsibility," Church History 32 (1963), 415-31, for a discussion of the historian's images of Hooker.

[43] Dwight, I, 172-73.

ciety still needs all the reason and charity its best men and women can provide, particularly so because these qualities can sometimes elude even the saints. (Although he engaged in none of the unseemly public rejoicings over Anne Hutchinson's tragic end or in the vitriolic harryings of Roger Williams in his Providence refuge, Hooker found it difficult to be charitable toward the Pequots.) Hooker's religion enriched the life of his imagination, and it educated his heart in the ways of sympathy and compassion. If the compassion could sometimes fail, his religion was still an objective standard of experience which held out the promise of something better than aimless human striving, something deeper and more lasting than phenomena or subjectivity. It gave majesty to his life and power to his language.

BIBLIOGRAPHICAL ESSAY

ALTHOUGH the footnotes to this study indicate the literature which was ultimately most important to me in studying Thomas Hooker, they do not reveal, first, the large background of scholarship on Puritanism which must be mastered before approaching any individual figure or problem, or, second, more specific studies, such as those on bibliographical questions, for example, which, like all good foundations, are essential but out of sight. Several recent bibliographies of the literature of Puritanism obviate the need for another, so I have concentrated on the second category of studies. In addition to works I found useful but did not have occasion to note before, I include some recent work which develops lines I have pursued here.

One exception to this principle of avoiding references to large backgrounds must be the works of Perry Miller, particularly *Orthodoxy in Massachusetts, 1630–1650* (Cambridge, Harvard Univ. Press, 1933); *The New England Mind: The Seventeenth Century* (New York, Macmillan, 1939); *The New England Mind: From Colony to Province* (Cambridge, Harvard Univ. Press, 1953); and the essays in *Errand into the Wilderness* (Cambridge, Harvard Univ. Press, 1956). As an undergraduate I was awed by the erudition and passion for ideas in his lectures; later I discovered with many others that one approached the New England Puritans first through his books. Miller's contentions have been amended by more recent scholarship, and both literary scholars and historians have felt constricted by his emphasis on the history of ideas to the exclusion of so much else, yet he raised the level of discourse for all of us. Useful bibliographies of scholarship on Puritanism since Miller include Darrett B. Rutman's bibliographical essay in his *American Puritanism: Faith and Practice* (Philadelphia, Lippincott, 1970); Michael McGiffert, "American Puritan Studies in the 1960's," *William and Mary Quarterly* 27 (1970), 36–67; and the "Selected Bibliography" in *The American Puritan Imagination: Essays in Revaluation*, ed. Sacvan Bercovitch (New York, Cambridge Univ. Press, 1974), 241–258. Rutman's and McGiffert's lists are oriented toward historical studies, Bercovitch's toward literary approaches. Just come to hand as this book goes to print is *Thomas Hooker: Writings in England and Holland, 1626–1633*, ed. George H. Williams, Norman Pettit, Winfried Herget, and Sargent Bush, Jr., Harvard Theological Studies, No. 28 (Cambridge, Harvard Univ. Press, 1975). This reprints early Hooker writings and contains a significant essay by each of the editors. Bush adds a bibliography which replaces all previous bibliographies.

The most convenient bibliography of Hooker's writings has been J. Hammond Trumbull's list, "Thomas Hooker's Published Works," in George Leon Walker, *Thomas Hooker: Preacher, Founder, Democrat* (New York, Dodd, 1891), 184–195. Less easily available is H. Clark Woolley, *Thomas Hooker Bibliography, together with a Brief Sketch of His Life* (Hartford, Center Church Monographs, 1932). Flaws and omissions in Trumbull's list have been pointed out by Hubert R. Pellman, "Thomas Hooker: A Study in Puritan Ideals," Diss., University of Pennsylvania 1958, x–xvi; Everett H. Emerson, "Notes on the Thomas Hooker Canon," *American Literature* 27 (1956), 554–555; Andrew Denholm, "Thomas Hooker: Puritan Preacher 1586–1647," Diss. Hartford Seminary Foundation 1961, 510–519; and in Sargent Bush, Jr., "Four New Works by Thomas Hooker: Identity and Significance," *Resources for American Literary Study* 4 (1974), 3–26. Denholm's dissertation is useful both for its bibliography and for its inclusion of transcriptions of manuscript notes by Hooker, his thanksgiving sermon of 1638, and Henry Wolcott's abstracts of some Hooker sermons. Everett Emerson has also published the thanksgiving sermon with a useful brief introduction, "A

Thomas Hooker Sermon of 1638," *Resources for American Literary Study* 2 (1972), 75–89. Sargent Bush, Jr.'s "The Growth of Thomas Hooker's *The Poor Doubting Christian*," *Early American Literature* 8 (1973), 3–20, provides an extensive account of that book's textual history.

Hooker's first biographer was Cotton Mather, *Piscator Evangelicus, or The Life of Mr. Thomas Hooker* (Boston, 1695); Mather's biography later became a part of the *Magnalia* (1702). His didactic intentions lead to various kinds of exaggeration; his Hooker is a figure larger than life who incidentally seems to offer support for Mather's espousal of ministerial associations. Although his illustrative anecdotes have little or no corroborative support, his portrait of Hooker seems to me to be true in its proportions, and he was able to talk about the past with one or two surviving contemporaries of Hooker like John Eliot. Later writers on Hooker confined themselves to Mather's biographical facts until George Leon Walker, *Thomas Hooker: Preacher, Founder, Democrat*, collected most of the verifiable details concerning Hooker's life. George Huntston Williams adds one or two facts in his extremely concise study, "The Pilgrimage of Thomas Hooker (1586–1647) in England, The Netherlands and New England," *Bulletin of the Congregational Library* 19 (October 1967, January 1968), 5–15, 9–13. Williams' "Called by Thy Name, Leave Us Not: The Case of Mrs. Joan Drake, A Formative Episode in the Pastoral Career of Thomas Hooker in England," *Harvard Library Bulletin* 16 (1968), 111–128, 278–300, illuminates Hooker's experience in Esher. Keith L. Sprunger, "The Dutch Career of Thomas Hooker," *New England Quarterly* 46 (1973), 17–44, goes over the ground covered by Raymond Phineas Stearns, *Congregationalism in the Dutch Netherlands* (Chicago, American Society of Church History, 1940), and Alice Clare Carter, *The English Reformed Church in Amsterdam in the Seventeenth Century* (Amsterdam, Scheltema, 1964). Sydney E. Ahlstrom, "Thomas Hooker—Puritanism and Democratic Citizenship: A Preliminary Inquiry into Some Relationships of Religion and American Civic Responsibility," Church History 32 (1962–1963), 415–431, discusses Hooker's historical reputation and considers the criteria which are essential for a biographical interpretation.

In addition to the titles footnoted in Chapter One useful studies of English education in the late sixteenth and early seventeenth centuries include Foster Watson, *The English Grammar Schools to 1660: Their Curriculum and Practice* (Cambridge, The Univ. Press, 1908); Mark H. Curtis, *Oxford and Cambridge in Transition 1558–1642* (Oxford, Clarendon Press, 1959); Hugh F. Kearney, *Scholars and Gentlemen, Universities and Society in Pre-Industrial Britain, 1500–1700* (Ithaca, Cornell Univ. Press, 1970); and Samuel Eliot Morison, *The Founding of Harvard College* (Cambridge, Harvard Univ. Press, 1935). Perry Miller first called attention to the importance of Ramism in *The New England Mind: The Seventeenth Century*, and Walter J. Ong's powerfully suggestive *Ramus, Method, and the Decay of Dialogue* (Cambridge, Harvard Univ. Press, 1958), is the authoritative study. Also useful is Rosemond Tuve, "Imagery and Logic: Ramus and Metaphysical Poetics," *Journal of the History of Ideas* 3 (1942), 365–400, and her subsequent treatment of Ramism in *Elizabethan and Metaphysical Imagery* (Chicago, Univ. of Chicago Press, 1947). Tuve's concentration on the rhetorical and poetical implications of Ramism is an important supplement to the more philosophical orientation of Miller and Ong. Of some interest are Keith L. Sprunger's chapters on "Technometria" and "The Marrow of Ames's Theology" in his *The Learned Doctor William Ames: Dutch Backgrounds of English and American Puritanism* (Urbana, Univ. of Illinois Press, 1972), 105–152.

Those interested in the backgrounds of Hooker's conception of pastoral care might consult John T. McNeill, *A History of the Cure of Souls* (New York, SCM Press, 1951), and Thomas

Wood, *English Casuistical Divinity During the Seventeenth Century* (London, S.P.C.K., 1952). Also useful are H. R. McAdoo, *The Structure of Caroline Moral Theology* (London, Longmans, 1949), and Sprunger's chapter, "Puritan Ethics," in *The Learned Doctor William Ames.* Thomas F. Merrill has provided an introduction to *William Perkins 1558–1602, English Puritanist: His Pioneer Works on Casuistry: A Discourse of Conscience and The Whole Treatise of Cases of Conscience* (Nieuwkoop, B. DeGraff, 1966). Everett H. Emerson discusses Hooker's ethical principles in "Thomas Hooker: The Puritan as Theologian," *Anglican Theological Review* 49 (1967), 190–203, and he treats the larger issue of theological background in "Thomas Hooker and the Reformed Theology," Diss. Louisiana State University 1955. Norman Pettit, *The Heart Prepared: Grace and Conversion in Puritan Spiritual Life* (New Haven, Yale Univ. Press, 1966), is authoritative on preparationist theology, and his "Hooker's Doctrine of Assurance: A Critical Phase in New England Spiritual Thought," *New England Quarterly* 47 (1974), 518–534 exetnds the discussion of Hooker's preparationism. David L. Parker examines Ramist underpinnings in "Peter Ramus and the Puritans: The 'Logic' of Preparationist Conversion Doctrine," *Early American Literature* 8 (1973), 140–162. I found little that was immediately helpful in treating Hooker's meditative concerns. Louis K. Martz, *The Poetry of Meditation* (New Haven, Yale Univ. Press, 1954), deals extensively with Ignatian meditative method but has little to say about Puritan meditation which he admits is very different. U. Milo Kaufmann, *The Pilgrim's Progress and Tradition in Puritan Meditation* (New Haven, Yale Univ. Press, 1966), is suggestive but focuses intensively on *Pilgrim's Progress* rather than taking a broader view of the tradition. John Rodney Fulcher, "Puritan Piety in Early New England: A Study in Spiritual Regeneration from the Antinomian Controversy to the Cambridge Synod of 1648 in the Massachusetts Bay Colony," Diss. Princeton University 1971, gives a good overview of the spiritual components of the New England Way, particularly as seen in the work of Hooker, Shepard, and Cotton.

David D. Hall, *The Faithful Shepherd: A History of the New England Ministry in the Seventeenth Century* (Chapel Hill, Univ. of North Carolina Press, 1966), goes well beyond theology to trace the idea itself of the Puritan ministry as he studies "the interaction of ideas and situation" (xi). His consideration of Puritan preaching should be supplemented with the literary considerations of Josephine K. Piercy, *Studies in Literary Types in Seventeenth Century America* (New Haven, Yale Univ. Press, 1939), and Kenneth Murdock, *Literature and Theology in Colonial New England* (Cambridge, Harvard Univ. Press, 1949). Still important is Babette May Levy, *Preaching in the First Half Century of New England History* (Hartford, American Society of Church History, 1945). Diane M. Darrow, "Thomas Hooker and the Puritan Art of Preaching," Diss. University of California at San Diego, 1968, provides an interesting if not always convincing examination of Hooker's sermonic art.

To study the creation of the New England Way of church government, Williston Walker's *The Creeds and Platforms of Congregationalism* (New York, Scribners, 1893) is still invaluable. Outstanding supplements to Perry Miller's work in this area are Larzer Ziff's *The Career of John Cotton: Puritanism and the American Experience* (Princeton, Princeton Univ. Press, 1962), and Edwin S. Morgan's *Visible Saints: The History of a Puritan Idea* (New York, New York Univ. Press, 1963). Morgan here and in the revised edition of his *The Puritan Family: Religion and Domestic Relations in Seventeenth-Century New England* (New York, Harper, 1966) overemphasizes the Puritan tendency toward tribalism, partly by not adequately weighing the significance of evangelically minded ministers like Hooker, Shepard, and John Eliot. Darrett B. Rutman, *Winthrop's Boston: A Portrait of a Puritan Town,*

1630–1649 (Chapel Hill, Univ. of North Carolina Press, 1965), puts the problems of creating a church polity into the larger context of creating a community. Ziff's *John Cotton* is also useful for its account of the antinomian crisis, which is treated more extensively by Emery Battis, *Saints and Sectaries: Anne Hutchinson and the Antinomian Controversy* (Chapel Hill, Univ. of North Carolina Press, 1962). Battis attempts to bring sociological and psychological points of view to bear but does not fully succeed. David D. Hall's *The Antinomian Controversy, 1636–1638: A Documentary History* (Middletown, Wesleyan Univ. Press, 1968) is an essential collection of the documents in the case along with informative introductions. Lyle Koehler's "The Case of the American Jezebels: Anne Hutchinson and Female Agitators during the Years of Antinomian Turmoil," *William and Mary Quarterly* 31 (1974), 55–78 is a feminist answer to Battis.

In discussing the settlement in Connecticut my focus on Hooker has not permitted me to go far into the roles of other important figures, particularly John Winthrop, Jr. Mary Jeanne Anderson Jones, *Congregational Commonwealth: Connecticut, 1636–1662* (Middletown, Wesleyan Univ. Press, 1968), provides a recent study, but Benjamin Trumbull's *A Complete History of Connecticut, Civil and Ecclesiastical* (Hartford, 1818) is still useful. Richard S. Dunn, *Puritans and Yankees: The Winthrop Dynasty of New England, 1630–1717* (Princeton, Princeton Univ. Press, 1962), and Robert C. Black III, *The Younger John Winthrop* (New York, Columbia Univ. Press, 1966), are informative. Charles M. Andrews, *The Colonial Period of American History*, 4 vols. (New Haven, Yale Univ. Press, 1934–1938), discusses the founding of Connecticut in volume II, 67–99. Richard Bushman, *From Puritan to Yankee: Character and the Social Order in Connecticut, 1690–1765* (Cambridge, Harvard Univ. Press, 1967), looks at a later period, but if one accepts with caution his contention that "in Connecticut the institutions inspired by the founders' piety persisted to the end of the nineteenth century," his first section (3–38) is suggestive.

My final chapter tracing Hooker's personal and intellectual influence and the mutations of some of his ideas is of necessity a mere sketch since to deal adequately with the issues touched on here would require one or more weighty volumes. One of the more controversial legacies of Perry Miller is his account of New England's spiritual and intellectual declension, presented most notably in *The New England Mind: From Colony to Province*. The title of Joseph Haroutounian's study, *Piety versus Moralism: The Passing of the New England Theology* (New York, Holt, 1932), indicates the direction of this supposed decline. A great deal of excellent recent scholarship has undertaken to revise or deny this version of New England history. Robert G. Pope, *The Half-Way Covenant: Church Membership in Puritan New England* (Princeton, Princeton Univ. Press, 1969), has shown how churches retained their vitality after 1660. Sacvan Bercovitch, "Horologicals to Chronometricals: The Rhetoric of the Jeremiad," *Literary Monographs*, III (Madison, Univ. of Wisconsin Press, 1970), 1–124, has given us a new way to read the jeremiads and fit them into a longer view of American culture. Cotton Mather has been rescued from his role as Puritan moralist by David Levin in his introduction to Mather's *Bonifacius: An Essay upon the Good* (Cambridge, Harvard Univ. Press, 1966), Robert Middlekauf, *The Mathers: Three Generations of Puritan Intellectuals, 1596–1728* (New York, Oxford Univ. Press, 1971), and Sacvan Bercovitch, "Cotton Mather," in *Major Writers of Early America*, ed. Everett H. Emerson (Madison, Univ. of Wisconsin Press, 1972). Recent useful work on Solomon Stoddard includes that of E. Brooks Holifield, "The Intellectual Sources of Stoddardeanism," *New England Quarterly* 45 (1972), 373–392, Robert L. Stuart, " 'Mr. Stoddard's Way' Church and Sacraments in Northampton," *American Quarterly* 24 (1972), 243–253, and Paul R. Lucas, " 'An Appeal to the

Learned': The Mind of Solomon Stoddard," *William and Mary Quarterly*, 30 (1973), 257–292. David D. Hall's *The Faithful Shepherd* examines the changing role of the ministry as it tried to adapt to new social conditions, as does Emery Elliott, *Power and the Pulpit in Puritan New England* (Princeton, Princeton Univ. Press, 1975), who is particularly sensitive to the effects of content and style in Puritan preaching. James W. Jones, *The Shattered Synthesis: New England Puritanism Before the Great Awakening* (New Haven, Yale Univ. Press, 1973), has difficulty escaping the limitations of a simplistic thesis, and Larzer Ziff, *Puritanism in America: New Culture in a New World* (New York, Viking, 1973), gives a tendentious reworking of the declension thesis. Sacvan Bercovitch, *The Puritan Origins of the American Self* (New Haven, Yale Univ. Press, 1975), is rewarding as he attempts to ground "the rhetoric of American identify" in the Puritan experience, taking Mather's life of John Winthrop as a kind of proof text.

INDEX

Saint Augustine, 39
Saint Paul, 21, 38, 39, 82, 89, 119,
134, 223, 294
Sallust, 8
Sassacus, 245
Schafer, Thomas A., 299n, 304n
separatism, 140, 144, 145, 146, 148,
186, 194, 270
Shepard, Samuel (son of Thomas),
278–79
Shepard, Thomas, 74, 75n, 125,
127, 131, 159, 174, 203, 227,
241, 242, 247n, 249, 252, 266,
273, 276–79, 280n, 283, 292–93,
303, 304
Sibbes, Richard, 37, 40, 42n, 56,
92, 96, 132, 133
Sidney Sussex College, 26
Skelton, Samuel, 171, 187
Spilsbury, John, 265n
Sprunger, Keith L., 134n
Stearns, Raymond P., 25n, 71n,
136, 138n, 141n, 143n, 151n
Stoddard, Solomon, 296–300, 301,
303
Stone, Samuel, 159, 160, 171, 177,
178, 180, 182, 212, 213, 214, 217,
219, 237, 245, 279, 280n
Stoughton, Israel, 190, 193
Suckiaug, 203, 214; settlement at,
211–13
Symmes, Zechariah, 240

Taylor, Jeremy, 107
Terence, 8
Tomson, William, 3
Tothill, William, 30
Tothill, Mrs. William, 30–31
Trumbull, J. Hammond, 230n,
282n
Tyndall, Humphrey, 11–12

Underhill, John, 235n, 237, 291
Ussher, James, 43

Vane, Sir Henry, 208, 241, 245
Venn, J., 11n
Venn, J. A., 11n

Virgil, 8
voluntarism, 85n, 254, 300, 304

Walker, George L., 6n, 7n, 28n,
124n, 171n, 282n
Walker, Williston, 267n, 290n
Walsh, James P., 299n
Ward, Nathaniel, 129, 275, 291,
295
Warham, John, 282
Warwick, Earl of, 102, 107, 128,
133, 138
Weld, Thomas, 74, 75, 129, 132,
188, 244
Wheelwright, John, 241, 242–44,
249, 250–51, 283
White, Mr., 72
Whiting, John, 283n
Willard, Samuel, 295
Williams, George H., 30n, 73n
Williams, Roger, 133, 245, 246,
307; as dissident in Massachu-
setts, 186–89, 192–96
Wilson, Dr. Edmund, 74
Wilson, John, 177, 208, 240, 242,
245
Wilson, Thomas, 14
Winslow, Edward, 72
Winslow, Ola Elizabeth, 171n,
187n
Winthrop, John, 76n, 133, 157,
158n, 161, 174, 175n, 176–77,
186n, 187n, 189, 191n, 192n, 193,
195, 198, 203n, 211n, 226, 233,
245, 251n, 266n, 277, 283; objects
to Newtown emigration, 199–
201; opposes antinomians, 238–
40, 242; political theory, 208–10,
230–31, 274–76; quarrels with
Dudley, 183–85; and settlement
at Newtown, 162–64
Wolsey, Cardinal, 28
Wood, William, 164
Woodbridge, John, Jr., 297n
Wright, Thomas G., 281n

Zeno, 14

Library of Congress Cataloging in Publication Data

Shuffelton, Frank, 1940–
    Thomas Hooker, 1586–1647.

    Includes bibliographical references and index.
    1. Hooker, Thomas, 1586–1647.   2. Con-
gregationalists—Connecticut—Hartford—Biography.
3. Clergy—Connecticut—Hartford—Biography.
4. Hartford—Biography.
BX7260.H596S55   285'.8'0924 [B]   76-45912
ISBN 0-691-05249-2